This book is a rare treasure of godly wisdom, totally scriptural, inspired by the Spirit, and born of practical experience. These principles will revolutionize and energize any church to reach its full potential. Every pastor *must* read this book! It is destined to be a classic.

Bill Bright, Founder, Campus Crusade for Christ International

I have hundreds of books and articles on the church. If I had to pick just one of them, I would choose Rick Warren's book. If I could, I'd make it required reading for every seminary student!

Jim Henry, President, Southern Baptist Convention

This is not just another "how to" book by a successful megachurch pastor. It shows just how far off the mark are many critics of "church growth" and seeker-sensitive" approaches. Study this book carefully! Rick Warren knows how *the Lord* builds the church.

George Brushaber, President, Bethel College and Seminary

The church has been waiting for this book for a long time, and it is worth every minute we've waited. It is destined to become a classic in the literature of the new paradigm of church health.

Leonard Sweet, Dean, Drew Theological Seminary

BALANCED! ... PRACTICAL! ... POWERFUL! You will want to read and use this book.

Ken Hemphill, President, Southwestern Baptist Theological Seminary

Rick Warren is the architect for the church of the 21st century, and this is the blueprint!

Bruce Larson, Minister at Large

This is the best book I've ever read on how to do church in today's world.

Lyle E. Schaller, Parish Consultant

Warren addresses *the* crucial question for churches: how to be both faithful and effective.

Marshall Shelley, Executive editor, *Leadership*

This is absolutely the best book I've read on church growth! It needs to be read by lay men and women, not just pastors. It can save your church from decline, division, and death. I want the core leadership of every new Southern Baptist congregation to study this book.

Charles Chaney, Vice President, New Churches, Home Mission Board, SB

In every era, God raises up leaders to pioneer new possibilities for God's people. God gave Rick Warren the gift of vision and discernment, and the results can be seen in Saddleback Church and in thousands of other congregations around the world that have applied his teaching. Oh! If we Methodists (and other mainline too) could realize how much we need to learn from Rick Warren!

Ezra Earl Jones, General Secretary, United Methodist Church Board of Discipleship

The Purpose-Driven Church is the most biblically and practically balanced book I've read on healthy church growth. It is compelling, convicting, and convincing.

Henry J. Schmidt, President, Mennonite Brethren Biblical Seminary

This book is the blueprint for the authentic church of the 21st century. It is probably the best practical application of genuine church growth principles in America. It will be required reading for all Nazarene pastors in the K-Church project.

Bill Sullivan, Director, Church Growth, International Church of the Nazarene

This book contains as much proven church growth wisdom as any book ever written from the local church experience.

George G. Hunter III, Dean, School of World Missions, Asbury Theological Seminary

Dr. Warren's insight that the critical issue facing the church is not church *growth*, but church *health* is revolutionary! This book is choc-o-bloc with ideas that are so practical and down-to-earth that any pastor who fails to correct his perspective on the church should probably leave the ministry.

Archibald Hart, Dean, School of Psychology, Fuller Seminary

This is the best book on church growth I've yet seen. It is biblical, practical, and visionary; it is Christ-centered; it focuses on church health; it dispels myths about how churches grow; it gives down-to-earth help and a truly scriptural model for ministry. Every pastor and church leader should read it—and I say this about few books.

Lewis Drummond, Professor of Evangelism, Beeson Divinity School, Samford University

I predict *The Purpose-Driven Church* will be *the* book for churches desiring to grow and prosper in the 21st century. It is required reading for all my classes. Put it at the top of your must-read list.

Gary McIntosh, Professor, Talbot School of Theology

I have waited for this book for a long time. It is the best of Rick Warren—his vision, clarity, energy, and effective articulation of concepts.

Joe Ellis, Distinguished Professor of Church Growth, Cincinnati Bible Seminary

One hundred years from now, young seminary students will have this book on their shelf beside their Bible and *Spurgeon's Lectures To My Students*. It will last for generations because its principles are timeless.

Bob Roberts, Pastor, Northwood Church, North Richland Hills, Texas

Destined to be a classic, the key to the greatness of this book is its passion and balance. Every student in the Billy Graham School of Missions and Evangelism will be required to read it.

Thom S. Rainer, Dean, Billy Graham School, Southern Baptist Theological Seminary

Every seminary graduate should be handed this book along with a diploma! I will see that every Golden Gate graduate gets a copy. Healthier, happier, and more fruitful churches will result from applying these principles. I wish Rick had written it forty years ago when I began my ministry.

William Crews, President, Golden Gate Baptist Theological Seminary

Rick Warren is building one of the great churches in America by getting back to biblical basics—not the *old methods* but the *eternal purposes* found in the Bible. Every pastor needs to read this book carefully to see how it is done.

Elmer L. Towns, Dean, School of Religion, Liberty University

This is the clearest, most comprehensive, and courageous book I've ever read on how to build a great church.

Walt Kallestad, Pastor, Community Church of Joy (ELCA), Glendale, Arizona

At the risk of sounding extravagant, I would, without hesitation, trade all my volumes on church life for this one book. Nobody does healthy church growth better than Rick Warren. He is its premier teacher and practitioner.

Jim Reeves, Faith Community Church, West Covina, California

The Purpose-Driven Church is perhaps the crown jewel of church growth literature. Every pastor and lay man who loves the church will do themselves a favor by reading this masterpiece.

Randy Pope, Pastor, Perimeter Church, Duluth, Georgia

If you want to dream great dreams, grow a healthy church, and accomplish God's purpose in your generation, this book is for you. The amazing story of Saddleback Church reads like a fresh encounter with the book of Acts.

Jack Graham, Pastor, Prestonwood Baptist Church, Dallas, Texas

Saddleback Church's growth is the miracle story of this century. I highly recommend *The Purpose-Driven Church* to every pastor who wants to build a great New Testament church.

Jerry Falwell, Chancellor, Liberty University

I'm praying that every pastor will read this book, believe it, be prepared to stand corrected by it, and change to match its sound, scriptural wisdom. Rick Warren is the one all of us should listen to and learn from.

Robert H. Schuller, Pastor, The Crystal Cathedral, Garden Grove, California

Rick Warren has been used to challenge my thinking in the area of church growth in an incredible way. This book is on the must-read list for every pastor.

Adrian Rogers, Pastor, Bellevue Baptist Church, Memphis, Tennessee

God has used Rick Warren as an effective instrument, and this book reveals why. He's kept grounded on eternal values and rooted in the Vine of ultimate truth—Christ Jesus.

Jack Hayford, Pastor, The Church On The Way, Van Nuys, California

Rick Warren's insights made me wish I could begin my ministry all over again. This book is so biblical, so well-organized, and so well-articulated, it made me exclaim, "I wish every Christian understood that!" I hope every United Methodist will read this book.

Richard B. Wilke, Bishop, United Methodist Church

This book could have as significant an impact on the future of Christianity as any book released in recent years. Every church leader in America needs to read it.

Ronnie W. Floyd, Pastor, First Baptist Church, Springdale, AR

No other pastor in America is more effective in cultivating both conversions and spiritual maturity than Rick Warren. This book should come with a triple-your-money-back guarantee—it's that good!. I'm making it required reading for every leader in our church.

David W. Miller, Pastor, The Church at Rocky Peak, Chatsworth, California

At last ... in print ... the real secret of Saddleback. And best of all, it is filled with practical and applicable principles to help us all become more contemporary without compromise.

O. S. Hawkins, Pastor, First Baptist Church, Dallas, Texas

This book is one of the finest books on ministry every written. It is *meat*, not theory. There isn't a church in America that can't benefit from its wisdom. I can't wait to take my board through it.

Larry Osborne, Pastor, North Coast Church (Evangelical Free), Vista, California

The Purpose-Driven Church gives us the comprehensive picture. It demonstrates biblical reflection, theological integrity, spiritual perception, evangelistic passion, pastoral concern, and refreshing common sense.

Eddie Gibbs, Associate Rector, All Saints' Parish, Beverly Hills, California

After all the church growth hype by people who've never done it, this book is a breath of fresh air. It's hard to argue with biblical principles and the voice of experience. Get this book and do what it says!

Jerry Sutton, Pastor, Two Rivers Baptist Church, Nashville, Tennessee

The chapter "Designing a Service for Seekers" alone is worth the price of this book. If only I had been taught these principles when I was in seminary!

James Merritt, 1995 President, SBC Pastors' Conference

If you want to examine the differences between healthy and unhealthy churches from a mature, experienced perspective, this is the book to read.

Paul D. Robbins, Exec. Vice President, Christianity Today, Inc.

I consider Rick Warren to be one of the greatest thinkers in the church today. In this book, he shows how passion, skill, and God's guidance can create a world-changing congregation. It will prove to be a classic!

Dwight "Ike" Reighard, Pastor, New Hope Baptist Church, Fayetteville, Georgia

The Purpose-Driven Church philosophy changed my life and the life of our church. Rick Warren is a genius with the ability to convert complex truths into understandable concepts.

Ed Young, Jr., Pastor, Fellowship of Las Colinas, Irving, Texas

This is a book we all need to *reread* once a year. Its insights will be applicable for generations to come. Each chapter causes you to pause often and pray.

Doug Murren, Pastor, Eastside Foursquare Church, Kirkland, Washington

THE
PURPOSE
DRIVEN™
CHURCH

Growth Without Compromising
Your Message & Mission

RICK WARREN

ZondervanPublishingHouse
Grand Rapids, Michigan

A Division of HarperCollinsPublishers

The Purpose-Driven™ Church
Copyright © 1995 by Rick Warren

Requests for information should be addressed to:

ZondervanPublishingHouse
Grand Rapids, Michigan 49530

Library of Congress Cataloging-in-Publication Data

Warren, Richard, 1954–
    The purpose-driven church: growth without compromising your message and mission / Rick
Warren.
       p.   cm.
    Includes bibliographical references.
    ISBN 0-310-20106-3 (hardcover: alk. paper)
    1. Church growth.   2. Evangelistic work. I. Title.
BV652.2.W38   1995
253—dc20   95-40707
                                                                   CIP

International Trade Paper Edition 0-310-20813-0

Edited by Jack Kuhatschek
Interior design by Joe Vriend

This edition printed on acid-free paper and meets the American National Standards Institute Z39.48
standard.

Printed in the United States of America

00 01 /DC/ 50 49 48 47 46 45

*I dedicate this book
to the bivocational pastors around the world:
shepherds who faithfully and lovingly serve
in churches that aren't large enough
to provide a full-time salary. You are the
true heroes of the faith in my view.
May this book encourage you.*

*I also dedicate this book
to seminary and Christian college professors:
educators called to prepare the next generation
of pastors. What an awesome, holy task you have!
May God bless and honor your ministry.*

*Finally, I dedicate this book
to the pastors and staff who have served
with me at Saddleback Church.
It has been a great adventure together.
I love you deeply.*

Contents

Part Five • Building Up the Church

Foreword

God could not have given me a more beloved and effective "son in the ministry" than Rick Warren. I first met Rick in 1974 when he was just a lad—a crazy college student who drove 350 miles to attend the California Baptist Convention in San Francisco. Through the message at that convention, God called Rick Warren to invest his life as a pastor-teacher. I am honored beyond words to be called his "father in the ministry."

In 1980, Rick graduated from the Southwestern Baptist Theological Seminary in Fort Worth, Texas, and moved with his wife to southern California to begin Saddleback Church in the living room of their home. He began with just one family. Now, fifteen years later, Saddleback Valley Community Church is recognized as the fastest-growing Baptist church in the *history* of America. It averages over 10,000 people in worship attendance each week on a beautiful, spacious seventy-four-acre campus. This is sufficient evidence that Rick Warren knows whereof he speaks. In 1995, Saddleback was selected as the Key Church of the Year by the Home Mission Board of the Southern Baptist Convention.

The Purpose-Driven Church is the exciting story of Saddleback. This book explains the convictions, principles, and practices that have been mightily used by God in building one of the most effective churches on the North American continent.

Rick Warren's ministry is grounded and rooted in the infallible and inerrant Word of God, Spirit-anointed servant leadership, and a genuine heart of love for his people. Some would call Saddleback a "megachurch," but this church has grown *without compromising the mission or the doctrine* of a New Testament church. What God has done at Saddleback is amazing.

During the past two to three decades, many churches have relied primarily on biological and transfer growth, but not

Saddleback. It is committed to the idea that vibrant churches in the twenty-first century must be wholeheartedly committed to conversion growth. Rick Warren understands the mind-set of the unchurched of this world. If churches are to be successful in evangelizing our society, which is becoming more pagan by the day, they must learn to think like an unbeliever.

To his credit, Rick discourages other churches from trying to become "photocopies" of Saddleback. Rather, he encourages local churches to penetrate our materialistic, humanistic society with the transforming message of Christ by using contemporary and relevant methods without compromising the truth of the Gospel. That's what this book is all about.

The Purpose-Driven Church will help *every* local church, regardless of size, to recapture the mission of the New Testament church. My prayer to God is that thousands of pastors, staff members, Sunday school teachers, and spiritual leaders will read this book. I heard a fellow say once, "Minds are like parachutes; they work best when they are open." That's the way to read this book!

May God bless you in whatever ministry assignment you have. Be faithful to Christ and his church until he returns.

W. A. Criswell, Pastor Emeritus
First Baptist Church
Dallas, Texas

Surfing Spiritual Waves

*I am the LORD your God, who churns up
the sea so that its waves roar.*

Isaiah 51:15

Southern California is well known for its beaches. It's the part of the country that popularized the music of the Beach Boys, beach party movies, and of course, surfing. Although the surfing fad has evolved into skateboarding for most American kids (who have no surf), the *real* sport is still popular in southern California. Many of our schools offer physical education courses in surfing.

If you take a class on surfing, you'll be taught everything you need to know about surfing: how to choose the right equipment; how to use it properly; how to recognize a "surfable" wave; how to catch a wave and ride it as long as possible; and, most important of all, how to get off a wave without wiping out. But you'll never find a course that teaches "How to Build a Wave."

Surfing is the art of riding waves that God builds. God makes the waves; surfers just ride them. No surfer tries to create waves. If the waves aren't there, you just don't surf that day! On the other hand, when surfers see a good wave, they make the most of it, even if that means surfing in the middle of a storm.

A lot of books and conferences on church growth fall into the "How to Build a Wave" category. They try to manufacture the wave of God's Spirit, using gimmicks, programs, or marketing techniques to create growth. *But growth cannot be produced by man!* Only God makes the church grow. Only God can breathe new life into a valley of dry bones. Only God can create waves—waves of revival, waves of growth, and waves of spiritual receptivity.

As Paul pointed out about the church at Corinth, "I planted the seed, Apollos watered it, *but God made it grow"* (1 Cor. 3:6, italics added). Notice the partnership: Paul and Apollos did their part, but God caused the growth. The sovereignty of God is a factor overlooked in almost all current church-growth literature.

Our job as church leaders, like experienced surfers, is to recognize a wave of God's Spirit and ride it. It is not our responsibility to *make* waves but to recognize how God is working in the world and join him in the endeavor.

Watching surfers from the shore makes catching waves look pretty easy. Actually, it is quite difficult and requires great skill and balance. Catching a spiritual wave of growth isn't easy, either. It takes more than desire or even dedication; it takes insight, patience, faith, skill, and most of all, *balance*. Pastoring a growing church, like surfing, may look easy to the uninitiated, but it isn't. It requires a mastery of certain skills.

Today, God is creating wave after wave of people receptive to the Gospel. Due to a plethora of problems in our world, more people seem to be open to the Good News of Christ than at any other time this century. Unfortunately, because our churches haven't been taught the needed skills, we are missing the spiritual waves that could bring revival, health, and explosive growth to our churches.

At Saddleback Church we've never tried to build a wave. That's God's business. But we *have* tried to recognize the waves God was sending our way, and we've learned to catch them. We've learned to use the right equipment to ride those waves, and we've learned the importance of balance. We've also learned to get off dying waves whenever we sensed God wanted to do something new. The amazing thing is this: *The more skilled we become in riding waves of growth, the more God sends!*

In my opinion, we live in the most exciting time in history for the church. Unparalleled opportunities and powerful technologies are available to our congregations. More importantly, we are experiencing an unprecedented movement of God's Spirit in many parts of the world today. More people are coming to Christ now than at any other time in history.

I believe God is sending waves of church growth wherever his people are prepared to ride them. The largest churches in the history of Christianity are in existence at this very moment. Most of them are not in the United States. While the stories of these churches are exciting to hear, I believe that the greatest churches are yet to be built. You may be the very person God chooses to use in that way.

God's Spirit is moving mightily in waves around the world. My prayer at the start of each day goes like this: "Father, I know you're going to do some incredible things in your world today. Please give me the privilege of getting in on some of what you're doing." In other words, church leaders should stop praying, "Lord, bless what I'm doing" and start praying, "Lord, help me to do what you are blessing."

In this book, I'll identify some of the principles and processes God is using to reach this generation for Christ. I would not presume to teach you how to create a wave of the Spirit. It can't be done. But I *can* teach you how to recognize what God is doing, how to cooperate with what God is doing, and how to become more skilled in riding a wave of God's blessing.

The problem with many churches is that they begin with the wrong question. They ask, "What will *make* our church grow?" This is a misunderstanding of the issue. It's like saying, "How can we build a wave?" The question we need to ask instead is, "What is *keeping* our church from growing?" What barriers are blocking the waves God wants to send our way? What obstacles and hindrances are preventing growth from happening?

All living things grow—you don't have to *make* them grow. It's the natural thing for living organisms to do if they are healthy. For example, I don't have to *command* my three children to grow. They naturally grow. As long as I remove hindrances such as poor nutrition or an unsafe environment, their growth will be automatic. If my kids don't grow, something has gone terribly wrong. Lack of growth usually indicates an unhealthy situation, possibly a disease.

> The wrong question: What will *make* our church grow? The right question: What is *keeping* our church from growing?

In the same way, since the church is a living organism, it is natural for it to grow if it is healthy. The church is a body, not a business. It is an organism, not an organization. It is alive. If a church is not growing, it is dying.

When a human body is out of balance we call that disease, which indicates *dis-ease* of the body. Likewise, when the body of Christ becomes unbalanced, disease occurs. Many of these diseases are illustrated and identified in the seven churches of Revelation. Health will occur only when everything is brought back into balance.

The task of church leadership is to discover and remove growth-restricting diseases and barriers so that natural, normal growth can occur. Seventy years ago Roland Allen, in his classic text on missions, called this kind of growth "the *spontaneous* expansion of the church." It is the kind of growth reported in the book of Acts. Is your church spontaneously growing? If that kind of growth is not happening in a church we should ask, "Why not?"

I believe the key issue for churches in the twenty-first century will be church *health*, not church growth. That's what this book is really about. Focusing on growth alone misses the point. When congregations are healthy, they grow the way God intends. Healthy churches don't need gimmicks to grow—they grow naturally.

Paul explained it like this: "It is from him that all the parts of the body are cared for and held together. So it grows in the way God wants it to grow" (Col. 2:19 NCV). Notice that God *wants* his church to grow. If your church is genuinely healthy, you won't have to worry about it growing.

> The key issue for churches in the twenty-first century will be church *health*, not church growth.

Twenty Years of Observing

For the past twenty years, I have been a student of growing churches, regardless of their size. In my travels as a Bible teacher, evangelist, and later as a trainer of pastors, I have visited hundreds of churches around the world. In each instance I made notes on why some were healthy and growing and why others were unhealthy, had plateaued, or were dying. I've talked to thousands of pastors and interviewed hundreds of church leaders, professors, and denominational leaders about what they've observed in churches. Years ago I wrote to the one hundred largest churches in America and spent a year researching their ministries. I've read nearly every book in print on church growth.

I've spent even more time going through the New Testament. I've read it over and over, studying it with "church-growth eyes," searching for principles, patterns, and procedures. The New Testament is the greatest church-growth book ever written. For the things that *really* matter, you can't improve on it. It's the owner's manual for the church.

I've also loved reading church history. It is amusing to me that many concepts currently labeled "innovative" or "contemporary" are not new ideas at all. Everything seems new if you are ignorant of history. Many methods parading under the banner of "change" have been used in the past in a slightly altered form. Some of them have worked and some of them haven't. It is a well-known truth that if we are ignorant of the lessons of the past, we usually end up making the same mistakes as the people did before us.

My greatest source of learning, however, has been watching what God has done in the church I pastor. It gave me an education that no book, no seminar, and no professor could have ever given me. I started Saddleback Valley Community Church in Orange County, California, in 1980, and spent the next fifteen years testing, applying, and refining the principles, processes, and practices in this book. Like a research and development center, we've experimented with all kinds of approaches to reaching, teaching, training, and sending out God's people. Saddleback has served as a laboratory for everything written in this book. The results have been very gratifying and have, I believe, brought glory to God. I am continually humbled by God's power to use ordinary people in extraordinary ways.

I've waited twenty years to write this book because I did not want to write it prematurely. Instead, I've let the concepts percolate and develop and mature. Nothing in this book is theory. The last thing we need is another church-growth theory. What is needed are answers to real problems that have been proven effective in actual church settings.

The principles in this book have been tested over and over, not only at Saddleback Church, but in many other purpose-driven churches of all sizes, shapes, locations, and denominations. While most of the illustrations are from Saddleback, that is only because I am most familiar with our church. It seems that every day I get a letter from another church that has adopted the purpose-driven church paradigm and has been able to ride waves of growth that God has sent their way.

To Pastors with Love

This book is written for anyone interested in helping his or her church grow, but because I am a pastor, my writing style is naturally slanted from a pastor's perspective to other pastors. I come from a long line of pastors. My great-grandfather was converted through Charles Spurgeon's historic ministry in London and came to the United States as a pioneer circuit-riding pastor.

Both my father and my father-in-law have been pastors. Both recently celebrated their fiftieth anniversaries in ministry. My sister is married to a pastor, and I spent part of my childhood growing up on a seminary campus where my father served on staff. So I have a deep love for pastors. I love being around them. I hurt with them when they hurt. I believe they are the most underrated leaders in our society.

> Pastors are the most strategic change agents to deal with the problems in our society.

My greatest admiration is for the thousands of *bivocational* pastors who support themselves with a second job in order to shepherd churches that are too small to provide a full-time salary. They are the heroes of the faith, in my view. They will receive great honor in heaven. Because I have been fortunate to afford training and experiences unavailable to them, I feel an obligation to share what I have learned with them in this book.

I also believe that pastors are the most strategic change agents to deal with the problems society faces. Even many politicians are coming to the conclusion that spiritual revival is our only solution. Recently I read this statement from former Cabinet member William Bennett in *American Enterprise* magazine: "The most serious problems afflicting our society today are manifestly moral, behavioral, and spiritual, and therefore are remarkably resistant to government cures." Does it seem ironic to you that at a time when politicians are saying we need a *spiritual* solution many Christians are acting like politics is the solution? While there is no doubt that the moral decline in our society has produced a battlefield, it also has given us an incredible mission field! We must remember that Christ also died for those on the other side of the cultural war.

It is a great privilege and an awesome responsibility to be a pastor of a local church. If I didn't believe pastors have the best chance of making a difference in our world, I'd be doing something else; I have no intention of wasting my life. Today the pastoral ministry is a hundred times more complex than it was just a generation ago. Even in the best circumstances, ministry is incredibly difficult. But there are also many more resources to help you if you avail yourself of them. The key is to never stop learning.

If you are a pastor, my prayer is that this book will encourage you. I hope it will be both instructional *and* inspirational. The books that have helped me most have blended facts and fire. My desire is that you'll grasp not only the principles I share, but also the passion I feel about God's purposes for his church.

I love the church of Jesus Christ with all my heart. Despite all its faults (due to *our* sinfulness) it is still the most magnificent concept ever created. It has been God's chosen instrument of blessing for two thousand years. It has survived persistent abuse, horrifying persecution, and widespread neglect. Parachurch organizations and other Christian groups come and go, but the church will last for eternity. It is worth giving our lives for and it deserves our best.

"I've Heard This Before!"

As you read through this book I'm sure you'll come across concepts and think, *I've heard this before.* I hope you have! This book contains many of the principles shared in the Purpose-Driven Church Seminar, which I've taught to over 22,000 pastors in the past fifteen years. In addition, church leaders from forty-two different countries and sixty different denominations have ordered tapes of the seminar, so some of the concepts are now well known.

My bookshelves contain more than a dozen books written by people I've trained who have put my ideas in print before I did. That doesn't matter to me. We're all on the same team. As long as pastors are helped, I'm pleased by it. Honestly, one of the reasons I waited twenty years to write this book is because I was too busy *doing* it!

Over one hundred doctoral theses have been written on the growth of Saddleback Church. We've been dissected, scrutinized, analyzed, and summarized by minds far better endowed than mine. "Hasn't enough been written already?" you may ask. "Why *another* book?" What I hope to offer in this book is the insider's perspective. What outsiders notice about a growing church rarely explains the real causes of growth.

You've heard that it is "wise to learn from experience." But it is wiser yet to learn from the experiences of others. It is less painful too! Life is too short to learn everything by personal experience. You can save yourself a lot of time and energy by gleaning from others the lessons they learned the hard way. That's the purpose of books like this one. If I can spare you the pain we experienced while learning these principles by trial and error, I'll be pleased.

When a surfer wipes out because he didn't ride a wave correctly, he doesn't give up surfing. He paddles back out into the ocean to wait for the next big wave God sends in. One thing I've observed about successful surfers: *They are persistent.*

You may have experienced a few "wipeouts" in your ministry. I certainly have. You may have missed a few waves. That doesn't mean you should quit. The ocean hasn't dried up. On the contrary, at this very moment God is creating in the world the best waves I've ever seen. It is my hope, as a fellow surfer, to share a few tips on how to ride what God is doing in his world. Let's go catch a wave.

Part One
Seeing the Big Picture

1

The Saddleback Story

One generation will commend your works
to another; they will tell of your mighty acts.

Psalm 145:4

Praise the greatness of the LORD,
who loves to see his servants do well.

Psalm 35:27 (NCV)

In November 1973, a buddy and I skipped out on our college classes and drove 350 miles to hear Dr. W. A. Criswell speak at the Jack Tar Hotel in San Francisco. Criswell was the renowned pastor of the largest Baptist church in the world, the First Baptist Church of Dallas, Texas. For me, as a young Southern Baptist, the opportunity to hear Criswell in person was the equivalent of a Catholic getting to hear the pope. I was determined to hear this living legend.

I had felt God's call to ministry three years earlier and had begun speaking as a youth evangelist while still in high school. Although I was just nineteen years old, I'd already preached revival meetings in about fifty churches. I had no doubt that God had called me to ministry, but I was unsure if God wanted me to become a pastor.

I believe W. A. Criswell is the greatest American pastor of the twentieth century. He pastored at First Baptist for fifty years, wrote fifty-three books, and developed the most widely copied church model of this century. Not only was he a powerful preacher and leader, he was an organizational genius. Most people think of tradition when they think of Criswell, but actually his ministry was incredibly innovative. It only became known as traditional after everyone copied him!

We often hear today about celebrity pastors whose stars flame bright for a few years and then fizzle out. It's easy to make an impressive start. But Criswell's ministry lasted half a century in *one* church! It was no flash in the pan. It withstood the test of time. To me that is genuine success: *loving and leading consistently and ending well*. Ministry is a marathon. It's not how you start out that matters but how you end. So, how do you make it to the end? The Bible says, "Love never fails" (1 Cor. 13:8). If you minister out of love you can never be considered a failure.

> Ministry is a marathon. It's not how you start that matters but how you end.

As I listened to this great man of God preach, God spoke personally to me and made it very clear that he was calling me to be a pastor. Then and there, I promised God I'd give my entire life to pastoring a single church if that was his will for me.

After the service, my buddy and I stood in line to shake hands with Dr. Criswell. When my turn finally arrived, something unexpected happened. Criswell looked at me with kind, loving eyes and said, quite emphatically, "Young man, I feel led to lay hands on you and pray for you!" Without delay, he placed his hands on my head and prayed these words that I will never forget: "Father, I ask that you give this young preacher a double portion of your Spirit. May the church he pastors grow to twice the size of the Dallas church. Bless him greatly, O Lord."

As I walked away with tears in my eyes, I said to my friend Danny, "Did he pray what I think he prayed?" "He sure did," said Danny, also with wet eyes. I could not possibly imagine that God could ever use me like Dr. Criswell had prayed, but that holy experience confirmed in my heart that God had called me to pastor a local church.

The Story Behind the Methods

Every theology has a context. You won't understand Luther's theology without understanding Luther's life and how God was sovereignly working in the world at that time. Likewise, you can't fully appreciate Calvin's theology without understanding the circumstances in which he forged his beliefs.

In the same way, every *methodology* has a story behind it. Many people look at the so-called "megachurches" and assume those churches have always been big. They forget that every large church started off as a small church. And no church becomes large without struggling through years of problems, setbacks, and failures. For instance, Saddleback met for fifteen years before being able to build our first building. This one factor alone helped shape our strategy of reaching, retaining, and growing believers in Christ. It kept our focus on people and created a church culture very open to change.

To understand many of the methods in this book, you need to understand the context in which they were developed. Otherwise you might be tempted to copy things we did without considering the context. *Please do not do this!* Instead, look beneath the methods to see the transferable principles on which they are based. I'll identify the principles, but first you need to know a little of Saddleback's history.

Very little of Saddleback's ministry was preplanned. I didn't have any long-range strategy before I started the church. I simply knew God had called me to plant a new church built on the five New Testament purposes, and I had a bag of ideas I wanted to try out. Each innovation we've developed was just *a response* to the circumstances in which we found ourselves. I didn't plan them in advance. Most people think of "vision" as the ability to see the future. But in today's rapidly changing world, vision is also the ability to accurately assess current changes and take advantage of them. Vision is being alert to opportunities.

> Vision is the ability to see the opportunities within your current circumstances.

Because Saddleback is a young church and I am the founding pastor, we've been able to experiment with far more ideas than the average church—mostly due to the fact that we didn't have decades of tradition to deal with. (However we had many *other* problems that older churches don't have!) In the early years we had nothing to lose, so we tried out all kinds of ideas. Some of our ideas were spectacular failures. And I wish I could claim that all our successes happened just the way we planned them—but it would be untrue. I'm not that smart. Most of our successes have been the result of trial and error and some of our discoveries were purely accidental.

One of my favorite movies is *Raiders of the Lost Ark.* At one cliff-hanging point in the story someone asks Indiana Jones, "What are we going to do now?" Jones replies, "How do I know? I'm making it up as we go along!" I have felt like that many, many times as pastor at Saddleback. We'd make up something and, if it worked, we'd pretend as though we'd planned it all along!

Mark Twain once said dryly, "I knew a man who grabbed a cat by the tail and learned forty percent more about cats than the man who didn't." We've been grabbing the cat by the tail since the beginning at Saddleback Church—and we have the cuts and scars to prove it.

The truth is, we've tried more things that *didn't* work at Saddleback than did. We've never been afraid of failure; we just call everything an "experiment." I could fill another book with stories of our failures and call it *1000 Ways to NOT Grow a Church*!

My Search for Principles

In 1974, I served as a student missionary to Japan. I lived with a Southern Baptist missionary couple in their home in Nagasaki. One day, while rummaging through the missionary's library, I picked up an old copy of *HIS*, a Christian student magazine published by InterVarsity Christian Fellowship.

As I thumbed through its pages, a picture of a fascinating older man with a goatee and sparkling eyes caught my attention. The article's subtitle said something like "Why Is This Man Dangerous?" As I sat there and read the article on Donald McGavran, I had no idea that it would dramatically impact the direction of my ministry as much as my encounter with Criswell had.

The article described how McGavran, a missionary born in India, had spent his ministry studying what makes churches grow. His years of research ultimately led him to write *The Bridges of God* in 1955 and a dozen more books on growing churches that are considered classics today.

Just as God used W. A. Criswell to sharpen the focus of my life mission from ministry in general to being a pastor, God used the writings of Donald McGavran to sharpen my focus from pastoring an already established church to planting the church that I would pastor. As Paul declared in Romans 15:20, "It has always been my ambition to preach the gospel where Christ was not known, so that I would not be building on someone else's foundation."

McGavran brilliantly challenged the conventional wisdom of his day about what made churches grow. With a biblical basis and simple but passionate logic, McGavran pointed out that God wants his church to grow; he wants his lost sheep found!

The issues raised by McGavran seemed especially relevant to me as I observed the painfully slow growth of churches in Japan. I made a list of eight questions that I wanted to find the answers to:

- How much of what churches do is really biblical?
- How much of what we do is just cultural?
- Why do some churches grow and others die on the vine?
- What causes a growing church to stop growing, plateau, and then decline?
- Are there common factors found in every growing church?
- Are there principles that will work in every culture?
- What are the barriers to growth?
- What are the conventional myths about growing churches that aren't true anymore (or never were)?

The day I read the McGavran article, I felt God directing me to invest the rest of my life discovering the principles—biblical, cultural, and leadership principles—that produce healthy, growing churches. It was the beginning of a lifelong study.

In 1979, while finishing my final year at Southwestern Baptist Seminary in Fort Worth, Texas, I decided to do an independent study of the one hundred largest churches in the United States at that time. First, I had to identify these churches, which was no small task. I was working as a grader for Dr. Roy Fish, professor of evangelism at Southwestern Seminary. Roy, also my mentor and friend, helped me identify many of these churches. Others I found by searching through denominational annuals and Christian magazines.

> To design the right strategy you must ask the right questions.

I then wrote to each of these churches and asked a series of questions I had prepared. Although I discovered that large, growing churches differ widely in strategy, structure, and style, there were some common denominators. My study confirmed what I already knew from Criswell's ministry: Healthy, large churches are led by pastors who have been there a long time. I found dozens of examples. A long pastorate does not *guarantee* a church will grow, but changing pastors every few years guarantees a church *won't* grow.

> Most healthy, large churches are led by a pastor who has been there a long time.

Can you imagine what the kids would be like in a family where they got a new daddy every two or three years? They would most likely have serious emotional problems. In the same way, the longevity of the leadership is a critical factor for the health and growth of a church family. Long pastorates make deep, trusting, and caring relationships possible. Without those kinds of relationships, a pastor won't accomplish much of lasting value.

Churches that rotate pastors every few years will never experience consistent growth. I believe this is one reason for the decline of some denominations. By intentionally limiting the tenure of pastors in a local congregation, they create "lame duck" ministers. Few people want to follow a leader who isn't going to be around a year from now. The pastor may want to start all sorts of new projects, but the members will be reticent because they will be the ones having to live with the consequences long after the pastor has been moved to another church.

Knowing the importance of longevity in growing a healthy church I prayed, "Father, I'm willing to go anyplace in the world you want to send me. But I ask for the privilege of investing my entire life in just one location. I don't care where you put me, but I'd like to stay wherever it is for the rest of my life."

Where in the World?

After that prayer, I tacked up a map of the world on our living room wall at home and began praying with my wife, Kay, for guidance about where we'd locate after seminary. This is the first step anyone should take in planting a new church: Pray for guidance. Proverbs 28:26 (LB) says, "A man is a fool to trust himself! But those who use God's wisdom are safe." Before anything else, you must first get God's perspective on your situation.

My wife and I originally thought that God was calling us to be missionaries overseas. Since I'd already served as a student missionary to Japan, we focused especially on countries in Asia. But as we prayed for guidance for about six months, God impressed upon us that we were not to serve overseas. Instead, we were to plant a new church in a major metropolitan area of the United States.

> A church's health is measured by its *sending* capacity, not its *seating* capacity.

Instead of becoming missionaries ourselves, Kay and I sensed God's leading to establish a *missionary-sending* church. God would use us to enlist and train others in America to become overseas missionaries. This was a disappointment to me, but looking back, I now see the wisdom of God's plan. Saddleback Church has already made a greater impact through the many missionaries we've sent out than if I'd gone myself.

I believe that you measure the health or strength of a church by its *sending* capacity rather than its *seating* capacity. Churches are in the sending business. One of the questions we must ask in evaluating a church's health is, "How many people are being mobilized for the Great Commission?"

This conviction, one I've held from Saddleback's beginning, led me to design the process described in this book for turning members into ministers and missionaries.

Focusing on America

Once we realized we wouldn't be serving overseas, Kay and I began to pray about where we'd begin a new church in the United States. Since I had no sponsor, it could be anywhere. So I once again tacked up a map on our living room wall (this time, a map of the United States) and circled every major metropolitan area outside of the South.

My background has been Southern Baptist for four generations, and I have relatives all across the South. But my thinking was that I would go someplace where most of my seminary buddies were unwilling to go. I prayed about beginning a church in Detroit, New York, Philadelphia, Chicago, Albuquerque, Phoenix, and Denver. Then I discovered that the three most unchurched states in America were Washington, Oregon, and California. So I narrowed my focus to four areas on the West Coast: Seattle, San Francisco, San Diego, and Orange County. These four metropolitan areas were all growing in the late 1970s, and that caught my attention.

During the summer of 1979, I practically lived in university libraries doing research on the United States census data and other demographic studies on these four areas. Proverbs 13:16 says, "Every prudent man acts out of knowledge." To me that meant I should find out all I could about an area before I committed to invest the rest of my life there. Before making any major decision it is important to ask, "What do I need to know first?"

Proverbs 18:13 (LB) says, "What a shame—yes, how stupid!—to decide before knowing the facts!" The reason many new churches fail is because they are started with uneducated enthusiasm. It takes more than enthusiasm to start a church; it takes wisdom. Having faith does not mean ignoring the facts about the community you have chosen.

I was twenty-five years old, five months away from seminary graduation, and Kay was nine months pregnant with our first child. I'd call her from the library several times each day to see if she'd started labor yet.

One afternoon I discovered that the Saddleback Valley, in Orange County, southern California, was the fastest-growing area in the fastest-growing county in the United States during the decade of the 1970s. This fact grabbed me by the throat and made my heart start racing. I knew that wherever new communities were being started at such a fast pace there would also be a need for new churches.

As I sat there in the dusty, dimly lit basement of that university library, I heard God speak clearly to me: "That's where I want you to plant a church!" My whole body began to tingle with excitement, and tears welled up in my eyes. I had heard from God. It didn't matter that I had no money, no members, and had never even seen the place. From that moment on, our destination was a settled issue. God had shown me where he was going to make some waves, and I was going to have the ride of a lifetime.

The next thing I did was find out the name of the Southern Baptist Director of Missions (District Superintendent) for Orange County, California. His name was Herman Wooten. I wrote him the following letter: "My name is Rick Warren. I am a seminary student in Texas. I am planning to move to south Orange County and start a church. I'm not asking for money or support from you; I just want to know what you think about that area. Does it need new churches?"

In the providence of God, an amazing thing happened. Although we'd never met, Herman Wooten had somehow heard about me and my desire to plant a new church after graduating. At the same time I was writing to him, he was writing to me this letter: "Dear Mr. Warren, I have heard that you may be interested in starting a new church in California after seminary. Have you ever considered coming to the Saddleback Valley in south Orange County?" Our letters crossed in the mail! When I opened the mailbox two days later and saw a letter from the same man I'd just written to, I began to cry. Kay and I both knew God was up to something.

Two months later, in October, I flew to Orange County and spent ten days seeing the area for the first time. During the day I talked to anyone I could. I consulted realtors, chamber of commerce people, bankers, county planning officials, residents, and other pastors in the area. I took copious notes on everything I learned. I was claiming the promise of Proverbs 20:18 (TEV), which says, "Get good advice and you will succeed."

At night I poured over local maps and brochures, spreading them out on the living-room floor of Dr. Fred Fisher, a retired Golden Gate Seminary professor who had invited me to stay in his home in the north part of Orange County. As I studied the materials I collected, I memorized the names of all the major streets in the Saddleback Valley.

After a week I flew Kay out to see the area for the first time. I have always relied on my wife's spiritual discernment to confirm God's leading in my life. If Kay had felt any reluctance toward moving, I would have taken that as a warning light from God. Happily, Kay's response was, "I'm scared to death, but I believe this is God's will, and I believe in you. Let's go for it." As Paul said in Romans 8:31, "If God is for us, who can be against us?" We climbed up on the highest hill we could find, and, looking over the Saddleback Valley filled with thousands of homes, committed to investing our lives in building the Saddleback Valley Community Church.

California, Here We Come

I graduated from seminary that December. In the final days of 1979, Kay and I packed what little we owned in a U-Haul truck and moved from Texas to southern California. Our furniture had been handed down from one newlywed couple to another. We were the fifth couple to have it. It was pretty pathetic looking stuff, but it was all we had. As we packed, it seemed implausible that this poor young couple was moving to one of the wealthiest communities in America.

We arrived in southern California full of hope. We had a new decade before us, a new ministry, a four-month-old baby, and God's promise to bless us. But we also arrived with no money, no church building, no members, and no home. We did not know a single person living in the Saddleback Valley. It was the greatest step of faith we had ever taken up to that time.

We made it to Orange County on a Friday afternoon, just in time to catch an infamous southern California traffic jam. I've never understood why they call the slowest traffic the rush hour! We inched along the freeway at a snail's pace, hungry and tired, with a crying infant.

Since I had grown up in a rural town of less than five hundred residents, I was completely unprepared for traffic like this. As I gazed out over miles and miles of cars at a complete standstill in freeway traffic I thought, *What in the world have I gotten myself into? God, you chose the wrong guy for this assignment! I think I've made a big mistake.*

Finally, at 5 P.M. we arrived at the Saddleback Valley. I pulled off the freeway and stopped at the first real estate office I could find. I walked in and introduced myself to the first realtor I met. His name was Don Dale. I said with a big smile, "My name is Rick Warren. I'm here to start a church. I need a place to live, but I don't have any money." Don grinned and laughed out loud. I laughed too. I had no idea what would happen next. Don said,

"Well, let's see what we can do." Within two hours Don found us a condo to rent, got us the first month's rent for free, and agreed to become the first member of Saddleback Church! God does provide.

While driving to the condo, I asked Don if he attended church anywhere. He said he didn't. I replied, "Great! You're my first member!" And that is exactly what happened. I began Saddleback Church with that realtor's family and mine. Two weeks later we held our first Bible study in our condo with seven people present.

After we moved on faith, it was exciting to see the financial support we needed begin to materialize. Pastor John Jackson led the Crescent Baptist Church in Anaheim, California, to become our official sponsoring church and provide six hundred dollars a month in financial support. Then, the First Baptist Church of Lufkin, Texas, and the First Baptist Church of Norwalk, California, both committed two hundred dollars a month toward our fledgling congregation.

One morning I received a phone call from a man I'd never met who offered to pay our rent for two months. He said he'd heard about the new church and wanted to help out. Another time, with a nearly empty checking account, Kay and I went scouting garage sales to buy nursery equipment for the first service. We found what we needed and wrote out a check, knowing we were spending our last food money. When we got home, I opened the mailbox and found a check from a woman in Texas who had heard me speak one time and somehow traced us to California. The check was the amount we'd just spent on nursery equipment: $37.50.

> God always uses imperfect people in imperfect situations to accomplish his will.

I would have preferred to have had the new church financially underwritten *before* we moved to California, but it didn't work out that way. Instead, we moved on faith. My sense of calling was so strong I was eager to get started. I love the Living Bible paraphrase of Ecclesiastes 11:4: "If you wait for perfect conditions, you will never get anything done." If you insist on solving all the problems before you make a decision, you'll never know the thrill of living by faith. God always uses imperfect people in imperfect situations to accomplish his will.

> Wherever God guides, he provides.

As we saw God confirm our decision to begin the church in many, many ways in those early days, we learned an important lesson: *Wherever God guides, he provides.* If you are a church planter, underline that previous sentence. It will be a great source of comfort and strength in your difficult days. Whatever he calls us to do, he will enable and equip us to do. God is faithful! He keeps his promises.

What Kind of Church Would We Be?

I had not been in southern California very long before I realized it was an area that already had many strong, Bible-believing churches. Some of the best-known pastors in America ministered within driving distance of our new church. On any Sunday you could go hear Chuck Swindoll, Chuck Smith, Robert Schuller, John MacArthur, E. V. Hill, John Wimber, Jack Hayford, Lloyd Ogilvie, Charles Blake, Greg Laurie, Ray Ortlund, or John Huffman. If you timed your arrival right, you could hear two or three of these guys on the same Sunday morning. And most of them could be heard on the radio or TV in southern California.

In addition, there were at least two dozen solid Bible-teaching churches in the Saddleback Valley when I arrived. I quickly concluded that all of the Christians in the area were already happily involved in a good church or at least had plenty of options.

I decided that we would make no effort at all to attract Christians from other churches to Saddleback. We would not even borrow workers from other area churches to start Saddleback. Since I felt called to reach unbelievers, I determined to *begin* with unbelievers, rather than with a core of committed Christians. This was not the way all the books on church starting said to do it, but I felt certain that it was what God was calling us to do. Our focus would be limited to reaching the unchurched for Christ, people who for one reason or another did not attend any existing church.

We've never encouraged other believers to transfer their membership to our church; in fact, we have openly discouraged it. We don't want transfer growth. In every membership class we say, "If you are coming to Saddleback from another church, you need to understand up front that this church was not designed for you. It is geared toward reaching the unchurched who do not attend anywhere. If you are transferring from another church you are welcome here only if you are willing to serve and minister. If all you intend to do is attend services, we'd rather save your seat for someone who is an unbeliever. There are plenty of good Bible-teaching churches in this area that we can recommend to you."

This position may sound harsh, but I believe we are following the example of Jesus. He defined his ministry target by saying, "It is not the healthy who need a doctor, but the sick. I have not come to call the righteous, but sinners" (Mark 2:17). At Saddleback we continually remind ourselves of this statement. It has helped us stay true to the original focus of our church: to bring the unchurched, irreligious people of our community to Christ.

In order to understand the mind-set of unchurched southern Californians, I spent the first twelve weeks after moving to the Saddleback Valley going door-to-door talking to people. Even though I knew what these people *really* needed most was a relationship to Christ, I wanted to listen first to what *they* thought their most pressing needs were. That's not marketing; it's just being polite.

I've learned that most people can't hear until they've first been heard. People don't care how much we know until they know how much we care. Intelligent, caring conversation opens the door for evangelism with nonbelievers faster than anything else I've used. It is *not* the church's task to give people whatever they want or even need. But the fastest way to build a bridge to the unchurched is to express interest in them and show that you understand the problems they are facing. Felt needs, whether real or imaginary, are a starting point for expressing love to people.

I didn't know enough to call my survey of the community a "marketing" study. To me, it was just a matter of meeting the people I intended to reach. Those who had been coming to our small Bible study helped me take the community survey. The irony was this: Many of those who came to our home Bible study and helped me survey the unchurched in our community were unbelievers themselves.

Setting the Date: E-DAY!

Next, we made the decision to begin Sunday services on Easter Sunday, which was a mere twelve weeks from the day Kay and I had moved to Orange County. I had no intention of staying in the home Bible study phase for longer than three months; I wanted to start public worship services as soon as possible. I also didn't want to miss the opportunity to begin the church on Easter Sunday.

I reasoned that if an unchurched family decided to attend just one service a year it would most likely be Easter Sunday. It was the ideal day to start a service designed to attract the unchurched. I realized that they might not come back the next week, but at least I'd have a crowd for the first service—and I'd get some names for a mailing list.

During the weeks prior to Easter, our home Bible study on Friday nights grew to about fifteen people. Each week I'd teach a Bible study, and then we'd work on preparations for our first public service. We also discussed our findings from our weekly community survey. After about eight weeks I summarized what we'd learned about the unchurched and their hang-ups about church in a philosophy of ministry statement. It became the blueprint for our evangelism strategy.

Next, I wrote an open letter to the unchurched of the community based on what we'd learned. I knew nothing about direct mail, marketing, or advertising. I just figured that an open letter to the community might be the fastest way to get the word out about our new church. I also knew that a large percentage of the Saddleback Valley lived behind "gated" communities and there was no way I'd be able to make cold-call visits to those homes.

I wrote and rewrote that letter about a dozen times. I kept thinking, *What would I say if I had one chance to speak to all of the unchurched of this community? How can I say it in a way that disarms their prejudices and objections to attending church?*

The first sentence of that letter clearly stated our focus and position. It said: "At last! A new church for those who've given up on traditional church services." It went on to explain the kind of church we were starting. We hand-addressed and hand-stamped 15,000 letters and mailed them out ten days before Easter. I guessed that if we could get a 1 percent response from the letter, then 150 people might show up on Easter.

Our First Service

I knew that if our church was going to attract and win the unchurched, it was going to take a different kind of service than

I grew up with. What *style* of worship would be the best witness to unbelievers? We spent a lot of time thinking through every element of the service. We even planned a "dress rehearsal" for our Easter service.

I said to the fifteen people attending our home Bible study group: "Next Sunday we'll meet at the high school and practice our service. We'll practice singing the songs, I'll preach like there's a crowd of 150 people, and we'll work out all the bugs in the order of service. This will insure that when all the visitors show up next week it will at least *appear* that we know what we're doing."

When Palm Sunday arrived, we expected only the fifteen Bible study attenders to show up for our "trial run" service. But God had other plans. The letter we had mailed out to 15,000 homes was delivered early to some of them. We hadn't expected the letter to arrive in homes until a few days before Easter. Due to an efficient post office, sixty people showed up at the dress rehearsal and five of them gave their lives to Christ that day!

At that trial run service I outlined the vision I believed God had given me for Saddleback Church. The first task of leadership is to define the mission, so I tried to paint, in attractive terms, the picture as clearly as I saw it. Over the years we've returned again and again to that vision statement for midcourse corrections. Our vision has never really focused on getting big or erecting buildings; instead, our vision has been to produce disciples of Jesus Christ.

I remember how scared I felt after sharing the vision at the dress rehearsal service. I was overwhelmed with the fear of failure. *What if it doesn't happen? Is this vision really from God, or is it just a wild dream of an idealistic twenty-six-year-old?* It was one thing to privately dream of what I expected God to do; it was another matter to publicly state that dream. In my mind, I had now passed the point of no return. In spite of my

The Saddleback Vision

From Pastor Rick's first sermon, March 30, 1980

It is the dream of a place where the hurting, the depressed, the frustrated, and the confused can find love, acceptance, help, hope, forgiveness, guidance, and encouragement.

It is the dream of sharing the Good News of Jesus Christ with the hundreds of thousands of residents in south Orange County.

It is the dream of welcoming 20,000 members into the fellowship of our church family—loving, learning, laughing, and living in harmony together.

It is the dream of developing people to spiritual maturity through Bible studies, small groups, seminars, retreats, and a Bible school for our members.

It is the dream of equipping every believer for a significant ministry by helping them discover the gifts and talents God gave them.

It is the dream of sending out hundreds of career missionaries and church workers all around the world, and empowering every member for a personal life mission in the world. It is the dream of sending our members by the thousands on short-term mission projects to every continent. It is the dream of starting at least one new daughter church every year.

It is the dream of at least fifty acres of land, on which will be built a regional church for south Orange County—with beautiful, yet simple, facilities including a worship center seating thousands, a counseling and prayer center, classrooms for Bible studies and training lay ministers, and a recreation area. All of this will be designed to minister to the total person—spiritually, emotionally, physically, and socially—and set in a peaceful, inspiring garden landscape.

I stand before you today and state in confident assurance that these dreams will become reality. Why? Because they are inspired by God!

fears, I now had to move full speed ahead. Convinced that my dream would bring glory to God, I decided to never look back.

Saddleback Church held its first public service the following Sunday, Easter, April 6, 1980. Two hundred five people showed up to attend. *We had caught a wave.* I will never forget the feeling of watching all those people I'd never seen before walking up the sidewalk to the Laguna Hills High School Theater. With a mixture of excitement, fear, and awe I said to Kay, "This is really going to work!"

A mother holding her newborn baby for the first time could not have felt more joy. The birth of a church was taking place. Yet I was also humbled by the awesome responsibility I sensed that God was assigning to me that day.

It was an unusual assembly for a beginning of a new church. There weren't more than about a dozen believers at that first service. Instead, it was filled with unchurched southern Californians. We had hit our target right in the bull's-eye.

Having so many unchurched people at the service actually made it quite comical. When I asked people to open their Bibles, nobody had one. When we tried to sing some songs, no one sang because they didn't know the tunes. When I said, "Let's pray," some of the people just looked around. I felt as if I was standing before a Kiwanis or Rotary meeting!

But, to my amazement, the people kept coming back week after week. Each time a few more would commit their lives to Christ. By the tenth week after we began services, eighty-two of the unchurched people who had attended at Easter had given their lives to Christ. We were riding the wave of God's Spirit as best we could. Our preparation had paid off. A congregation was beginning to form.

Our first membership class drew twenty people. Eighteen of them were unbelievers, so I had to begin by teaching the most elementary truths of the Christian life. By the end of the six-week class, all eighteen unbelievers had accepted Christ, were baptized, and were welcomed into membership.

Baptisms have always been unique at Saddleback. We've used pools, the Pacific Ocean, and other churches' baptistries, but most frequently we've used the spas and hot tubs that are standard equipment in many Orange County homes. Thousands have been baptized in what we fondly refer to as "Jacuzzis for Jesus."

Those being baptized are encouraged to invite as many of their unbelieving friends as possible to witness their baptism. Some have even sent out embossed invitations. Our monthly baptisms are always big events. One time we baptized 367 people on a single morning. My skin was wrinkled by the time the other pastors and I climbed out of the heavily chlorinated high school pool. I remember joking that, if we weren't Baptists, I could have just sprayed everyone with a fire hose!

Growing Pains

Saddleback has experienced continuous growing pains throughout its brief history. To accommodate our continuous growth we used seventy-nine different facilities in the first fifteen years of Saddleback's history. Each time we'd outgrow a building, we'd move that program or service somewhere else. We often said that Saddleback was the church you could attend—if you could find us. We would joke that this was the way we attracted only really smart people.

> Saddleback used seventy-nine different locations to meet in during its first fifteen years.

We used four different high schools, numerous elementary schools, bank buildings, recreation centers, theaters, community centers, restaurants, large homes, professional office buildings, and stadiums, until finally we erected a 2,300-seat high-tech tent. We were filling the tent for four services each weekend before we built our first building. I feel that most churches build too soon and too small. The shoe must never tell the foot how big it can grow.

I'm often asked, "How big can a church grow without a building?" The answer is, "I don't know!" Saddleback met for fifteen years and grew to 10,000 attenders without our own building, so I know it's possible to grow to at least 10,000! A building, or lack of a building, should never be allowed to become a barrier to a wave of growth. People are far more important than property.

During Saddleback's first fifteen years, over 7,000 people gave their lives to Christ through our evangelism efforts. If you found yourself up to your neck in baby Christians, what would *you* do? Our sanity and survival depended upon developing a workable process to turn seekers into saints, turn consumers into contributors, turn members into ministers, and turn an audience into an army. Believe me, it is an incredibly difficult task to lead people from self-centered consumerism to being servant-hearted Christians. It is not a task for fainthearted ministers or those who don't like to get their religious robes wrinkled. But it *is* what the Great Commission is all about and it has been the driving force behind all that has happened so far at Saddleback.

2

Myths About Growing Churches

*Get the facts at any price, and hold on
tightly to all the good sense you can get.*

Proverbs 23:23 (LB)

Children growing up in America learn many myths: Santa
Claus brings presents via reindeer; the tooth fairy exchanges
money for teeth; the Easter Bunny hides candy and eggs;
when the groundhog sees his shadow, we're in for more bad
weather; the moon is made of Swiss cheese. Some of these
myths are harmless, but others can cause great harm.

I have always loved the passages in the gospels where Jesus
challenged the popular myths, or "conventional wisdom," of his
day. The New Testament records twenty times where Jesus used
the phrase "You have heard it said. . . . but I say to you. . . ." I
once preached a series of messages based on these instances
called "Myths That Make Us Miserable." Only when we base our
lives on the bedrock of God's Word will we know "the truth
that sets us free."

Many myths about large, growing churches are circulated
among pastors and church leaders. While many people have
heard about the so-called *megachurches* (a designation I
dislike), few outside these churches know what is actually happening inside them. Inaccurate assumptions are made, some-

times out of envy, sometimes out of fear, and sometimes due to ignorance.

If you are serious about seeing your own church grow, you must be willing to challenge much of the conventional wisdom about large and growing churches that you hear today.

Myth #1: The Only Thing That Large Churches Care About Is Attendance

The truth is, you *won't* grow large if that is all you care about. In the entire history of Saddleback's growth we've only set two attendance goals—and both were in our first year. We do not focus on attendance; we focus on assimilating all the people God brings to us.

Attendance campaigns and advertising may bring people to your church once. But they will not come back unless your church delivers the goods. To maintain consistent growth, you must offer people something they cannot get anywhere else.

If you are preaching the positive, life-changing Good News of Christ, if your members are excited by what God is doing in your church, if you are providing a service where they can bring unsaved friends without embarrassment, and if you have a plan to build, train, and send out those you win to Christ, attendance will be the least of your problems. People flock to that kind of church. It's happening all around the world.

> The church must offer people something they cannot get anywhere else.

Healthy, lasting church growth is multidimensional. My definition of genuine church growth has five facets. Every church needs to grow *warmer* through fellowship, *deeper* through discipleship, *stronger* through worship, *broader* through ministry, and *larger* through evangelism.

In Acts 2:42–47, these five facets of growth are described in the first church at Jerusalem. The first Christians fellowshiped, edified each other, worshiped, ministered, and evangelized. As a result, verse 47 says, "And the Lord added to their number daily those who were being saved." Note a couple of things about this verse. First, God added the growth (his part) when the church did its part (fulfill the five purposes). Second, the growth was daily, which means, at a minimum, this healthy church had 365 conversions a year! What if this was the evangelistic standard every church had to meet in order to call itself a healthy "New Testament" church? How many churches do you think would qualify?

Church growth is the natural result of church health. Church health can only occur when our message is *biblical* and our mission is *balanced*. Each of the five New Testament purposes of the church must be in equilibrium with the others for health to occur. Balance in a church does not occur naturally; in fact, we must continually correct imbalance. It is human nature to overemphasize the aspect of the church we feel most passionate about. Intentionally setting up a strategy and a structure

Five Dimensions of Church Growth

Churches grow *warmer* through fellowship.

Churches grow *deeper* through discipleship.

Churches grow *stronger* through worship.

Churches grow *broader* through ministry.

Churches grow *larger* through evangelism.

to force ourselves to give equal attention to each purpose is what being a purpose-driven church is all about.

Myth #2: All Large Churches Grow at the Expense of Smaller Churches

Some large churches have grown at the expense of smaller churches, but that certainly is not true in Saddleback's case. The Saddleback statistic I'm most pleased about is the fact that 80 percent of our members found Christ and were baptized at Saddleback. We have not grown at the expense of other churches. At this writing we have about 5,000 adult members, 4,000 of whom were converted and baptized at Saddleback. Our growth has been by conversion, not by transferring Christians from other churches.

Transferring Christians from one church to another is not what Jesus had in mind when he gave us the Great Commission. God called us to be fishers of men, not to swap fish between aquariums. A church that grows larger only by transfers from other churches is not experiencing genuine growth—it is only reshuffling the card deck.

Myth #3: You Must Choose Between *Quality* and *Quantity* in Your Church

This is, unfortunately, a widely promoted myth that simply isn't true. Part of the problem is that no one ever defines what they mean by the terms *quality* and *quantity*. Let me give you my definitions.

Quality refers to the *kind* of disciples a church is producing. Are people being genuinely transformed into the likeness of Christ? Are believers grounded in the Word? Are they maturing in Christ? Are they using their talents in service and ministry? Are they sharing their faith regularly with others? These are just a few ways to measure the quality of a church.

Quantity refers to the *number* of disciples a church is producing. How many people are being brought to Christ, developed to maturity, and mobilized for ministry and missions?

Once the terms are defined, it's obvious that quality and quantity are not in opposition of each other. They are not mutually exclusive. You do not have to choose between the two. Every church should want both. In fact, an exclusive focus on either quality or quantity will produce an unhealthy church. Don't be fooled by either/or thinking.

When you go fishing, do you want quality or quantity? I want both! I want to catch the biggest fish I can, and I want to catch as many as I can. Every church should desire to reach as many people for Christ as possible as well as desire to help those people become as spiritually mature as possible.

> *Quality* refers to the *kind* of disciples a church produces. *Quantity* refers to the *number* of disciples a church produces.

The fact that many pastors wish to ignore is this: *Quality produces quantity.* A church full of genuinely changed people attracts others. If you study healthy churches you'll discover that when God finds a church that is doing a quality job of winning, nurturing, equipping, and sending out believers, he sends that church plenty of raw material. On the other hand, why would God send a lot of prospects to a church that doesn't know what to do with them?

In any church where lives are being changed, marriages are being saved, and love is flowing freely, you'll have to lock the doors to keep people from attending. People are attracted to churches with quality worship, preaching, ministry, and fellowship. Quality attracts quantity. Every pastor needs to ask a very tough question: If most of our members never invite anyone to come to our church, what are they saying (by their actions) about the quality of what our church offers?

It is also true that *quantity creates quality* in some areas of church life. For instance, the bigger your church gets, the better your music gets. Would you rather sing with eleven people or eleven hundred people? Would you rather be a part of a single-adult program with two people or two hundred people?

Some churches excuse their lack of growth by insisting that the smaller a church is, the more quality it can maintain. This reasoning is faulty. If quality is inherent in smallness, then, logically, the highest quality churches would consist of only one person! On the contrary, having spent much of my life prior to Saddleback in small churches, I have observed that one reason many churches remain small is because there is little quality in the life and ministry of those churches. There is no correlation between the size and the quality of a ministry.

What if your parents had applied the quality versus quantity myth to having children? What if, after their first child, they had said, "One kid is enough. Let's focus on making this child a quality kid. Let's not worry about quantity." Most of us wouldn't be here if our parents had thought that!

A church that has no interest at all in increasing its number of converts is, in essence, saying to the rest of the world, "You all can go to hell." If my three kids were lost on a wilderness trip, my wife and I would be consumed with finding them. We'd spare no expense to seek and save our lost children. And when we found one child, we wouldn't think of calling off the search and just focusing on the one "quality" kid we had left. We'd keep looking as long as any child was still lost.

In the church's case, as long as there are lost people in the world we *must* care about quantity as well as quality. At Saddleback, we count people because people count. Those numbers represent people Jesus died for. Anytime someone says,

"You can't measure success by numbers," my response is, "It all depends on what you're counting!" If you're counting marriages saved, lives transformed, broken people healed, unbelievers becoming worshipers of Jesus, and members being mobilized for ministry and missions, numbers are extremely important. They have eternal significance.

Myth #4: You Must Compromise the Message and the Mission of the Church in Order to Grow

This popular myth implies that the leaders of growing churches are somehow "selling out" the Gospel in order to grow. The assumption is that if a church is attracting people, it must be shallow and lacking in commitment. It assumes that the presence of a large crowd indicates a "watered-down" message.

Of course, there are examples of churches that have grown large with faulty theology, shallow commitment, and worldly gimmicks. But the presence of a large crowd doesn't automatically indicate that this is the case. While a few large churches *have* compromised their message and mission, many others, like Saddleback, are unfairly placed in the same category due to our size. This guilt by association is unfortunate.

Jesus' ministry attracted enormous crowds. Why? Because the Gospel is good news! It has an attractive power when clearly presented. Jesus said, "When I am lifted up from the earth, [I] will draw all men to myself" (John 12:32). Not only did crowds of adults want to be around Jesus, so did young children. A Christlike church will have the same drawing effect on people.

Jesus drew large crowds yet he never compromised the truth. No one accused him of watering down the message except the jealous chief priests, who criticized him out of envy (Mark 15:12). Frankly, I suspect that same ministerial jealousy motivates some today who criticize churches that attract large crowds.

Don't confuse expectations

Another reason many people think large churches are shallow is because they confuse what is expected of unbelieving attenders with what is expected of the actual church members. These are two very different groups. At Saddleback we use the terms "the Crowd" and "the Congregation" to distinguish between the groups.

At Saddleback Church we do not expect unbelievers to act like believers until they are. We do not expect visitors in the crowd to act like members of the congregation. We expect very little from the seeker who is investigating the claims of Christ. We simply say, as Jesus did in his first encounter with the disciples, "Come and see!" We invite unbelievers to check us out, to see for themselves what the church is all about.

On the other hand, we require a major commitment from those who want to *join* our church. I'll share these details in chapter 17. All prospective members must complete a membership class and are required to sign a membership covenant. By signing the covenant, members agree to give financially, serve in a ministry, share their faith, follow the leadership, avoid gossip, and maintain a godly lifestyle, among other things. Saddleback practices church discipline—something rarely heard of today. If you do not fulfill the membership covenant, you are dropped from our membership. We remove hundreds of names from our roll every year.

New members also agree to take additional classes where they will sign growth covenants that include tithing, having a daily quiet time, and participating weekly in a small group. One of the reasons Saddleback has not had a lot of transfer growth is because we expect so much more from our members than most other churches do.

I've discovered that challenging people to a serious commitment actually attracts people rather than repels them. The greater the commitment we ask for, the greater the response we get. Many unbelievers are fed up and bored with what the world offers. They are looking for something greater than themselves, something worth giving their lives to.

Asking for commitment doesn't turn people off; it is the *way* many churches ask for it. Too often, churches fail to explain the purpose, value, and benefits of commitment, and they have no process to help people take gradual steps in their commitment.

Being contemporary without compromising

Anyone who is serious about *doing* ministry, not just theorizing about it, must be willing to live with the tension of what Bruce and Marshall Shelley call "our ambidextrous calling." On the one hand we are obligated to remain faithful to the unchanging Word of God. On the other hand we must minister in an ever-changing world. Sadly, many Christians unwilling to live with this tension retreat to one of two extremes.

Some churches, fearing worldly infection, retreat into isolation from today's culture. While most do not retreat as far back as the Amish have, many churches seem to think that the 1950s was the golden age, and they are determined to preserve that era in their church. What I admire about the Amish is at least they are honest about it. They freely admit that they have chosen to preserve the lifestyle of the

> Asking for commitment doesn't turn people off; it is the *way* many churches ask for it.

1800s. In contrast, churches that try to perpetuate the culture of the 1950s usually deny their intent or they try to prove with proof-texts that they are doing it the way it was done in New Testament times.

Then there are those who, fearing irrelevance, foolishly imitate the latest fad and fashion. In their attempt to relate to today's culture they compromise the message and lose all sense of being set apart. Too often, these churches offer a message that emphasizes the benefits of the Gospel while ignoring the responsibility and cost of following Christ.

> Jesus never lowered his standards, but he always started where people were.

Is there a way to minister in our culture without compromising our convictions? I believe there is and I will discuss this more fully in chapter 12. The solution is to follow Christ's example of ministering to people. Jesus never lowered his standards, but he always started where people were. He was contemporary without compromising the truth.

Myth #5: If You Are Dedicated Enough, Your Church Will Grow

This is a favorite myth promoted at pastors' conferences, where speakers piously imply that if your church is not growing, the problem is your lack of dedication. They say, "If you'll just stay doctrinally pure, preach the Word, pray more, and be dedicated, then your church will explode with growth." It sounds so simple and so spiritual, but it just isn't true. Instead of being encouraged by these conferences, many pastors leave feeling more guilty, more inadequate, and more frustrated.

I know hundreds of dedicated pastors whose churches are not growing. They are faithful to God's Word, they pray earnestly and consistently, they preach solid messages, and their dedication is unquestioned—but still their churches refuse to grow. It is an insult to say that their problem is a lack of dedication. Few things infuriate me faster. These are good, godly pastors who serve God wholeheartedly.

It takes more than dedication to lead a church to grow; it takes *skill.* One of my favorite verses is Ecclesiastes 10:10: "If the ax is dull and its edge unsharpened, more strength is needed but skill will bring success." Notice that God says *skill,* not just dedication, will bring success. If I have wood to chop, I'll do a better job by sharpening my ax first. The point is, work smarter, not harder.

Take the time to learn the skills you need in ministry. You'll save time in the long run and be far more successful. Sharpen your ministry ax by reading books, attending conferences, listening to tapes, and by observing working models. You're never wasting time when you're sharpening your ax. Skill brings success.

In our church there are a number of professional pilots who fly for the major airlines. They tell me that no matter how long they've been pilots, the airlines require that twice a year they spend a week retraining and sharpening their skills. When I asked them why retraining is required so often, the answer was, "Because people's lives depend on how skilled we are." That's true of ministry as well. Should we be any less concerned about keeping our skills up-to-date?

At Saddleback, we offer a basic training conference for church leaders and pastors at least once a year. Even though our staff is thoroughly acquainted with Saddleback's vision, strategy, and structure, I require each of them to attend the conference. We all need to have our vision reenergized and our skills sharpened on a regular basis.

The reason the apostle Paul was so effective in planting and developing churches was because he was skilled at it. He admits this in 1 Corinthians 3:10: "By the grace God has given me, I laid a

> It takes more than dedication to lead a church to grow; it takes skill.

foundation as an *expert* builder" (italics added). Paul was an expert at building churches. He was not a haphazard builder who did shoddy work. Not only was he dedicated to his task, he was skilled at using the right tools. We too must learn to use the right tools in building a church. If all you have is a hammer in your ministry toolbox, you'll tend to treat everything as a nail!

The Bible also compares ministry to farming, another profession that requires skill. A farmer can be a dedicated and hard worker but he must also be skilled in using the right equipment. If he tries to harvest a corn field with a wheat harvester, he's bound to fail. If he tries to harvest tomatoes with a cotton picker, he'll end up with a mess! Successful ministry, like farming, requires more than dedication and hard work; it takes skill, timing, and the right tools.

Many simplistic solutions for church growth are couched in such pious terms that it makes it difficult for anyone to challenge them without seeming unspiritual. Somebody needs to boldly state the obvious: Prayer alone will not grow a church. Some of the greatest prayer warriors I know are pastors and members of dying churches.

Of course, prayer *is* absolutely essential. Every step of Saddleback's development has been bathed in prayer. In fact, I have a prayer team that prays for me *while I speak* at each of our four weekend services. A prayerless ministry is a powerless ministry. But it takes far more than prayer to grow a church. It takes skilled action. One time God told Joshua to stop praying about his failure and get up and correct the cause of it instead (Josh. 7). There is a time to pray, and there is a time to act responsibly.

We must always be careful to avoid two extreme positions in ministry. One extreme is to assume all responsibility for the growth of the church. The other extreme is to abdicate all responsibility for it. I am deeply indebted to Joe Ellis for identifying these two extremes and helping me sort out the issues of responsibility and faithfulness in ministry. Joe identifies the first error as "practical humanism" and the second as "pious irre-sponsibility." Both are fatal to a church.

First, we must avoid the error that all it takes to grow a church is organization, management, and marketing. The church is not a business! I've talked to some pastors who act as if the church is merely a human enterprise with a few prayers thrown in for good measure. After listening to them, I've wondered, *Where is the Holy Spirit in all of this?*

Unfortunately, many churches can be explained away in terms of a standard Sunday school, an efficient organization, and a balanced budget. Nothing supernatural ever happens in these churches, and few lives are genuinely changed.

All of our plans, programs, and procedures are worthless without God's anointing. Psalm 127:1 says, "Unless the LORD builds the house, its builders labor in vain." A church cannot be built by human effort alone. We must never forget whose church it is. Jesus said, "*I* will build *my* church" (Matt. 16:18, italics added).

On the other hand, we must avoid the error that there is *nothing* we can do to help a church grow. This misconception is just as prevalent today. Some pastors and theologians believe that any planning, organizing, advertising, or effort is presumptuous, unspiritual, or even sinful, and that our only role is to sit back and watch God do his thing. You will find a lot of this teaching in literature on

> Churches grow by the power of God through the skilled effort of people.

revival. In a sincere desire to emphasize God's work in revival, all human effort is disparaged. This way of thinking produces passive believers and often uses spiritual-sounding excuses to justify a church's failure to grow.

The Bible clearly teaches that God has given us a critical role to play in accomplishing his will on earth. Church growth is a partnership between God and man. Churches grow by the power of God through the skilled effort of people. Both elements, God's power and man's skilled effort, must be present. We cannot do it *without God* but he has decided not to do it *without us!* God uses people to accomplish his purposes.

> # While we wait for God to work *for* us, God is waiting to work *through* us!

Paul illustrated this partnership between God and man when he said, "I planted the seed, Apollos watered it, but God made it grow ... we are God's *fellow workers* ..." (1 Cor. 3:6, 9 LB, italics added). God did his part after Paul and Apollos did their part.

The New Testament is full of analogies of church growth that teach this principle: planting and cultivating God's garden (1 Cor. 3:5–9); building God's building (1 Cor. 3:10–13); harvesting God's fields (Matt. 9:37–38); growing Christ's body (Rom. 12:4–8; Eph. 4:16).

For an Old Testament example, we can look to the book of Joshua. God told the Israelites to take possession of the land; he did not do it for them. He offered them a partnership and gave them a role to play. But because of their fear and passivity, the Israelites died in the wilderness. While we wait for God to work *for* us, God is waiting to work *through* us.

Myth #6: There Is *One* Secret Key to Church Growth

Church growth is a complex matter. It is seldom caused by just one factor. Anytime you hear a pastor attribute the growth of his church to one single factor, realize that he is either oversimplifying what has occurred, or he may not be recognizing the real reason his church is growing.

Through my interactions with church leaders who've taken the Saddleback training, I've identified a few basic facts about churches that my staff call "Rick's Rules of Growth."

First, *there is more than one way to grow a church*. I could show you churches that are using strategies exactly opposite of each other, yet both are growing. Some churches grow through their Sunday schools; others use small groups in homes. Some churches grow by using contemporary music; others grow using traditional music. Some growing churches have an organized visitation program; others have never had one.

Second, *it takes all kinds of churches to reach all kinds of people*. Thank God we're not all alike! God loves variety. If every church was like all the others we'd only reach one small segment of this world. In just the area of music alone, imagine all the styles of music needed to reach all the different cultures of our world. Every once in a while I hear someone say that all churches should get together under one denomination where we would all be the same. I couldn't disagree more. I think diversity in style is a strength, not a weakness. God uses different approaches to reach different groups of people.

I'm not talking about churches deviating from biblical truth. The message of Christ must never change. It is, as Jude said, ". . . the truth which God gave, once for all, to his people to keep *without change* through the years" (Jude 1:3 LB, italics added). Don't con-

> Never confuse methods with the message. The message must never change, but the methods must change with each new generation.

fuse methods with the message. The message must never change, but the methods must change with each new generation.

Third, *never criticize what God is blessing,* even though it may be a style of ministry that makes you feel uncomfortable. It is amazing to me how God often blesses people I disagree with or don't understand. So I've adopted this attitude: If lives are being changed by the power of Jesus Christ—then I like the way you are doing it! We are all trophies of God's grace.

Myth #7: All God Expects of Us Is Faithfulness

This statement is only half true. God expects both faithfulness *and* fruitfulness. Fruitfulness is a major theme of the New Testament. Consider the following:

- *We are called by Christ to bear fruit.* "You did not choose me, but I chose you and appointed you to go and bear fruit—fruit that will last" (John 15:16). God wants to see *lasting* fruit come from our ministry.
- *Being fruitful is the way we glorify God.* "This is to my Father's glory, that you bear much fruit, showing yourselves to be my disciples" (John 15:8). An unfruitful ministry does not bring glory to God, but a fruitful ministry is the proof that we are Christ's disciples.
- *Being fruitful pleases God.* "We pray this in order that you may live a life worthy of the Lord and may please him in every way: bearing fruit in every good work" (Col. 1:10).
- *Jesus reserved his severest judgment for the unfruitful tree.* He cursed it because it didn't bear fruit. "Seeing a fig tree by the road, he went up to it but found nothing on it except leaves. Then he said to it, 'May you never bear fruit again!' Immediately the tree withered" (Matt. 21:19). Jesus did not do this to show off but to make a point: He expects fruitfulness!

- *The nation of Israel lost its privilege because of unfruitfulness.* "Therefore I tell you that the kingdom of God will be taken away from you and given to a people who will produce its fruit" (Matt. 21:43). This same principle can be applied to individual churches. I have seen God remove his hand of blessing from churches—churches that had been greatly blessed in the past—because they became self-satisfied and self-absorbed and stopped bearing fruit.

What is fruitfulness? The word *fruit*, or a variation of it, is used fifty-five times in the New Testament and refers to a variety of results. Each one of the following is considered by God to be fruit: repentance (Matt. 3:8; Luke 13:5–9), practicing the truth (Matt. 7:16–21; Col. 1:10), answered prayer (John 15:7–8), an offering of money given by believers (Rom. 15:28), Christlike character, and winning unbelievers to Christ (Rom. 1:13). Paul said he wanted to preach in Rome "in order that I might obtain some fruit among you also, even as among the rest of the Gentiles" (Rom. 1:13 NASB). The fruit of a believer is another believer.

Considering the Great Commission that Jesus gave to the church, I believe that the definition of fruitfulness for a local church must include growth by the conversion of unbelievers. Paul referred to the first converts in Achaia as the "first fruit of Achaia" (1 Cor. 16:15 NASB).

The Bible clearly identifies numerical growth of the church as fruit. Many of the kingdom parables of Jesus emphasize the unavoidable truth that God expects his church to grow. In addition, Paul connected fruit bearing with church growth. Colossians 1:6 says, "All over the world this gospel is *bearing fruit* and *growing*, just as it has been doing among you since the day you heard it . . ." (italics added). Is your church bearing fruit and growing? Are you seeing the fruit of new converts being added to your congregation?

God wants your church to be *both* faithful and fruitful. One without the other is only half the equation. Numerical results are no justification for being unfaithful to the message, but neither can we use faithfulness as an excuse for being ineffective! Churches that have few or no conversions often attempt to justify their ineffectiveness with the statement, "God has not called us to be successful. He has just called us to be faithful." I strongly disagree because the Bible clearly teaches that God expects both.

> Ministry must be *both* faithful and fruitful. God expects both from us.

The sticking point is how you define the terms *successful* and *faithful*. I define being *successful* as fulfilling the Great Commission. Jesus has given the church a job to do. We will either succeed or fail at it. Using this definition, every church should want to be successful! What is the alternative? The opposite of success is not faithfulness, but *failure*. Any church that is not obeying the Great Commission is failing its purpose, no matter what else it does.

What is *faithfulness*? Usually we define it in terms of beliefs. We think that by holding orthodox beliefs we are fulfilling Christ's command to be faithful. We call ourselves "defenders of the faith." But Jesus meant far more than adherence to beliefs when he used the term. He defined faithfulness in terms of behavior—a willingness to take risks (that require faith) in order to be fruitful.

The clearest example of this is the parable of the talents in Matthew 25:14–30. The two men who doubled the talents the master gave them were called "good and faithful servants." In other words, they proved their faithfulness by taking risks that produced fruit. They were successful at the task that they had been assigned, and they were rewarded for it by the master.

The passive, fearful servant who did nothing with the talent he was given produced no results for the master because he would not take a risk. He was called "wicked and lazy" in contrast to the two men called "faithful" for producing results. The point of the story is clear: God expects to see results. Our faithfulness is demonstrated by our fruit.

Faithfulness is accomplishing as much as possible with the resources and talents God has given you. That's why comparing churches is an illegitimate way to measure success. Success is not being larger than some other church; it is bearing as much fruit as possible given your gifts, opportunities, and potential.

Christ doesn't expect us to produce *more* than we can, but he does expect us to produce *all* that we can by his power within us. That is a lot more than most of us think is possible. We expect too little from God, and we attempt too little for him. If you're not taking any risks in your ministry, then it is not requiring that you have faith. And if your ministry doesn't require any faith, then you are being unfaithful.

How do *you* define faithfulness? Are you being faithful to God's Word if you insist on communicating it in an outdated style? Are you being faithful if you insist on doing ministry in a way that is *comfortable* for you, even though it doesn't produce any fruit? Are you being faithful to Christ if you value man-made traditions more than reaching people for him? I contend that when a church continues to use methods that no longer work, it is being unfaithful to Christ!

Sadly, there are many churches today who are completely orthodox in their

> Success is bearing as much fruit as possible given your gifts, opportunities, and potential.

beliefs but are still unfaithful to Christ because they refuse to change programs, methods, styles of worship, buildings, or even locations in order to reach a lost world for Christ. Vance Havner used to say, "A church can be straight as a gun barrel doctrinally and just as empty spiritually." We must be willing to say, with unreserved commitment to our Lord and Savior, "We'll do *whatever it takes* to reach people for Christ."

Myth #8: You Can't Learn from Large Churches

Saddleback's story of growth is a sovereign act of God that cannot be replicated. However, we *should* extract the lessons and principles that are transferable. To ignore what God has taught our church would be unwise stewardship. "Remember today what you have learned about the LORD through your experiences with him" (Deut. 11:2 TEV). Every church should not have to reinvent the wheel.

> Saddleback's growth is a sovereign act of God that cannot be replicated. However, we should extract the lessons and principles that are transferable.

Anytime I see a program working in another church, I try to extract the principle behind it and apply it in our church. Because of this, our church has benefited from many other models that we've studied, both contemporary and historical. I'm very grateful for the models that have helped me. I learned a long time ago that I don't have to originate everything for it to work. God has not called us to be original at everything. He has called us to be effective.

To reduce the risk of copying the wrong things, however, I want to identify what is transferable from Saddleback's example and what isn't.

What you can't copy

First, you won't be able to transfer our context. Every church operates in a unique cultural setting. Saddleback is located in the middle of a busy, southern California suburban area, filled with well-educated young couples. It isn't Peoria, Illinois; Muleshoe, Texas; or even Los Angeles, California. Every community is unique. To artificially plant a Saddleback clone in a different environment is a formula for failure. Despite my clear warning, some have tried this anyway and then wondered why things didn't work out.

Second, you won't be able to replicate our staff. God uses people to do his work. The leadership of any program is always more crucial than the program itself. I've spent fifteen years building a staff team that together is more effective than any one of us would be on our own.

> God has not called us to be original at everything. He has called us to be effective.

Individually, we're all pretty ordinary folk. But when you put us together, somehow our mixture of gifts, personalities, and backgrounds creates a powerful synergy that baffles management experts and has allowed us to accomplish some amazing tasks.

Third, you can't be me. (No one in his right mind would want my weaknesses.) Only I can be me, and only you can be you. That's the way God intended it. When you get to heaven, God is not going to say, "Why weren't you more like Rick Warren (or Jerry Falwell or Bill Hybels or John MacArthur or anyone else)?" God is likely to say, "Why weren't you more like you?"

God made you to be yourself. He wants to use your gifts, your passion, your natural abilities, your personality, and your experiences to impact your part of the world. All of us start out as originals. Unfortunately, many end up as carbon copies of someone else. You cannot grow a church trying to be someone else.

What you can learn

First, you can learn principles. As the old cliché says, "Methods are many, principles are few; methods change often, principles never do." If a principle is biblical, I believe it is transcultural. It will work anywhere. It's wise to learn and apply principles from watching how God is working around the world. While you cannot grow a church trying to be someone else, you *can* grow a church by using principles someone else discovered and then filtering them through your personality and context.

I've never been interested in producing clones of Saddleback. That's one reason I chose a local name for our church rather than a generic name that could be copied. Unless you live in our community, the name "Saddleback" won't work for you. Not one of the twenty-five daughter churches we've started is doing ministry exactly like Saddleback. I encourage them to filter what they've learned from us through their context and personality.

> You can learn from other churches without becoming a clone.

God has a custom ministry for every church. Your church has a unique thumbprint that God has given it. But you can learn from models without becoming a clone! We learn best and fastest by observing models. After all, most of what we learn in life is learned by watching someone model it. Never be embarassed to use a model; it is a sign of intelligence! Proverbs 18:15 (LB) says, "The intelligent man is always open to new ideas. In fact, he looks for them."

Paul was certainly not afraid of using models for the churches he started. He told the church at Thessalonica, "You became imitators of us and of the Lord. . . . And so you became a model to all the believers in Macedonia and Achaia" (1 Thess. 1:6–7). This is my prayer for your church. I hope you'll be able to learn from Saddleback's model, and that you will, in turn, become a model for other churches.

Saddleback is by no means a perfect church, but it is a healthy church (as my children will never be perfect, but they are healthy). A church doesn't have to be perfect to be a model. If perfection were a requirement for being a model, you can forget trying to learn anything from *any* church. There are no perfect churches.

Let me warn you: If you implement the strategy and ideas in this book in your church, someone is bound to say, "You got that from Saddleback." You should respond, "So what! They got what they know from hundreds of other churches." Remember, we're all on the same team.

I believe that people who can't learn from models have an ego problem. The Bible says, "God opposes the proud but gives grace to the humble" (James 4:6). Why does God do this? One reason is that when people are full of pride they are unteachable: They think they know it all. I've found that when people think they have all the answers, it usually means they don't even know all the questions. My goal is to learn as much as I can, from as many people as I can, as often as I can. I try to learn from critics, from people I disagree with, and even from enemies.

Second, you can learn a process. This book is about a process, not programs. It offers a system for developing the people in your church and balancing the purposes of your church. Having watched Saddleback's strategy of assimilating people who work under the heavy demands of a rapidly growing church, I'm confident the purpose-driven process can work in other churches where the pace of growth is more reasonable.

We've now seen it produce strong, fruitful believers in thousands of small and medium-sized churches. It is not a strategy for just the megachurch.

People forget that Saddleback was once a very small church. It grew large by using the purpose-driven process. I've had many church leaders say to me after I've explained the process to them, "Why, anybody can do this!" I reply, "That's the point!" Healthy churches are built on a process, not on personalities.

Finally, you can learn some methods. No method is meant to last forever or work everywhere, but that doesn't make it worthless. Recently, church-growth methods have gotten a bad reputation. In some circles, they are considered unspiritual, even carnal. Because some church-growth enthusiasts have overemphasized methods to the neglect of sound doctrine and the supernatural work of the Holy Spirit, others have gone just as far to the other extreme and are ready to throw out all talk of methods.

Every church uses some type of methodology, intentionally or unintentionally, so the question isn't whether or not to use methods. The issue is what kind of methods you use, and whether or not they are biblical and effective.

Methods are just expressions of principles. There are many different ways to express biblical principles in different cultural settings. The book of Acts has many examples of how the first Christians used different methods for different situations.

If you study the churches of today, it is obvious that God uses all kinds of methods, and that he blesses some methods more than others. It is also obvious that some methods that worked in the past are no longer effective. Fortunately, one of the great strengths of Christianity has been its ability to change methods when confronted with new cultures and times. History dramatically illustrates the church's continuous creation of "new wineskins." God gives the church new methods to reach each new generation. Ecclesiastes 3:6 says, "[There is] a time to keep and a time to throw away." This verse can be applied to methodology. Each generation of the church must decide which methods to keep using and which ones should be thrown away because they are no longer effective.

You probably won't like some of the methods we use at Saddleback. That's okay. I don't expect you to since I don't even like everything we're doing! Read this book like you'd eat fish: Pick out the meat and throw away the bones. Adopt and adapt what you can use. One of the most important skills of leadership is learning to distinguish between what is essential and what isn't. The method must always be subservient to the message. Whenever you read a book about church health or growth, don't confuse primary issues with secondary ones.

The primary issues of church health and growth:
- Who is our master?
- What is our message?
- What is our motive?

Secondary issues of church health and growth:
- Who is our market?
- What are our models?
- What are our methods?

Albert Einstein once lamented that one of the great weaknesses of the twentieth century is that we habitually confuse the means with the end. For the church, this is especially dangerous. We must never become so enamored with methods that we lose sight of our mission and forget our message.

Unfortunately, many churches operate on the misconceptions and myths I've identified in this chapter. This prevents them from being healthy and growing to their full potential. Churches need *truth* to grow. Cults may grow without truth but churches can't. First Timothy 3:15 talks about "the pillar and foundation of the truth." In the next section of this book we'll look at how to lay a foundation of truth on which God can build his church.

Part Two

Becoming a Purpose-Driven Church

3

What Drives Your Church?

*Many are the plans in a man's heart, but
it is the LORD's purpose that prevails.*

Proverbs 19:21

Steve Johnson called the monthly church council meeting of Westside Church to order at exactly 7 P.M. "We've got a lot to cover tonight, folks, so we'd better get started," said Steve. "As you know, our agenda is to agree on a unified church program for the new year. We're supposed to present it to the congregation in two weeks."

As chairman, Steve was feeling quite anxious over what happened. Only the annual budget meeting provoked more disagreement and debate than this program-planning meeting. "Who wants to go first?" asked Steve.

"This ought to be easy," said Ben Faithful, a deacon who'd been a member for twenty-six years. "Last year was a good year. Let's just repeat all the good things we did last year. I've always believed that the tried and true is better than a lot of newfangled ideas."

"Well, I'd have to disagree with that," said Bob Newman. "Times have changed, and I think we need to reevaluate *everything* we're doing. Just because a program worked in the past doesn't automatically mean it's going to continue working next year. I'm especially interested in starting another worship service with a different style. We've all seen the growth that Calvary Church has had since they started a contemporary service to reach out to the unchurched."

"Yes, some churches will do *anything* to get a crowd," replied Ben. "They forget who the church is for: It's for us Christians! We're supposed to be *different* and separate from the world. We're not to pander to whatever the world wants. I sure don't intend to see that happen at Westside!"

Over the next two hours a worthy list of programs and causes was presented for inclusion in the church calendar. Karen Doer passionately insisted that Westside church take a more active role in Operation Rescue and the pro-life movement. John Manly gave a moving testimony about how Promise Keepers had changed his life and suggested a full slate of men's activities. Linda Loving spoke of the need to develop various support groups. Bob Learner made his usual pitch for the church to begin a Christian school. And of course, Jerry Tightwad kept asking, "How much will it cost?" as each proposal was presented. They were *all* valid suggestions. The problem was there seemed to be no standard of reference by which the council could evaluate and decide which programs would be adopted.

Finally Clark Reasoner spoke up. Clark was the voice everyone was waiting for at this point. Whenever issues became confused at church business meetings, he'd usually make a short speech, and a majority would vote his way. It wasn't that his ideas were better; in fact, people often disagreed with him. But the sheer force of his personality made whatever he said seem sensible at the time.

What is the problem in this scenario? Multiple driving forces in this church are competing for attention. This results in conflict and a church that is trying to head in several different directions at the same time.

If you were to look up the word *drive* in a dictionary, you'd find this definition: "to guide, control, or direct." When you drive a car, it means you guide, control, and direct it down the street. When you drive a nail, you guide, control, and direct it into the wood. When you drive a golf ball, you hope to guide, control, and direct it down the fairway!

Every church is driven by something. There is a guiding force, a controlling assumption, a directing conviction behind everything that happens. It may be unspoken. It may be unknown to many. Most likely it's never been officially voted on. But it is there, influencing every aspect of the church's life. What is the driving force behind your church?

Churches Driven by Tradition

In the tradition-driven church the favorite phrase is "We've always done it this way." The goal of a tradition-driven church is to simply perpetuate the past. Change is almost always seen as negative, and stagnation is interpreted as "stability."

Older churches tend to be bound together by rules, regulations, and rituals, while younger churches tend to be bound together by a sense of purpose and mission. In some churches, tradition can be such a driving force that everything else, even God's will, becomes secondary. Ralph Neighbour says the seven last words of the church are, "We've never done it that way before."

Churches Driven by Personality

In this church the most important question is, "What does the leader want?" If the pastor has served the church for a long time, he is most likely the driving personality. But if the church has a history of changing pastors every few years, a key layperson is likely to be the driving force. One obvious problem with a personality-driven church is that its agenda is determined more by the background, needs, and insecurities of the leader than by God's will or the needs of the people. Another problem is that the personality-driven church comes to a standstill when its driving personality leaves or dies.

Churches Driven by Finances

The question at the forefront of everyone's mind in a finance-driven church is, "How much will it cost?" Nothing else ever seems quite as important as finances. The most heated debate in a finance-driven church is always over the budget. While good stewardship and cash flow are essential for a healthy church, finances must never be the controlling issue. The greater issue should be what God wants the church to do. Churches do not exist to make a profit. The bottom line in any church should not be "How much did we save?" but "Who was saved?" I've noticed that many churches are driven by faith in their early years and driven by finances in later years.

Churches Driven by Programs

The Sunday school, the women's program, the choir, and the youth group are examples of programs that are often driving forces in churches. In program-driven churches, all the energy is focused on maintaining and sustaining the programs of the church. Often, the program-driven church's goal subtly shifts from developing people to just filling positions, and the nominating committee becomes the most crucial group in the church. If results from a program diminish, the people involved blame themselves for not working hard enough. No one ever questions if a program still works.

Churches Driven by Buildings

Winston Churchill once said, "We shape our buildings, and then they shape us." Too often a congregation is so anxious to have a nice building that the members spend more than they can afford. Paying for and maintaining the building becomes the biggest budget item. Funds needed to operate ministries must be diverted to pay the mortgage, and the actual ministry of the church suffers. The tail ends up wagging the dog. In other situations, churches allow the smallness of their building to set the limit for future growth. Staying with a historic, but inadequate, building should never take priority over reaching the community.

Churches Driven by Events

If you look at the calendar of an event-driven church, you might get the impression that the goal of the church is to keep people busy. Something is going on every night of the week. As soon as one big event is completed, work begins on the next one. There is a lot of activity in churches like this, but not necessarily productivity. A church may be busy without having a clear purpose for what it does. Someone needs to ask, "What is the purpose behind each of our activities?" In the event-driven church, attendance becomes the sole measurement of faithfulness and maturity. We must be wary of the tendency to allow meetings to replace ministry as the primary activity of believers.

Churches Driven by Seekers

In an honest attempt to reach unbelievers for Christ and be relevant in today's culture, some churches allow the needs of the unbelievers to become their driving force. The primary question asked is, "What do the unchurched want?" While we must be sensitive to the needs, hurts, and interests of seekers, and while it is wise to design evangelistic services that target their needs, we cannot allow seekers to drive the total agenda of the church.

God's purposes for his church include evangelism—but not to the exclusion of his other purposes. Attracting seekers is the first step in the process of making disciples, but it should not be the driving force of the church. While it is fine for a business to be market driven (give the customer whatever he wants), a

> The church should be *seeker sensitive*, but it must not be *seeker driven*.

church has a higher calling. The church should be *seeker sensitive* but it must not be seeker driven. We must adapt our communication style to our culture without adopting the sinful elements of it or abdicating to it.

A Biblical Paradigm: Purpose-Driven Churches

What is needed today are churches that are driven by purpose instead of by other forces. This book is written to offer a new paradigm, the purpose-driven church, as a biblical and healthy alternative to traditional ways that churches have organized and operated.

There are two essential elements of this paradigm. First, it requires a new *perspective*. You must begin to look at everything your church does through the lens of five New Testament purposes and see how God intends for the church to balance all five purposes.

Second, this paradigm requires a *process* for fulfilling the purposes of the church. In this book, I'll explain the process we've used at Saddleback Church that has enabled our congregation to experience fifteen years of healthy, consistent growth.

This is not some "ivory tower" theory; it has been field tested in a real church for fifteen years and has produced one of the largest and fastest-growing churches in American history. It is also producing exciting results in thousands of other churches in America, Australia, Europe, and Asia. Your church, regardless of its size or location, will be healthier, stronger, and more effective by becoming a purpose-driven church.

The apostle Paul said that God will judge whatever we build on the basis of whether it will last: "The fire will test the quality of each man's work. If what he has built survives, he will receive his reward" (1 Cor. 3:13–14). Paul also tells us that the key to building something that lasts is to build it on the right foundation: "But each one should be careful how he builds. For no one can lay any foundation other than the one already laid, which is Jesus Christ" (1 Cor. 3:10–11).

Strong churches are built on purpose! By focusing equally on all five of the New Testament purposes of the church, your church will develop the healthy balance that makes lasting growth possible. Proverbs 19:21 says, "Many are the plans in a man's heart, but it is the LORD's purpose that prevails." Plans, programs, and personalities don't last. But God's purposes *will* last.

> Plans, programs, and personalities don't last. But God's purposes *will* last.

The importance of being purpose driven

Nothing precedes purpose. The starting point for every church should be the question, "Why do we exist?" Until you know what your church exists for, you have no foundation, no motivation, and no direction for ministry. If you are helping a new church get started, your first task is to *define* your purpose. It's far easier to set the right foundation at the start of a new church than it is to reset it after a church has existed for years.

However, if you serve in an existing church that has plateaued, is declining, or is simply discouraged, your most important task is to *redefine* your purpose. Forget everything else until you have established it in the minds of your members. Recapture a clear vision of what God wants to do in and through your church family. Absolutely nothing will revitalize a discouraged church faster than rediscovering its purpose.

As I prepared to start Saddleback Church, one of the most important factors I discovered in my research was that growing, healthy churches have a clear-cut identity. They understand their reason for being; they are precise in their purpose. They know exactly what God has called them to do. They know what their business is, and they know what is none of their business! Does your church have a clear-cut identity?

If you ask typical church members why their church exists, you'll get a wide variety of answers. Most churches do not have a clear consensus on this issue. Win Arn, a consultant to churches, once told me about a survey he took. He surveyed members of nearly a thousand churches asking the question, "Why does the church exist?" The results? Of the church members surveyed, 89 percent said, "The church's purpose is to take care of my family's and my needs." For many, the role of the pastor is simply to keep the sheep who are already in the "pen" happy and not lose too many of them. Only 11 percent said, "The purpose of the church is to win the world for Jesus Christ."

> Absolutely nothing will revitalize a discouraged church faster than rediscovering its purpose.

Then, the *pastors* of the same churches were asked why the church exists. Amazingly, the results were exactly opposite. Of the pastors surveyed, 90 percent said the purpose of the church was to win the world and 10 percent said it was to care for the needs of the members. Is it any wonder why we have conflict, confusion, and stagnation in many churches today? If the pastor and congregation can't even agree on why the church exists, conflict and disagreement on everything else is inevitable.

Churches are started for many different reasons. Sometimes those reasons are inadequate: competition, denominational pride, the need for recognition by a leader, or some other unworthy motivation. Unless the driving force behind a church is biblical, the health and growth of the church will never be what God intended. Strong churches are not built on programs, personalities, or gimmicks. They are built on the eternal purposes of God.

4

The Foundation for a Healthy Church

Jesus: "...I will build my church."

Matthew 16:18

Paul: "By the grace God has given me, I laid a foundation as an expert builder."

1 Corinthians 3:10

A few years ago I bought some property in the mountains behind Yosemite National Park and built a log cabin. Even with the help of my father and some friends it took two years to complete, since I couldn't work on it full-time. When I began building, it took me an entire summer just to lay the foundation. First I had to clear a pad in the forest by cutting down and uprooting thirty-seven towering pine trees. Then I had to dig over sixty feet of five-foot-deep French drains and fill them with gravel because the ground was wet from a nearby underground spring.

After ten exhausting weeks, all I had to show for my effort was a leveled and squared concrete foundation. I was very discouraged. But my father, who has built over 110 church buildings in his lifetime, said, "Cheer up, son! When you've finished laying the foundation, the most critical work is behind you."

The foundation determines both the size and the strength of a building. You can never build larger than the foundation can handle. The same is true for churches. A church built on an inadequate or faulty foundation will never reach the height that God intends for it to reach. It will topple over once it outgrows its base.

> Your church's foundation will determine both its size and strength. You can never build larger than your foundation can handle.

If you want to build a healthy, strong, and growing church you *must* spend time laying a solid foundation. This is done by clarifying in the minds of everyone involved exactly why the church exists and what it is supposed to do. There is incredible power in having a clearly defined purpose statement. If it is short enough for everyone to remember, your statement of purpose will yield five wonderful benefits for your church.

A Clear Purpose Builds Morale

Morale and mission always go together. First Corinthians 1:10 (LB) says, "Let there be real harmony so that there won't be splits in the church. . . . Be of one mind, united in thought and purpose." Notice Paul says that the key to harmony in the church is to be united in purpose. If your mission is unclear, your morale will be low.

Saddleback Church has an unusually high morale and atmosphere of harmony. People working together for a great purpose don't have time to argue over trivial issues. When you're helping row the boat, you don't have time to rock it! We've been able to maintain a warm fellowship in spite of the enormous growth our church has experienced because our members are committed to a common purpose.

Proverbs 29:18 (KJV) says, "Where there is no vision, the people perish." I believe it is also true that where there is no vision, *people leave for another parish!* Many churches are barely surviving because they have no vision. They limp along from Sunday to Sunday because they've lost sight of their purpose for continuing. A church without a purpose and mission eventually becomes a museum piece of yesterday's traditions.

Nothing discourages a church more than not knowing why it exists. On the other hand, the quickest way to reinvigorate a plateaued or declining church is to reclaim God's purpose for it and help the members understand the great tasks the church has been given by Christ.

A Clear Purpose Reduces Frustration

A purpose statement reduces frustration because it allows us to forget about things that don't really matter. Isaiah 26:3 (TEV) says that God "give[s] perfect peace to those *who keep their purpose firm* and put their trust in [him] (italics added)." A clear purpose not only defines what we do, it defines what we do not do. I'm sure you'd agree that your church does not have time to do everything. The good news is that God doesn't *expect* you to do everything. Besides, there are only a few things really worth doing in the first place! The secret of effectiveness is to know what really counts, then do what really counts, and not worry about all the rest.

As a pastor I've learned that everybody has their own agenda for the church. To rephrase the first spiritual law: God loves me and everybody else has a wonderful plan for my life! People are

> A clear purpose not only defines what we do, it defines what we *don't* do.

always saying "The church ought to do this" or "The church ought to do that." Many of these suggestions are noble activities, but that is not the real issue. The filter must always be: Does this activity fulfill one of the purposes for which God established this church? If the activity meets that criterion, you must consider it. If it doesn't pass this test, you must not let it distract you from God's agenda for the church.

Without a purpose statement it is easy to be frustrated by all the distractions around us. Maybe you've felt the way Isaiah did: "I have labored to no purpose; I have spent my strength in vain and for nothing" (Isa. 49:4). Trying to lead a church without a clearly defined purpose is like trying to drive a car in the fog. If you can't see clearly where you're headed, you are likely to crash.

James 1:8 (PHILLIPS) says, ". . . the life of a man of divided loyalty will reveal instability at every turn." When a church forgets its purpose, it has a difficult time deciding what's important. An indecisive church is an unstable church. Almost anything can get it off course. It will vacillate between priorities, purposes, and programs. It will head one direction, then another, depending on who is leading at the time. Sometimes churches just move in circles.

In a purpose-driven church, once your course is set, decision making becomes far easier and less frustrating. Define your roles then set your goals. Once your church's purposes have been clarified, any goal that fulfills one of those purposes gets automatic approval. Anytime someone suggests an activity or an event or a new program you should simply ask, "Will this fulfill one of our purposes?" If it does, do it. If it doesn't, don't do it.

A Clear Purpose Allows Concentration

Focused light has tremendous power. Diffused light has no power at all. For instance, by focusing the power of the sun through a magnifying glass, you can set a leaf on fire. But you can't set a leaf on fire if the same sunlight is unfocused. When light is concentrated at an even higher level, like a laser beam, it can even cut through a block of steel.

The principle of concentration works in other areas too. A focused life and a focused church will have far greater impact than unfocused ones. Like a laser beam, the more focused your church becomes, the more impact it will have on society.

The reason for this is that a clear purpose allows you to concentrate your effort. Paul knew this. He said, "I am bringing all my energies to bear on this one thing, forgetting what is behind and looking forward to what lies ahead" (Phil. 3:13 LB).

One of the common temptations I see many churches falling for today is the trap of majoring in the minors. They become distracted by good, but less important, agendas, crusades, and purposes. The energy of the church is diffused and dissipated; the power is lost.

If you want your church to make an impact on the world, you must major in the majors. It is amazing to me how many Christians have no idea what the main objective of their church is. As the old cliché says, "The main thing is to keep the main thing the main thing!"

In my opinion, most churches try to do too much. This is one of the most overlooked barriers to building a healthy church: We wear out people. Too often, small churches involve themselves in all kinds of activities, events, and programs. Instead of concentrating like Paul did, they dabble in forty different things and miss being good at any of them.

The older a church gets, the truer this becomes. Programs and events continue to be added to the agenda without ever cutting anything out. Remember, no program is meant to last forever. A good question to keep in mind when dealing with programs in your church is, "Would we begin this today if we were not already doing it?" A bloated church calendar diffuses the energy of your church. It is essential to the health of your church that you periodically "clean house"—abandon programs that have outlived their purpose. When the horse is dead—dismount!

When I started Saddleback Church, all we offered for the first year was a worship service and a limited children's church program. We didn't attempt to be a full-service church. For instance, we didn't have a youth program until we were averaging over 500 in worship attendance, and we didn't have a singles program until attendance had grown to nearly 1,000.

We determined that we would never begin a new ministry without first having someone to lead it. If no leader emerged, we would wait on God's timing before beginning a ministry. When the right leader would finally appear on the scene, we would initiate the new ministry. This plan helped us to concentrate on doing a few things very well. Only after we got a ministry to an acceptable level of performance did we consider adding another one to our menu. We didn't try to do everything at once.

Being *efficient* is not the same as being *effective*. Peter Drucker says, "Efficiency is *doing things right*. Effectiveness is *doing the right things*." Many churches are efficient in that they are well organized and maintain a full slate of programs. But while they generate a lot of *activity*, there is little *productivity*. Energy is wasted on trivial issues. It's like rearranging deck chairs on the Titanic; everything may look nice and organized, but it doesn't matter because the ship is still sinking! It is not enough for a church to be well organized; it must be well organized to do the right things.

God wants churches to be effective. Those few churches that are really effective concentrate on their purpose. By continually reviewing your purpose, you can keep your priorities straight and your church focused.

A Clear Purpose Attracts Cooperation

People want to join a church that knows where it's going. When a church clearly communicates its destination, people are eager to get on board. This is because everyone is looking for something that gives meaning, purpose, and direction to life. When Ezra told the people exactly what God expected them to do the people responded, "Tell us how to proceed in setting things straight, and we will fully cooperate" (Ezra 10:4 LB).

The apostle Paul was always clear in his purpose. As a result, people wanted to be a part of what he was doing. This was especially true of the church at Philippi. The Philippians were so captivated by Paul's mission that they gave him ongoing financial support (see Phil. 4:15). If you want your members to get excited about the church, actively support it, and generously give to it, you must vividly explain up front exactly where the church is headed.

Have you ever boarded a wrong plane? Once I got on a plane I thought was going to St. Louis but instead was headed to Kansas City. I learned an important lesson: Check the destination *before* the plane takes off. Bailing out later is painful! You wouldn't dare get on a bus without first knowing where it's going, so neither should you expect people to join your church without knowing its destination.

I want prospective members to make sure they know exactly where Saddleback Church is headed, so our purpose statement is explained in detail to every person who wants to join our church family—*before* they join. No one can join Saddleback Church without attending the membership class and signing the membership covenant, which includes a commitment to support the purposes of Saddleback.

Proverbs 11:27 (TEV) says, "If your goals are good, you will be respected." Tell people up front where your church is headed, and it will attract cooperation. Spell out your church's purposes and priorities in a membership class. Clearly explain your strategy and structure. This will keep people from joining the membership with false assumptions.

If you allow people to become members of your church without their understanding your purposes *you're asking for trouble*. New members, especially those transferring from other churches, often have personal agendas and preconceptions about the church. Unless you deal with them up front in a forthright manner, these issues will eventually cause problems and conflict.

People who transfer their membership to your church carry cultural baggage from their previous church, and they may have certain expectations your church has no intention of fulfilling. This fact became evident to me in the early days of Saddleback, even before we started public worship services. One of the men in our home Bible study group had been a member of a well-known large church in our area for twelve years. Every time we started to plan something he'd say, "Now, at my old church they did it like this." This became his recurring refrain.

After about eight weeks of this, I finally said, "You know, if you want a church just like your old church, why don't you go back there? It's only thirteen miles up the road." He took my advice and left with his family of five. That was thirty percent of our fellowship at that time—and he was a tither!

At the time, his action shocked me, but now I look back on that situation and believe it was one of the crucial decisions that determined the destiny of Saddleback Church. If I had listened to that fellow, Saddleback would have ended up just being a clone of that other church. Our future would have turned out very differently.

I also learned two important lessons about leadership: First, you cannot let whiners set the agenda for the church. That is an abdication of leadership. Unfortunately, the smaller a church is, the more influence the most negative member has. That experience also taught me that the best time to discover anyone's conflict with your church's philosophy of ministry is *before* they join. Explaining your church's purposes to people before they join will not only reduce conflict and disappointment in your church, it will also help some people realize they should join another church because of philosophy or personal taste.

A Clear Purpose Assists Evaluation

Second Corinthians 13:5 says, "Examine yourselves to see whether you are in the faith; test yourselves." How does a church evaluate itself? Not by comparing itself to other churches, but by asking, "Are we doing what God intends for us to do?" and "How well are we doing it?" As Peter Drucker says, "What is our business?" and "How's business?" These are the two most critical questions for evaluating your church. Your church's purpose statement must become the standard by which you measure your congregation's health and growth.

There is absolutely no correlation between the size and the strength of a church. A church can be big and strong, or big and flabby. Likewise a church can be small and strong, or small and wimpy. Big is not necessarily better, nor is being small necessarily better. *Better is better!*

The purpose of this book is not to make your church as large as Saddleback. Size is not the issue. The important issue is this: Your church will be stronger and healthier by being purpose driven.

Becoming a purpose-driven church takes time—it doesn't happen all at once, or even over six months. It may even take your church several years to make the transition. If you want your church to become purpose

> Evaluate your church by asking, "What is our business?" and then, "How's business?"

driven, you will have to lead it through four critical phases: First, you must *define* your purposes. Next, you must *communicate* those purposes to everyone in your church—on a regular basis. Third, you must *organize* your church around your purposes. Finally, you must *apply* your purposes to every part of your church. I'll describe each of these tasks in the following chapters.

5

Defining Your Purposes

Let there be real harmony so that there won't be splits in the church.... Be of one mind, united in thought and purpose.

1 Corinthians 1:10 (LB)

While I was a seminary student in Texas, I once agreed to help some leaders of a large church evaluate their total church program. The church had been a strong, vibrant witness for Christ in the past, and it had a historic reputation. I was a little intimidated as I drove up to the massive red brick structure for my first experience at church consulting. The hall to the conference room was filled with the portraits of the men who had pastored the church in the past one hundred years. This was a church with a history!

As we sat down for our first meeting I asked the group of leaders gathered, "How do you *feel* about your church?" Most of the comments expressed a quiet sense of satisfaction. One man summed it up by saying, "We have a *sound* church." But as I probed deeper I discovered that the church was *sound asleep!* While the church was theologically sound, nothing of spiritual significance was taking place there. The buildings were all paid for, and the church leaders had become lazy and lethargic. They were, as the prophet Amos would have said, "at ease in Zion" — and their "at ease" disease was slowly killing the church. Since they'd hired me to be their doctor, I gave them a simple prescription: Rediscover your purpose.

Leading Your Church to Define Its Purposes

Leading your congregation through a discovery of the New Testament purposes for the church is an exciting adventure. Don't rush through the process. And don't spoil the joy of discovery by simply telling everyone what the purposes are in a sermon. Wise leaders understand that people will give mental and verbal assent to what they are told, but they will hold with conviction what they discover for themselves. You're building a foundation for long-term health and growth.

It's thrilling to see apathetic members become enthusiastic as they rediscover how God desires to use them and their church. Below, I will explain the four steps to take in leading your church to define, or redefine, its purposes.

Study what the Bible says

Begin by involving your congregation in a study of the biblical passages on the church. Prior to starting Saddleback Church I took six months to do an extensive, personal Bible study on the church, using the methods described in my book *Dynamic Bible Study Methods* (Victor Books, 1980). During the first months of the new church, I led our young congregation through the same study. Together we studied all the relevant Scripture about the church.

Some of the Scriptures you may want to include in your study are: Matt. 5:13–16; 9:35; 11:28–30; 16:15–19; 18:19–20; 22:36–40; 24:14; 25:34–40; 28:18–20; Mark 10:43–45; Luke 4:18–19; 4:43–45; John 4:23; 10:14–18; 13:34–35; 20:21; Acts 1:8; 2:41–47; 4:32–35; 5:42; 6:1–7; Rom. 12:1–8; 15:1–7; 1 Cor. 12:12–31; 2 Cor. 5:17–6:1; Gal. 5:13–15; 6:1–2; Eph. 1:22–23;

2:19–22; 3:6; 3:14–21; 4:11–16; 5:23–24; Col. 1:24–28; 3:15–16; 1 Thess. 1:3; 5:11; Heb. 10:24–25; 13:7, 17; 1 Peter 2:9–10; 1 John 1:5–7; 4:7–21.

Gene Mims has written a great little book entitled *Kingdom Principles for Church Growth* (Convention Press) that can be used as a churchwide study course on the purposes of the church. As you lead your congregation in a study, there are several topics that you should consider.

- *Look at Christ's ministry on earth.* Ask, "What did Jesus do while he was here? What would he do if he were here today?" Whatever Jesus did while he was on earth, we are to continue today. The different elements of Christ's ministry should be evident in his church today. Whatever he did while here in a physical body, he wants continued in his spiritual body, the church.
- *Look at the images and names of the church.* The New Testament offers many analogies for the church: a body, a bride, a family, a flock, a community, and an army. Each of these images has profound implications for what the church should be, and what the church should be doing.
- *Look at the examples of the New Testament churches.* Ask, "What did the first churches do?" There are many different models given in Scripture. The Jerusalem church was very different from the church at Corinth. The Philippian church was very different from the church at Thessalonica. Study each of the local congregations found in the New Testament, including the seven churches listed in Revelation.
- *Look at the commands of Christ.* Ask, "What did Jesus tell us to do?" In Matthew 16:18 Jesus said, "I will build my church." He obviously has a specific purpose in mind. It isn't our job to *create* the purposes of the church but to *discover* them.

Remember, it's Christ's church, not ours. Jesus founded the church, died for the church, sent his Spirit to the church, and will someday return for his church. As the owner of the church, he has already established the purposes, and they're not negotiable.

> It isn't our job to *create* the purposes of the church but to *discover* them.

Our duty is to understand the purposes Christ has for the church and to implement them. While the programs must change in every generation, the purposes never change. We may be innovative with the *style* of ministry, but we must never alter the *substance* of it.

Look for answers to four questions

As you review what the Bible says about the church, watch for the answers to the questions below. As you formulate your answers, focus on both the *nature* and the *tasks* of the church.

1. Why does the church exist?
2. What are we to *be* as a church? (Who and what are we?)
3. What are we to *do* as a church? (What does God want done in the world?)
4. How are we to do it?

Put your findings in writing

Write down everything you've learned through your study. Don't worry about trying to be brief. Say everything you think needs to be said about the nature and purposes of the church. When we did this in the first year of Saddleback, I used a flip chart and felt-tipped marker to record all the findings that came out of our group study. Then we typed up everything that had been written down on the chart. The result was a ten-page document containing our random insights on the church.

Don't try to come up with a purpose statement at this point: Just collect information. It is always easier to edit and condense than to create. Focus only on getting all of the purposes clearly identified. I want to reemphasize this for pastors: Don't rush through this process! You're building a foundation that will support everything else you do for years to come. Even though *you* already know the New

> We may be innovative with the *style* of ministry, but we must never alter the *substance* of it.

Testament purposes, it is vital for your congregation to review all that the Bible has to say about the church and write down *their* conclusions.

Summarize your conclusions in a sentence

From our collection of typed insights from our Bible study, we eventually distilled a single sentence that summarized what we believe are the biblical purposes of the church. That's what you need to do as well. First, condense what you've discovered about the church by grouping similar concepts together under major headings such as evangelism, worship, fellowship, spiritual maturity, and ministry. Next, try to state all these major themes in a single paragraph. Then begin to edit out unnecessary words and phrases to reduce that paragraph to a single sentence.

Condensing your purpose statement into a single sentence is absolutely important. Why? Because it will have limited value if people can't remember it! Dawson Trotman used to say, "Thoughts disentangle themselves when they pass through the lips and the fingertips." In other words, if you can *say it* and *write it*, then you've clearly thought it through. If you haven't put your purposes on paper, you haven't really thought them out.

Francis Bacon, the English essayist, once said, "Reading makes a broad man, but writing makes an *exact* man." When it comes to communicating the purposes of the church, we want to be as precise as we can be.

What Makes an Effective Purpose Statement?

It is biblical

An effective purpose statement expresses the New Testament doctrine of the church. Remember, we don't decide the purposes of the church—we *discover* them. Christ is the head of his church. He established the purposes long ago. Now each generation must reaffirm them.

It is specific

Purpose statements need to be simple and clear. The biggest mistake a church can make when developing a purpose statement is trying to cram too much into it. The temptation is to add in all kinds of good, but unnecessary, phrases because you are afraid of leaving out something important. But the more you add to your statement, the more diffused it becomes, and the more difficult it is to fulfill.

A narrow mission is a clear mission. Disneyland's purpose statement is "To provide people happiness." The original mission of the Salvation Army was to "Make citizens of the rejected." Many purpose statements are so vague, they have no impact at all. Nothing becomes dynamic until it becomes specific. Some church statements say, "Our church exists to glorify God." Of course it does! But exactly *how* do you accomplish that?

A specific purpose statement forces you to focus your energy. Don't be detoured by peripheral issues. Ask the questions, "What are the very few things that will make the most difference for Jesus' sake in our world? What can we do that only the church can do?"

It is transferable

A purpose statement that is transferable is short enough to be remembered and passed on by everyone in your church. The shorter it is, the better. Although the purpose statement of every biblical church will include the same elements, there is nothing to keep you from saying it in a fresh, creative way. Try to make it memorable.

As a pastor I hate to admit this, but people don't remember sermons or speeches—they don't even remember paragraphs. What people remember are simple statements, slogans, and phrases. I don't remember any speech John F. Kennedy gave, but I do remember his statements, "Ask not what your country can do for you, ask what you can do for your country" and "I am a Berliner!" Neither do I remember any sermon preached by Dr. Martin Luther King Jr., but I do remember his famous phrase, "I have a dream!"

It is measurable

You must be able to look at your purpose statement and evaluate whether your church is doing it or not. Will you be able to *prove* you've accomplished it at the end of each year? You cannot judge the effectiveness of your church unless your mission is measurable.

A great purpose statement will provide a specific standard by which you can review, revise, and improve everything your church does. If you can't evaluate your church by your purpose statement, go back to the drawing board. Make it measurable. Otherwise your purpose statement is just a public relations piece.

Two Great Scriptures

In the first months of Saddleback I led our new church in the process I have just explained to you. Finally, we concluded that although many passages describe what the church is to be and do, two statements by Jesus summarize it all: the Great Commandment (Matt. 22:37–40) and the Great Commission (Matt. 28:19–20).

> Love the Lord your God with all your heart and with all your soul and with all your mind. . . . Love your neighbor as yourself. All the Law and the Prophets hang on these two commandments.
>
> Matthew 22:37–40

> Go and make disciples of all nations, baptizing them in the name of the Father and of the Son and of the Holy Spirit, and teaching them to obey everything I have commanded you.
>
> Matt. 28:19–20

The Great Commandment was given by Jesus in response to a question. One day, Jesus was asked to identify the most important command. He responded by saying, "Here is the entire Old Testament in a nutshell. I'm going to give you the *Cliff Notes* summary of God's Word. All the Law and all the Prophets can be condensed into two tasks: Love God with all your heart, and love your neighbor as yourself."

A Great Commitment to the Great Commandment and the Great Commission will grow a Great Church!

Later, in some of his last words to his disciples, Jesus gave the Great Commission to them and assigned them three more tasks: Go make disciples, baptize them, and teach them to obey everything he had taught.

I believe that every church is defined by what it is committed to, so I came up with this slogan: "A Great Commitment to the Great Commandment and the Great Commission will grow a Great Church." It became Saddleback's motto.

These two passages summarize everything we do at Saddleback Church. If an activity or program fulfills one of these commands, we do it. If it doesn't, we don't. We are driven by the Great Commandment and the Great Commission. Together, they give us the primary tasks the church is to focus on until Christ returns.

The Five Purposes of the Church

A *purpose-driven* church is committed to fulfilling all five tasks that Christ ordained for his church to accomplish.

Purpose #1: Love the Lord with all your heart

The word that describes this purpose is *worship*. The church exists to worship God. How do we love God with all our heart? By worshiping him! It doesn't matter if we're by ourselves, with a small group, or with 100,000 people. When we express our love to God, we're worshiping.

The Bible says, "Worship the Lord your God, and serve him only" (Matt. 4:10). Notice that worship comes before service. Worshiping God is the church's first purpose. Sometimes we get so busy working for God, we don't have time to express our love for him through worship.

Throughout Scripture we're commanded to celebrate God's presence by magnifying the Lord and exalting his name. Psalm 34:3 (NASB) says, "O magnify the LORD with me and let us exalt his name together." We shouldn't worship out of duty; we should worship because we want to. We should enjoy expressing our love to God.

Purpose #2: Love your neighbor as yourself

The word we use to describe this purpose is *ministry.* The church exists to minister to people. Ministry is demonstrating God's love to others by meeting their needs and healing their hurts in the name of Jesus. Each time you reach out in love to others you are ministering to them. The church is to minister to all kinds of needs: spiritual, emotional, relational, and physical. Jesus said that even a cup of cold water given in his name was considered as ministry and would not go unrewarded. The church is to ". . . equip the saints for the work of ministry" (Eph. 4:12 NRSV).

Unfortunately, very little actual ministry takes place in many churches. Instead, much of the time is taken up by meetings. Faithfulness is often defined in terms of attendance rather than service, and members just sit, soak, and sour.

Purpose #3: Go and make disciples

This purpose we call *evangelism.* The church exists to communicate God's Word. We are ambassadors for Christ, and our mission is to evangelize the world. The word *go* in the Great Commission is a present participle in the Greek text. It should read "as you are going." It is every Christian's responsibility to share the Good News wherever we go. We are to tell the whole world of Christ's coming, his death on the cross, his resurrection, and his promise to return. Someday each of us will give an account to God regarding how seriously we took this responsibility.

The task of evangelism is so important, Christ actually gave us *five* Great Commissions, one in each of the gospels, and one in the book of Acts. In Matthew 28:19–20, Mark 16:15, Luke 24:47–49, John 20:21, and Acts 1:8 Jesus commissions us to go and tell the world the message of salvation.

Evangelism is more than our responsibility; it is our great privilege. We are invited to be a part of bringing people into

God's eternal family. I don't know of a more significant cause to give one's life to. If you knew the cure for cancer, I'm sure you'd do everything you could to get the news out. It would save millions of lives. But you already know something better: You've been given the Gospel of eternal life to share, which is the greatest news of all!

As long as there is one person in the world who does not know Christ, the church has a mandate to keep

> As Christians we're called to *belong*, not just to *believe*.

growing. Growth is not optional; it is commanded by Jesus. We should not seek church growth for our own benefit, but because God wants people saved.

Purpose #4: Baptizing them

In the Greek text of the Great Commission there are three present participle verbs: *going, baptizing*, and *teaching.* Each of these is a part of the command to "make disciples." Going, baptizing, and teaching are the essential elements of the disciple-making process. At first glance you might wonder why the Great Commission gives the same prominence to the simple act of baptism as it does to the great tasks of evangelism and edification. Obviously, Jesus did not mention it by accident. Why is baptism so important to warrant inclusion in Christ's Great Commission? I believe it is because it symbolizes one of the purposes of the church: *fellowship*—identification with the body of Christ.

As Christians we're called to *belong*, not just to *believe.* We are not meant to live lone-ranger lives; instead, we are to belong to Christ's family and be members of his body. Baptism is not only a symbol of salvation, it is a symbol of fellowship. It not only symbolizes our new life in Christ, it visualizes a person's incorporation into the body of Christ. It says to the world, "This person is now one of us!" When new believers are baptized, we welcome them into the fellowship of the family of God. We are not alone. We have each other for support. I love the way Ephesians 2:19 is phrased in the Living Bible: "You are members of God's very own family ... and you belong in God's household with every other Christian." The church exists to provide fellowship for believers.

Purpose #5: Teaching them to obey

The word we commonly use to refer to this purpose is *discipleship*. The church exists to edify, or educate, God's people. Discipleship is the process of helping people become more like Christ in their thoughts, feelings, and actions. This process begins when a person is born again and continues throughout the rest of his life. Colossians 1:28 (NCV) says, "We continue to preach Christ to each person, using all wisdom to warn and to teach everyone, in order to bring each one into God's presence *as a mature person in Christ*" (italics added).

As the church we are called not only to reach people, but also to teach them. After someone has made a decision for Christ, he or she must be discipled. It is the church's responsibility to develop people to spiritual maturity. This is God's will for every believer. Paul writes: ". . . so that the body of Christ may be built up until we all reach unity in the faith and in the knowledge of the Son of God and become mature, attaining to the whole measure of the fullness of Christ" (Eph. 4:12b–13).

If you examine the earthly ministry of Jesus, it is apparent that he included all five of these elements in his work (for a summary see John 17). The apostle Paul not only fulfilled these purposes in his ministry, he also explained them in Ephesians 4:1–16. But the clearest example of all five purposes is the first church at Jerusalem described in Acts 2:1–47. They taught each other, they fellowshiped together, they worshiped, they ministered, and they evangelized. Today our purposes are unchanged: The church exists to *edify, encourage, exalt, equip,* and *evangelize.* While each church will differ in *how* these tasks are accomplished, there should be no disagreement about *what* we are called to do.

Saddleback's Purpose Statement

At Saddleback we use five key words to summarize Christ's five purposes for his church.

Magnify: We celebrate God's presence in worship

Mission: We communicate God's Word through evangelism

Membership: We incorporate God's family into our fellowship

Maturity: We educate God's people through discipleship

Ministry: We demonstrate God's love through service

These key words, representing our five purposes, have been incorporated into our mission statement, which reads as follows:

Saddleback's Purpose Statement

To bring people to Jesus and *membership* in his family, develop them to Christlike *maturity,* and equip them for their *ministry* in the church and life *mission* in the world, in order to *magnify* God's name.

There are three important distinctives I want you to notice about Saddleback's purpose statement. First, it is stated *in terms of results* rather than in terms of activity. Five measurable results are listed. Most churches, if they have a purpose statement, usually state it in terms of activities ("we edify, evangelize, worship," etc.). This makes it harder to evaluate and quantify.

At Saddleback, we identify the results we expect to see coming from fulfilling each of the five purposes of the church. For each result we can ask questions like: How many? How many more than last year? How many were brought to Christ?

How many new members are there? How many are demonstrating spiritual maturity? What are the signs of maturity we look for? How many have been equipped and mobilized for ministry? How many are fulfilling their life mission in the world? These questions measure our success and force us to evaluate if we are really fulfilling the Great Commandment and the Great Commission.

Second, I want you to notice that Saddleback's purpose statement is stated in a way that *encourages participation* by every member. People must be able to see how they can make a contribution toward the goals of your church. The mission must be stated in a way that everyone can not only believe in it—they can participate in it. If your statement doesn't allow individual participation, very little will get done.

Third, and most importantly, notice that we've arranged the five purposes into a *sequential process*. This is absolutely crucial. To be a purpose-driven church your purposes must be put into a process. That way they can be acted on every day. Every purpose statement needs a process to fulfill it; if not, you simply have a theological statement that sounds good but produces nothing.

Instead of trying to grow a church with programs, focus on growing people with a process. This concept is the heart of being a purpose-driven church. If you will set up a process for developing disciples and *stick with it*, your church's growth will be healthy, balanced, and consistent. Benjamin Disraeli once observed that "constancy to purpose is the secret of success."

> Don't focus on growing a *church* with *programs*, focus on growing *people* with a *process*.

Our process for implementing the purposes of God involves four steps: We bring people in, build them up, train them, and send them out. We bring them in as *members,* we build them up to *maturity*, we train them for *ministry,* and we send them out on *mission*, *magnifying* the Lord in the process. That's it! This is our total focus at Saddleback. We don't do anything else.

If I were to use business terms I'd say that our church is in the "disciple-development" business, and that our product is changed lives—Christlike people. If it is the church's objective to develop disciples, then we must think through a process that will accomplish that goal. Your church must define both your purposes and a process for fulfilling those purposes. To do less is to leave to chance the great responsibility we've been given by our Lord Jesus Christ.

Every great church has defined its purposes and then somehow figured out a process or system for fulfilling those purposes. The Central Church of Seoul, Korea, was built on a cellgroup system. First Baptist Church, Dallas, was built on a fully graded Sunday school system. Coral Ridge Presbyterian Church in Fort Lauderdale, Florida, grew due to a personal evangelism system. In the early 1970s, many churches were built around a system of bringing attenders to church on buses. In each of these cases, church leaders clearly defined their purposes and then developed a process to fulfill those purposes.

I cannot overemphasize the importance of defining your church's purposes. It is not merely a target that you aim for; it is your congregation's reason for being. A clear purpose statement will provide the direction, the vitality, the boundaries, and the driving force for everything you do. Purpose-driven churches will be the churches best equipped to minister during all the changes we will face in the twenty-first century.

6

Communicating Your Purposes

An unreliable messenger can cause a lot of trouble.
Reliable communication permits progress.

Proverbs 13:17 (LB)

I n Nehemiah's story of rebuilding the wall around Jerusalem, we learn that halfway through the project the people got discouraged and wanted to give up. Like many churches, they lost their sense of purpose and, as a result, became overwhelmed with fatigue, frustration, and fear. Nehemiah rallied the people back to work by reorganizing the project and recasting the vision. He reminded them of the importance of their work and reassured them that God would help them fulfill his purpose (Neh. 4:6–15). The wall was completed in fifty-two days.

Although the wall took only fifty-two days to complete, the people became discouraged at the halfway point: just twenty-six days into the project! Nehemiah had to renew their vision. From this story we get what I call the "Nehemiah Principle": *Vision and purpose must be restated every twenty-six days to keep the church moving in the right direction*. In other words, make sure you communicate your purpose at least monthly. It is amazing how quickly human beings — and churches — lose their sense of purpose.

Once you have defined the purposes of your church, you must continually clarify and communicate them to everyone in your congregation. It is not a task you do once and then forget about. This is the foremost responsibility of leadership. If you fail to communicate your statement of purpose to your members, you may as well not have one.

Ways to Communicate Vision and Purpose

There are several ways to communicate the vision and purpose of your church.

Scripture

Teach the biblical truth about the church. I've already mentioned that the greatest church-growth textbook is the Bible. Teach the doctrine of the church passionately and frequently. Show how every part of your church's vision is biblically based by giving Bible verses that explain and illustrate your reasoning.

Symbols

Great leaders have always understood and harnessed the tremendous power of symbols. People often need visual representations of concepts in order to grasp them. Symbols can be powerful communication tools because they elicit strong passions and emotions. For instance, you would be outraged to find a swastika painted on your church wall, while an American flag brings out feelings of honor and pride.

Continents have been conquered under the sign of Christianity's cross, Communism's hammer and sickle, and Islam's crescent moon. At Saddleback we've used two symbols—five concentric circles and a baseball diamond—to illustrate our purposes. These will be explained in the next two chapters.

Slogans

Slogans, maxims, mottoes, and pithy phrases are remembered long after sermons are forgotten. Many key events in history have hinged on a slogan: "Remember the Alamo!" "Sink the Bismarck!" "Give me liberty or give me death!" History has proven that a simple slogan, repeatedly shared with conviction, can motivate people to do things they would normally never do—even to give up their lives on a battlefield.

We've developed and used dozens of slogans at Saddleback to reinforce our church's vision: "Every member is a minister," "All leaders are learners," "We're saved to serve," "Evaluate for excellence," "Win the lost at any cost," and many others. I periodically set aside time to think of new ways to communicate old ideas in fresh, succinct ways.

Stories

Jesus used simple stories to help people understand and relate to his vision. Matthew 13:34 (LB) says, "Jesus constantly used . . . illustrations when speaking to the crowds. . . . He never spoke to them without at least one illustration."

Use stories to dramatize the purposes of your church. For example, when I speak about the importance of evangelism, I tell stories of Saddleback members who have recently shared their faith with friends and led them to Christ. When I speak about the importance of fellowship, I read actual letters from people whose loneliness was relieved by getting involved in our church family. When I speak about the importance of discipleship, I may use a testimony of how a couple's spiritual growth saved their marriage, or how someone resolved a personal problem by applying biblical principles.

At Saddleback we have certain "legends," stories that I tell over and over, that powerfully illustrate a purpose of our church. One of my favorites is the story of how five different lay pastors beat me to a hospital visit, and when I got there the nurse would not let me see the patient because "too many pastors have already seen him!" I've bragged on those five lay pastors ever since then. People tend to do whatever gets rewarded, so make heroes of people in your church when they do the work of the church. Tell their stories.

Specifics

Always give practical, clear, concrete action steps that explain how your church intends to fulfill its purposes. Offer a detailed plan for implementing your purposes. Plan programs, schedule events, dedicate buildings, and hire staff for each purpose. These are the specifics that people care about.

Remember, nothing becomes dynamic until it becomes specific. When a vision is vague it holds no attraction. The more specific your church's vision is, the more it will grab attention and attract commitment. The most specific way to communicate the purposes is to apply them personally to each member's life.

Personalize the Purposes

In communicating the purposes of your church it is important to personalize them. The way to personalize the purposes is to show how there is both a privilege and a responsibility connected to each of them. Colossians 3:15 (LB) says, "This is your responsibility and privilege as members of his body." There are both responsibilities and privileges of being a member of a church family. I try to personalize the purposes of our church by showing how they are our *responsibility to fulfill* and how they are our *privilege to enjoy.*

The purposes of the church can be personalized as God's five goals for every believer. These goals express what God wants each of us to do with our lives while on earth.

My responsibilities as a believer

God wants me to be a member of his family. This is the purpose of fellowship stated in a personal way. The Bible is very clear that following Christ is not just a matter of believing—it also includes belonging. The Christian life is not a solo act. We are meant to live in relationship with each other. First Peter 1:3 (LB) says "[He] has given us the privilege of being born again, so that we are now members of God's own family." God has given us the church as a spiritual family for our own benefit. Ephesians 2:19 (LB) says, "You are members of God's very own family, . . . and you belong in God's household with every other Christian."

God wants me to be a model of his character. This is the personalized goal of discipleship. God wants every believer to grow up to become like Christ in character. Becoming like Christ is the biblical definition of "spiritual maturity." Jesus has established a pattern for us to follow. "To this you were called, because Christ suffered for you, leaving you an example, that you should follow in his steps" (1 Peter 2:21).

In 1 Timothy 4:12, Paul gives us several specific areas in which we are to model the character of Christ: "Set an example for the believers in speech, in life, in love, in faith and in purity." Notice that maturity is not measured by one's learning but by one's lifestyle. It is possible to be well versed in the Bible and still be immature.

God wants me to be a minister of his grace. A third responsibility of every Christian is the personalized purpose of service, or ministry. God expects us to use the gifts, talents, and opportunities he gives us to benefit others. First Peter 4:10 says, "Each one should use whatever gift he has received to serve others, faithfully administering God's grace in its various forms."

God intends for every believer to have a ministry. At Saddleback we are very up front about this expectation when witnessing to unbelievers. We don't "bait and switch." I tell unbelievers, "When you give your life to Christ, you are signing up to minister in his name for the rest of your life. It's what God made you for." Ephesians 2:10 (LB) says, "It is God himself who has made us what we are and given us new lives from Christ

Jesus; and long ages ago he planned that we should spend these lives in helping others."

God wants me to be a messenger of his love. This is the church's purpose of evangelism stated in a personal way. Part of the job description for each believer is that once we have been born again, we become messengers of the Good News to others. Paul says, "Life is worth nothing unless I use it for doing the work assigned me by the Lord Jesus—the work of telling others the Good News about God's mighty kindness and love" (Acts 20:24 LB). This is an important responsibility of every Christian. Second Corinthians 5:19–20 (LB) says, "God was in Christ, restoring the world to himself, no longer counting men's sins against them but blotting them out. This is the wonderful message he has given us to tell others. We are Christ's ambassadors. God is using us to speak to you." We are to plead with unbelievers to receive the love he offers—to be reconciled to God.

Have you ever wondered why God leaves us here on earth, with all its pain, sorrow, and sin, after we accept Christ? Why doesn't he just zap us immediately to heaven and spare us from all this? After all, we can worship, fellowship, pray, sing, hear God's Word, and even have fun in heaven. In fact, there are only two things you can't do in heaven that you can do on earth: sin, and witness to unbelievers. I ask our church members which of these two they think Christ has left us here to do. We each have a mission on earth and part of it includes telling others about Christ.

God wants me to be a magnifier of his name. Psalm 34:3 (NASB) says, "O *magnify* the LORD with me, and let us exalt His name together" (italics added). We each have a personal responsibility to worship God. The very first commandment says, "Thou shalt have no other gods before me" (Exodus 20:3 KJV). There is an inborn urge in each person to worship. If we don't worship God we will find something else to worship, whether it be a job, a family, money, a sport, or even ourselves.

My privileges as a believer

While fulfilling the five purposes of the church are a responsibility of every Christian, they also provide spiritual, emotional, and relational benefits. In fact, the church provides people with things they cannot find anywhere else in the world: Worship helps people focus on God; fellowship helps them face life's problems; discipleship helps fortify their faith; ministry helps them find their talents; and evangelism helps them fulfill their mission.

State It Over and Over

Don't assume that a single sermon on the church's purposes will permanently set the direction of your church. Don't suppose that by printing your purposes in the bulletin everyone has learned them, or even read them! One widely known law of advertising is that a message must be communicated seven times before it really sinks in.

My Church Family Gives Me

- God's *purpose* to live for (mission)
- God's *people* to live with (membership)
- God's *principles* to live by (maturity)
- God's *profession* to live out (ministry)
- God's *power* to live on (magnify)

At Saddleback we use as many different channels as we can think of to keep our purposes before our church family. I've already mentioned that our purposes and vision are communicated in each monthly membership class. Once a year, usually in January, I also preach an annual "state of the church" message. It is always a review of our five purposes. It's the same message every year; only the illustrations are updated.

Many pastors do not understand the power of the pulpit. Like a rudder on a ship, it will determine the direction of a church either intentionally or unintentionally. If you are a pastor, use your pulpit on purpose! Where else do you get everyone's undivided attention on a weekly basis? Whenever you speak, always look for the opportunity to say something like, "And that's why the church exists." Don't be afraid to repeat yourself, because nobody gets it the first time. I call repeating things over and over in fresh ways "creative redundancy."

On the opposite page you will find a chart that shows several different angles I've used to present the purposes of the church. Feel free to use any of these outlines. They are just different ways of saying the same thing.

In addition to communicating our purposes through preaching and teaching, we've used brochures, banners, articles, newsletters, bulletins, videos, and cassettes, and we've even written songs. At the entrance to our worship center, our purposes and corresponding verses are etched into the glass foyer for all to read as they enter. We believe that if we keep saying the same thing in different ways, one of those ways will capture the attention of every member. Often, after presenting the purposes in a new way, someone will say that they just understood for the first time. Our goal is for every member to be able to explain our purposes to others.

The vision of any church always fades with time unless it is reinforced. This is because people become distracted by other things. Restate your purposes on a regular basis. Teach them over and over. Utilize as many different media as you can to keep them before your people. By continually fanning the fire of your purposes you can overcome the tendency of your church to become complacent or discouraged. Remember the Nehemiah Principle!

Explaining the Church's Purposes

Purpose	Task	Acts 2:42-47	Objective	Target	Life Component	Basic Human Need	The Church Provides	Emotional Benefit
Outreach	Evangelize	"…added to their number daily those who were being saved."	Mission	Community	My **Witness**	**Purpose** to Live For	A **Focus** for Living	Significance
Worship	Exalt	"They devoted themselves to… breaking of bread and prayers.… praising God."	Magnify	Crowd	My **Worship**	**Power** to Live On	A **Force** for Living	Stimulation
Fellowship	Encourage	"…devoted to the fellowship…all the believers were together …they ate together."	Membership	Congregation	My **Relationships**	**People** to Live With	A **Family** for Living	Support
Discipleship	Edify	"They devoted themselves to the apostles' teaching."	Maturity	Committed	My **Walk**	**Principles** to Live By	A **Foundation** for Living	Stability
Service	Equip	"They gave to anyone as he had need."	Ministry	Core	My **Work**	**Profession** to Live Out	A **Function** for Living	Self-expression

?

Organizing Around Your Purposes

New wine must be poured into new wineskins.

Luke 5:38

The two most influential preachers of the eighteenth century were George Whitefield and John Wesley. Although they were contemporaries of each other, and both were greatly used by God, they differed widely in theology, personality, and how they organized their ministries.

Whitefield was best known for his preaching. In his lifetime, he preached over 18,000 sermons, averaging ten a week! He once spoke to nearly 100,000 people near Glasgow, Scotland, and his preaching tours in America stimulated the revival known as the Great Awakening. However, biographers have pointed out that Whitefield often left his converts without any organization so the results of his work were of short duration. Today, very few Christians would recognize George Whitefield's name.

In contrast, John Wesley's name is still recognized by millions of Christians. Why is this? Wesley was an itinerant preacher just like Whitefield, engaging in large, outdoor evangelistic meetings. But Wesley was also an organizer. He created an organizational structure to fulfill his purpose that far outlasted his lifetime. That organization is called the Methodist Church!

For any renewal to last in a church, there must be a structure to nurture and support it. It is not enough to merely define a purpose statement and communicate it, you must also organize around your church, around your purposes. In this chapter I'll discuss how to set up a structure that insures equal emphasis is given to all five purposes. Remember, balance is the key to a healthy church.

Most evangelical churches already do the five purposes of the church—*sort of.* But they don't do them all equally well. One church may be strong in fellowship, yet weak in evangelism. Another church may be strong in worship, yet weak in discipleship. Still another may be strong in evangelism, yet weak in ministry. Why is this?

> Without a *system* and a *structure* to balance the five purposes, your church will overemphasize the purpose that expresses the gifts and passion of its pastor.

It is the natural tendency of leaders to emphasize what they feel strongly about and neglect whatever they feel less passionate about. Around the world you can find churches that have become an extension of their pastor's giftedness. Unless you set up a *system* and a *structure* to intentionally balance the five purposes, your church will tend to overemphasize the purpose that best expresses the gifts and passion of its pastor.

Historically, churches have taken on five basic shapes, depending on which purpose they emphasize the most.

Five Kinds of Churches

The Soul Winning Church. If the pastor sees his primary role as an evangelist, then the church becomes a "soul winning" church. Because this church's main goal is to save souls, it is always reaching out to the lost. The terms you're likely to hear most often in this church are *witnessing, evangelism, salvation, decisions for Christ, baptisms, visitation, altar calls*, and *crusades*. In the soul winning church, anything other than evangelism is relegated to a secondary role.

The Experiencing God Church. If the pastor's passion and gifts lie in the area of worship, he will instinctively lead the church to become an "experiencing God" church. The focus of this church is on experiencing the presence and power of God in worship. Key terms for this church are *praise, prayer, worship, music, spiritual gifts, spirit, power*, and *revival*. In this type of church, the worship service receives more attention than anything else. I've found both charismatic and non-charismatic varieties of the experiencing God church.

The Family Reunion Church. A church that focuses primarily on fellowship is what I call the "family reunion" church. This church is shaped by the pastor who is highly relational, loves people, and spends most of his time caring for members. He serves more as a chaplain than anything else. Key terms for this church are *love, belonging, fellowship, caring, relationships, potlucks, small groups*, and *fun*. In the family reunion church, the gathering is more important than the goals.

Most churches of this type have less than 200 members, since that's about all one pastor can personally care for. I estimate that about 80 percent of American churches fall into this category. A family reunion church may not get much done, but it is almost indestructible. It can survive poor preaching, limited finances, lack of growth, and even church splits. Relationships are the glue that keep the faithful coming.

The Classroom Church. A "classroom" church occurs when the pastor sees his primary role as being a teacher. If teaching is his primary gift, he will emphasize preaching and teaching and de-emphasize the other tasks of the church. The pastor serves as the expert instructor, and members come to church with notebooks, take notes, and go home. Key words for the classroom church are *expository preaching, Bible study, Greek and Hebrew, doctrine, knowledge, truth,* and *discipleship*. It is not unheard of for a classroom church to have the word *Bible* in its name.

The Social Conscience Church. The pastor of the "social conscience" church sees his role as prophet and reformer. This kind of church is out to change society. It is full of activists who are "doers of the Word," and comes in both a liberal and a conservative version. The liberal version tends to focus on the injustice in our society, while the conservative version tends to focus on the moral decline in our society. Both liberal and conservative versions feel the church should be a major player in the political process, and its members are always involved in some current crusade or cause. Important terms in this church are *needs, serve, share, minister, take a stand,* and *do something*.

I realize that I have painted these pictures with broad strokes. Generalizations never tell the whole story. Some churches are a blend of two or three of these categories. The point is that unless there is an intentional plan to balance all five purposes, most churches will embrace one purpose to the neglect of the others.

There are some interesting things we can observe about these five categories of churches. The members of each of these churches will usually consider their church as *the most spiritual.* That's because people are attracted to join the type of church that corresponds to their own passion and giftedness. We all want to be a part of a church that affirms what we feel is most important. The truth is, all five of these emphases are important purposes of the church and must be balanced if a church is to be healthy.

Much of the conflict occurring in congregations is caused when a church calls a pastor whose gifts and passion do not

Most Churches Tend to Focus On Only One Purpose

Paradigm	Primary Focus	Pastor's Role	People's Role	Primary Target	Key Term	Central Value	Tools Used	Source of Legitimacy
Soul Winning Church	Evangelism	Evangelist	Witnesses	The Community	Save	Decisions for Christ	Visitation & Altar Call	Number Baptized
Experiencing God Church	Worship	Worship Leader	Worshipers	The Crowd	Feel	Personal Experience	Music & Prayer	"The Spirit"
Family Reunion Church	Fellowship	Chaplain	Family Members	The Congregation	Belong	Loyalty & Tradition	Fellowship Hall & Potluck	Our Heritage
Bible Classroom Church	Edification	Instructor	Students	The Committed	Know	Bible Knowledge	Notebooks & Overheads	Verse by Verse Teaching
Social Conscience Church	Ministry	Reformer	Activists	The Core	Care	Justice & Mercy	Petitions & Placards	Number of Needs Met
Purpose Driven Church	**Balance All Five**	**Equipper**	**Ministers**	**All Five**	**Be & Do**	**ChristLike Character**	**Life Development Process**	**Changed Lives**

match what the church has been in the past. For example, if a family reunion church thinks they are calling a pastor to be their chaplain and they get an evangelist or a reformer, you can expect sparks to fly. That is a recipe for disaster!

Five Major Parachurch Movements

I've found it interesting to observe that most of the parachurch movements begun in the past forty years tend to specialize in one of the purposes of the church. From time to time God has raised up a parachurch movement to reemphasize a neglected purpose of the church. I believe it is valid, and even helpful to the church, for parachurch organizations to focus on a single purpose. It allows their emphasis to have greater impact on the church.

The Lay Renewal Movement. This movement has refocused the church on the ministry of all Christians. Organizations such as Faith at Work, Laity Lodge, and The Church of the Savior, and authors such as Elton Trueblood, Findley Edge, and David Haney have been used by God to reemphasize that he has called and gifted *every* believer for service.

The Discipleship/Spiritual Formations Movement. A reemphasis on developing believers to full maturity has been the focus of this movement. Organizations such as the Navigators, Worldwide Discipleship, and Campus Crusade for Christ, and authors such as Waylon Moore, Gary Kuhne, Gene Getz, Richard Foster, and Dallas Willard have underscored the importance of building up Christians and establishing personal spiritual disciplines.

The Worship/Renewal Movement. This movement has taken on the task of refocusing the church on the importance of worship. It began with the Jesus Movement in the early 1970s and was followed by the charismatic and liturgical renewals. Most recently, the contemporary worship emphasis has brought us new music, new worship forms, and a greater emphasis on corporate worship. Organizations like Maranatha! Music and

Hosanna/Integrity have played a major role in shaping how worship styles have changed and multiplied.

The Church Growth Movement. This movement has refocused the church on evangelism, missions, and corporate growth. Beginning with the books of Donald McGavran, Peter Wagner, Elmer Towns, Win Arn, and numerous seminary professors, the movement grew larger in the 1980s through growth consultants, seminars, and well-known pastors.

The Small Group/Pastoral Care Movement. It has been the task of the small group/pastoral care movement to refocus the church on fellowship and caring relationships within the body. The Korean cell-church model and organizations such as Touch Ministries, Serendipity, Care Givers, and Stephen's Ministry have shown us the value of using small groups and the importance of caring for individuals.

We should be thankful to God for each of these movements, organizations, and authors. Each movement has had a valid message for the church. Each has given the body of Christ a wake-up call. Each has emphasized a different purpose of the church.

Keeping Your Church Balanced

Movements, by nature, *specialize* in order to have an impact. There is nothing wrong with specializing. When I need surgery, I want a doctor who specializes in the surgery I'm having. But no one specialist can adequately explain everything that goes on in my body.

> There is no single key to church health and church growth.

Likewise, no single parachurch movement can offer everything the body of Christ needs to be healthy. Each one emphasizes just a *part* of the big picture. It is important to have a larger perspective of the whole church which recognizes the importance of balancing all five purposes.

For instance, a friend of mine who is a pastor went to a seminar where he was taught that small groups were *the* key to church growth. So he went home and instituted a plan to completely overhaul the structure of his church and rebuild around a network of small cell groups. But about six months later he went to another popular seminar where he was told that seeker services were *the* key to growth. So he went home and rearranged the order and style of his worship service. Then he got really confused when he got three seminar brochures in the same week. One boldly proclaimed, "Sunday school is the growth agent of the church." Another said, "One-on-one disciple making: the secret of growth." The third brochure was about a conference on "Expository preaching for church growth." Eventually, he got so frustrated about what *the* key to growth was, he quit going to seminars. I don't blame him! I've often felt the same way. Each time he went to a conference he'd be given a true, but *partial* picture of what the church should be doing. It is simplistic and inaccurate to suggest that only one factor is the secret of church growth.

> A balanced church will be a healthy church.

There is no single key to church health and church growth; there are many keys. The church is not called to do one thing; it is called to do many things. That's why balance is so important. I tell my staff that the ninth Beatitude is "Blessed are the balanced; for they shall outlast everyone else."

As Paul points out so vividly in 1 Corinthians 12, the body of Christ has many parts to it. It's not just a hand or a mouth or an eye; it is a system of interworking parts and organs. Actually, your body is made up of different systems: respiratory, circulatory, nervous, digestive, skeletal, and so forth. When all of these systems are in balance with each other, that is called "health." Imbalance is illness. Likewise, balancing the five New Testament purposes brings health to the body of Christ, the church.

Saddleback Church is organized around two simple concepts to insure balance. We call them the "Circles of Commitment" and the "Life Development Process." These two concepts symbolize how we apply the five purposes of the church at Saddleback. The Life Development Process (a baseball diamond) illustrates *what we do* at Saddleback. The Circles of Commitment (five concentric circles) illustrate *who we do it with.*

I developed these concepts in 1974, as a youth pastor, before beginning Saddleback. Today, with nearly 10,000 attending, we still build everything we do around these two diagrams. They have served us well.

The concentric circles represent a way of understanding the different levels of commitment and maturity in your church. The baseball diamond represents a process for moving people from little or no commitment to deeper levels of commitment and maturity. In this chapter we'll look at the concentric circles. I'll explain the baseball diamond in chapter 8.

Look at your church from a new perspective. Is everyone in your church equally committed to Christ? Are all your members at the same level of spiritual maturity? Of course not. Some of your members are highly committed and very mature. Others are uncommitted and spiritually immature. Between these two groups are other people at various stages of spiritual growth. In a purpose-driven church we identify five different levels of commitment. These five levels correlate to the five purposes of the church.

In the graphic of the five concentric circles on the next page, each circle represents a different level of commitment, ranging from very little commitment (such as agreeing to attend services occasionally) to a very mature commitment (such as the commitment to use your spiritual gifts in ministering to others). As I describe these five different groups of people at Saddleback, you'll recognize that they exist in your church too.

5 Circles of Commitment

The Life Development Process

You may have seen a version of either of these diagrams in many places. I first published them in *Discipler* magazine in 1977. Since that time, they have been adopted by thousands of churches and reprinted in many books.

The Circles of Commitment

The goal of your church is to move people from the outer circle (low commitment/maturity) to the inner circle (high commitment/maturity). At Saddleback we call this "moving people from the community into the core."

The Community

The community is your starting point. It is the pool of lost people that live within driving distance of your church that have made no commitment at all to either Jesus Christ or your church. They are the unchurched that you want to reach. Your community is where the purpose of *evangelism* takes place. It is the largest circle because it contains the most people.

As Saddleback Church has grown, we have narrowed our definition of the community to refer to people we call "unchurched, occasional attenders." If you visit a Saddleback service at least four times in a year (and indicate it with a registration card or offering envelope), your name gets put on the "Community" database in our computer. These are our hottest evangelistic prospects. As I write this, we have over 31,000 names of occasional attenders of Saddleback. This represents about 10 percent of our area. Our ultimate goal, of course, is total penetration of our community, giving everyone a chance to hear about Christ.

The Crowd

The next circle inward represents the group of people we call the "Crowd." The crowd includes everyone who shows up on Sundays for services. They are your regular attenders. The crowd is made up of both believers and nonbelievers—all they may have in common is that they are committed to attending a *worship* service every week. That isn't much of a commitment, but at least it's something you can build on. When someone moves from your community into your crowd you've made major progress in his or her life. Currently we have about 10,000 "crowd" people attending our services at Saddleback each weekend.

While an unbeliever cannot truly worship, he can watch others worship. I'm convinced that genuine worship is a powerful witness to unbelievers if it is done in a style that makes sense to them. I will discuss this in detail in chapter 13. If an unbeliever makes a commitment to regular attendance at Saddleback, I believe it will be just a matter of time until he accepts Christ. Once a person has received Christ, our goal is to move him into the next level of commitment: the "Congregation."

The Congregation

The congregation is the group of official members of your church. They have been baptized and have made a commitment to be a part of your church family. They are now more than attenders, they are committed to the purpose of *fellowship*. This is a critical commitment. The Christian life is not just a matter of believing; it includes belonging. Once people have made a commitment to Christ they need to be encouraged to take the next step and commit themselves to Christ's body, the church. At Saddleback, only those who have received Christ, been baptized, taken our membership class (Class 101: "Discovering Saddleback Membership"), and signed the membership covenant are considered a part of the congregation (membership).

At Saddleback we see no use in having nonresident or inactive members on a roll. As a result, we remove hundreds of names from our membership each year. We are not interested in a large membership, just a legitimate membership of genuinely active and involved people. Currently, our congregation is formed by about five thousand active members.

I once spoke in a church that had over a thousand members on its roll but had less than two hundred people attending services! What is the value of having that kind of membership? If you have more members on your church roll than you have in attendance you should seriously consider redefining the meaning of membership in your congregation.

Having more attenders than members means the church is being effective in attracting the unchurched and building a pool for evangelism. A good indicator of a church's evangelistic effectiveness is when you have at least 25 percent more people attending as part of the crowd than you have members in the congregation. For example, if you have 200 members, you ought to have at least 250 in average attendance. If you don't, it means almost no one in your church is inviting unbelievers to come with them. Currently at Saddleback, the crowd is 100 percent larger than the congregation. Our 5,000 members are bringing their unsaved friends, so we're averaging 10,000 in attendance.

The Committed

Do you have people in your church who are godly and growing—people who are serious about their faith—who for one reason or another are not actively serving in a ministry of your church? We call these people the "Committed." They pray, give, and are dedicated to growing in *discipleship*. They are good people, but they have not yet gotten involved in ministry.

At Saddleback, we consider those who have taken Class 201: "Discovering Spiritual Maturity" and have signed a maturity covenant card to be in this group. The maturity covenant card indicates a commitment to three spiritual habits: (1) having a daily quiet time, (2) tithing ten percent of their income, and (3) being active in a small group. We consider these three habits essential for spiritual growth. At the time of this writing, about 3,500 people at Saddleback have signed maturity covenant cards and are considered a part of our "committed" group.

The Core

The "Core" is the smallest group, because it represents the deepest level of commitment. They are the dedicated minority of workers and leaders, those who are committed to *ministering* to others. They are people that lead and serve in the various ministries of your church as Sunday school teachers, deacons, musicians, youth sponsors, and so forth. Without these people your church would come to a standstill. Your core workers form the heart of your church.

At Saddleback we have a very intentional process for helping people find their best ministry niche. This includes taking Class 301: "Discovering My Ministry," filling out a SHAPE profile, having a personal ministry interview, being commissioned as a lay minister in the church, and attending a core-only monthly training meeting. Currently we have about 1,500 people in the core at Saddleback. I would do anything for these people. They are the secret of our strength. If I were to drop dead, Saddleback would continue to grow because of this base of 1,500 lay ministers.

What happens when people finally get to the core? We move them back out into the community for ministry!

Jesus Recognized Different Levels of Commitment

Jesus realized that every person is at a different level of spiritual commitment. I've always been fascinated by a conversation Jesus had with a spiritual seeker. Jesus made the comment, "You are *not far* from the kingdom of God"(Mark 12:34, italics added). Not far? I take that to mean that Jesus recognized degrees of spiritual understanding and commitment, even among unbelievers.

Jesus' ministry included ministering to the *Community*, feeding the *Crowd*, gathering a *Congregation*, challenging the *Committed,* and discipling the *Core*. All five tasks are evident in the gospels. We need to follow his example! Jesus began at the level of commitment of each person he met. Often he would simply capture their interest and create a desire to know more. Then, as people would continue to follow him, Jesus would slowly, gently define more clearly the kingdom of God and ask for a deeper commitment to it. But, he did this only when the followers had reached the previous stage.

At the first encounter Jesus had with John and Andrew, he simply said, "Come and . . . see!" (John 1:39). He didn't lay any heavy requirement on those early followers; he just invited them to check him out. He allowed them to watch his ministry without asking for a lot of commitment. This wasn't watering down the Gospel. He was just creating an interest.

As that group of early followers grew into a crowd, Jesus began to slowly turn up the heat. Eventually, after three years of public ministry among them, just six days before the Transfiguration, Jesus gave his ultimate challenge to the crowd: "Then he called the crowd to him along with his disciples and said: 'If anyone would come after me, he must deny himself and take up his cross and follow me'"(Mark 8:34).

> Jesus started where people were—at their level of commitment—but he never left them there.

Jesus was able to ask for that kind of commitment from the crowd only after demonstrating his love for them and earning their trust. To a stranger or first-time visitor at a church I believe Jesus would be more likely to say, "Come to me, all you who are weary and burdened, and I will give you rest. Take my yoke upon you and learn from me, for I am gentle and humble in heart, and you will find rest for your souls" (Matt. 11:28–29).

Jesus took into account that people have different cultural backgrounds, understanding, and levels of spiritual commitment. He knew that it doesn't work to use the same approach with all people. The same idea is behind the Circles of Commitment. It is a simple strategy that acknowledges we minister to people at different levels of commitment. People are not all alike: They have different needs, interests, and spiritual problems, depending on where they are in their spiritual journey. We must not confuse what we do with the community and the crowd with what we do with the core. Each group requires a different approach. A crowd is not a church—but a crowd can be turned into a church.

By organizing your church around the five purposes and identifying people in your church in terms of their commitment to each of those purposes, you will be well on the way to balancing your ministry and producing a healthy church. You are now ready for the final step in becoming a purpose-driven church—applying your purposes to every area of your church. That is the focus of the next chapter.

8

Applying Your Purposes

We trust the Lord that you are putting into
practice the things we taught you.

2 Thessalonians 3:4 (LB)

Now we come to the most difficult part of becoming a purpose-driven church. Many churches have done all I've talked about in the previous chapters: They have defined their purposes and developed a purpose statement; they regularly communicate their purposes to their membership; some have even reorganized their structure around their purposes. However, a purpose-driven church must go one step further and rigorously apply its purposes to every part of the church: programming, scheduling, budgeting, staffing, preaching, and so forth.

Integrating your purposes into every area and aspect of your church's life is the most difficult phase of becoming a purpose-driven church. Making the leap from a purpose statement to purpose-driven actions requires leadership that is totally committed to the process. The application of your purposes will require months, maybe even years, of praying, planning, preparing, and experimenting. Take it slow. Focus on progress, not perfection. The end result in your church will look different from Saddleback and every other purpose-driven church.

There are ten areas you must consider as you begin to reshape your church into a purpose-driven church.

Ten Ways to Be Purpose Driven

1. Assimilate new members on purpose

Use the Circles of Commitment as your strategy for assimilating people into the life of your church. Begin by moving the unchurched from the community to your crowd (for worship). Then move them from the crowd into the congregation (for fellowship). Next, move them from your congregation into the committed (for discipleship), and from the committed into the core (for ministry). Finally, move the core back out into the community (for evangelism). This process fulfills all five purposes of the church.

Notice that I suggest you grow the church from the outside in, rather than from the inside out. Start with your community, not your core! This is opposite the advice given by most books on church planting. The traditional approach to beginning a new church is to build a committed core of mature believers first, and then start reaching out to the community.

> Grow the church from the *outside in*, rather than from the *inside out*.

The problem I have found with an "inside-out" approach is that by the time the church planter has "discipled" his core, they have often lost contact with the community and are actually afraid of interacting with the unchurched. It's easy to get what Peter Wagner calls "koinonitis"—developing such a close-knit fellowship that newcomers are afraid or unable to break into it. Too often, a core group planning a new church spends so long in the small group stage that they become comfortable with it and lose their sense of mission. The fire of evangelism dies out.

The problem with most small churches is that they are all core and nothing else. The same fifty people come to everything the church does. They've all been Christians for so long they have few, if any, unbelieving friends to witness to. A church with this problem needs to learn how to develop the other four circles.

When I began Saddleback, I started by totally focusing on the community, specifically the unchurched in my community. I personally met hundreds of unchurched people by spending twelve weeks going door-to-door listening to people who didn't go to church and surveying their needs. I developed relationships and built bridges of friendship with as many unbelievers as I could.

I then gathered a crowd out of the community by writing a letter announcing the beginning of our church and mailing it to 15,000 homes. I wrote the letter based on what I learned about the community from my survey. We also used a lot of advertising that first year because we didn't have enough relationships to rely only on word of mouth to build a crowd. This is true of most small churches. Today, with thousands of members inviting friends to our church, advertising is unnecessary.

For that first year, about all we tried to do was build a crowd and introduce them to Christ. Just as it takes an enormous amount of energy to move a rocket off a launch pad, it requires an incredible amount of effort to gather a crowd out of nothing. Our focus was very narrow. I preached very simple, straightforward evangelistic series such as "Good News About Common Problems" and "God's Plan for Your Life." At the end of the year we had about 200 in average attendance, and most of them were brand-new believers.

In our second year, I began working on turning the believers in our crowd into a congregation. We continued reaching out to the community and increasing the size of the crowd, but we added a strong emphasis on building relationships within our fellowship. We focused on converting attenders into members. I began to talk more about the value of church membership, the benefits of belonging to a church family, and the responsibilities included in membership. I preached messages with titles like "We're in This Together," "All in God's Family," and "Why Do We Have Church Anyway?" I still remember the excitement of watching how God began transforming a crowd of self-absorbed attenders into a loving congregation of members.

The third year, I instituted a plan to raise the commitment level of our members. I repeatedly challenged those in the congregation to deepen their dedication to Christ. I taught them how to establish the spiritual disciplines and habits that build spiritual maturity. I preached a series on commitment called "Together We Grow" and a basic doctrine series called "Questions I've Wanted to Ask God." Of course, I taught these things to new believers in the first and second years, but the third year was when it became a major emphasis.

> **Build a multidimensional ministry by focusing on one level of commitment at a time.**

As people became solidly established in the faith, I began to give greater emphasis to involvement in ministry through messages like "Every Member Is a Minister" and a series called "Making the Most of What God Gave You." I stressed that a non-ministering Christian was a contradiction in terms and exploded the myth that spiritual maturity is an end in itself. I stressed that maturity is for ministry.

Although we had lay ministries existing in our church from the start, we now began to organize them better into a recognizable core. I added staff to assist me in leading regular meetings for training, encouraging, and supervising the leaders of our lay ministries.

Do you see the natural progression? You build a multidimensional ministry by assimilating new members in a purposeful way, focusing on one level of commitment at a time. Don't feel that you have to do everything all at once. Even Jesus didn't do everything at once! Build from the outside in. And once you've got all five groups up and running, you then continue by giving equal emphasis to each one.

Some may criticize the slow speed at which we moved people to deeper levels of commitment at first. But you need to remember that we began with the hard-core unchurched and were designing an entire philosophy of ministry from scratch at the same time.

I've always viewed the building of Saddleback Church as a lifetime task. My desire has been, like Paul, to "[lay] a foundation as an expert builder" (1 Cor. 3:10). It takes time to build commitment, to develop quality, and to move people through the Circles of Commitment. I can tell you how to build a balanced, healthy church, but I *can't* tell you how to do it quickly.

Solid, stable churches are not built in a day. When God wants to make a mushroom he takes six hours. When God wants to build an oak tree he takes sixty years. Do you want your church to be a mushroom or an oak tree?

2. Program around your purposes

You need to choose or design a program to fulfill each of your purposes. Remember, each Circle of Commitment also corresponds to a purpose of the church. If you use the five circles as a strategy for programming, you'll identify both your targets (community, crowd, congregation, committed, and core) and your objective with each target (evangelism, worship, fellowship, discipleship, and ministry).

Always clarify the purpose for every program in your church. Kill any program that doesn't fulfill a purpose. Replace a program when you find one that does a better job than the one you're using. Programs must always be the servants of your purposes.

Bridge events. At Saddleback, the primary program we use to impact the community is an annual series of community-wide events. We call these our "bridge events" because they are designed to build a bridge between our church and our community. They are usually quite large, in order to capture the attention of the entire community. These events include: a Harvest party as a safe alternative for children at Halloween, community-wide Christmas Eve services, community-wide Easter services, and Western Day near the Fourth of July, as well as other seasonal emphases, concerts, and productions. Some of our bridge events are overtly evangelistic while others we consider "pre-evangelism"—they simply make the unchurched in our community aware of our church.

Seeker services. The main program for the crowd is our weekend seeker services. These are designed as services to which our members can bring any unsaved friends to whom they are witnessing. The purpose of the seeker service is to assist personal evangelism, not replace it. Studies have shown that people make a decision for Christ sooner when there is group support.

The main program for the congregation is our small group network. Fellowship, personal care, and a sense of belonging are all benefits of being in a small group. We tell people, "You won't really feel a part of this church family until you join a small group."

Life Development Institute. The main program for the committed is our Life Development Institute. The Life Development Institute offers a wide variety of opportunities for spiritual growth: Bible studies, seminars, workshops, mentoring opportunities, and independent study programs. A person may earn credits for the classes they take and eventually receive a diploma. Our midweek worship service is a vital part of the Life Development Institute.

SALT. The main program for the core is our monthly SALT meeting, which stands for Saddleback Advanced Leadership Training. This two-hour rally, held on the first Sunday evening of each month, includes reports and testimonies from all the lay ministries, vision-casting by the pastor, skill-building, leadership training, prayer, and the commissioning of new lay ministers. As a pastor, I consider my monthly meeting with the core of lay ministers to be the most important meeting I prepare for and lead. It is an invaluable opportunity to instruct, inspire, and express appreciation to the people who make Saddleback happen.

The thing to remember about programming is that no single program, no matter how great it is or how well it has worked in the past, can adequately fulfill all the purposes of your church. Likewise, no single program can minister to all the people who compose each circle in your church. It takes a variety of programs to minister to the five levels of commitment and fulfill the five different purposes of the church.

3. Educate your people on purpose

Saddleback's Christian education program is purpose-driven. Our goal is to help people develop a lifestyle of evangelism, worship, fellowship, discipleship, and ministry. We want to produce doers of the Word, not hearers only—to transform, not merely inform. One of our slogans is "You only believe the part of the Bible that you DO."

Transformation will not happen by chance. We must establish a disciplemaking, or educational, process that encourages people to act on what they learn and rewards them when they do. At Saddleback we call this the "Life Development Process."

The Life Development Process

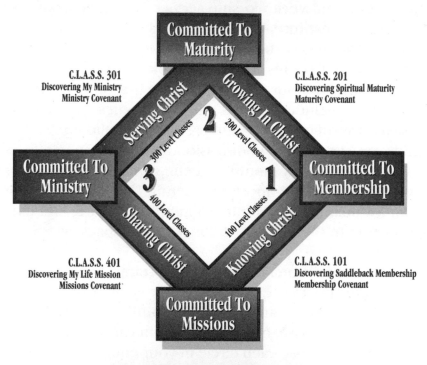

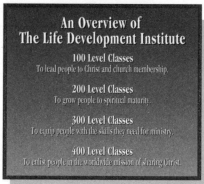

We use the simple diagram of a baseball diamond to visually explain our education and assimilation process to our members. Each base represents a completed class and a deeper level of commitment.

You get to first base by completing Class 101 and committing to Saddleback's membership covenant. You arrive at second base after completing Class 201 and committing to a spiritual growth covenant. You make it to third base by completing Class 301 and committing to serve in a ministry of the church. And you finally get back to home plate by completing Class 401 and committing to sharing your faith both at home and on mission trips. These steps will be explained in detail later.

As in baseball, no credit is given for runners left on base. We tell new members that our goal for them is to become "Grand Slam Disciples." We want them to complete all sixteen hours of basic training and to commit to the covenants explained at each base. There is a written covenant at each base that we expect people to sign and commit to before moving ahead. No member may proceed to the next base until he has committed to the requirements of each covenant.

Most churches do a fairly good job getting people to first base or maybe even second base. People will receive Christ, be baptized, and join the church (that's getting them to first base). Some churches also do an excellent job of helping believers develop the habits that lead to spiritual maturity (that's getting to second base). But few churches have a plan to insure that every believer finds an appropriate ministry (third base), and even fewer equip members to win others to Christ and fulfill their life mission (home plate).

> You don't get credit for runners left on base.

Our ultimate goal at Saddleback is to turn an audience into an army. You don't judge the strength of an army by how many soldiers sit and eat in the mess hall but by how they perform on the front line. Likewise a church's strength is not seen in how many show up for services (the crowd) but how many serve in the core.

In the early 1980s I used to joke that my objective was to turn "Yuppies" (Young Urban Professionals) into "Yummies," (Young Urban Missionaries)! As I've said before, I believe the church is to be a missionary-sending station. Only as we move members completely around the bases to home plate can we fulfill the Great Commission.

4. Start small groups on purpose

We don't expect each small group to do the same things; we allow them to specialize.

Seeker groups. Our seeker groups are formed exclusively for evangelism. They provide a nonthreatening environment for nonbelievers to ask questions, express doubts, and investigate the claims of Christ.

Support groups. We have support groups for the purpose of congregational care, fellowship, and worship. Many of our support groups are related to providing support and fellowship during a specific stage of life, such as new parents, college students, or empty nesters. Others deal with healing specific hurts encountered by those who have lost a mate by death or divorce. We also have a full menu of recovery groups.

Service groups. These groups are formed around a specific ministry such as our orphanage in Mexico, our prison ministry, or our divorce recovery ministry. Groups such as these naturally find fellowship together through a common task, project, or ministry.

Growth groups. Our growth groups are dedicated to nurturing, discipleship training, and in-depth Bible study. We offer about fifty different curriculum choices, and some of these groups do a more in-depth study of the previous week's sermon subject.

Rather than force everyone to conform to a "one size fits all" mentality, we allow people to choose the type of small group that best fits their needs, their interests, their stage of life, or their spiritual maturity. We do not expect each small group to fulfill every purpose of the church, but we do require that each one must be organized around at least one purpose of the church.

5. Add staff on purpose

Each person we hire onto our church staff is given a purpose-based job description. While interviewing, we use some standard questions in order to discover which of the church's purposes an applicant feels most passionate about, and then we place them accordingly. We don't look just for character and competence when interviewing staff; we look for a passion about one of the purposes of the church. People who are passionate about something they are doing are self-motivated.

If I were starting a new church today I would begin by recruiting five volunteers for five unpaid staff positions: a music/magnification director to help prepare the worship services for the crowd; a membership director to teach Class 101 and oversee the care of members in the congregation; a maturity director to teach Class 201 and oversee the Bible study programs for the committed; a ministry director to teach Class 301, interview people for ministry placement, and supervise the lay ministries of the core; and a mission director to teach Class 401 and oversee our evangelism and missions programs in the community. As the church grew I would move these people to part-time paid staff and eventually full-time. With this plan, you can be purpose driven regardless of the size of your church.

> Any church can be purpose driven, regardless of its size.

6. *Structure on purpose*

Rather than organizing by traditional departments, organize around purpose-based teams. At Saddleback every lay ministry and every staff member is assigned to one of our five purpose-based teams. In turn, each team is led by a team pastor, assisted by a team coordinator, and composed of a combination of paid staff ministers and volunteer lay ministers. Together they lead the programs, ministries, and events that fulfill the particular purpose assigned to that team.

The Missions Team. The missions team is assigned the purpose of evangelism. Their target is the community. Their job is to plan, promote, and oversee all of the church's bridge events, seeker groups, evangelism training (including Class 401), evangelistic activities and programs, and mission projects. They are to organize whatever it takes to reach our community and our world for Christ.

The church is in the sending business. It is our goal that eventually 25 percent of our membership will do some kind of mission project each year. I'd love to see our attendance go down every summer, not because people are on vacation but because they are out on the mission field serving. Another goal is to send out 200 career missionaries from Saddleback in the next twenty years. This past year we sent adult members on mission projects to five continents, and our youth did mission projects at our orphanage in Mexico and at a rescue mission in inner-city Los Angeles.

The Magnification/Music Team. This team is assigned the purpose of worship. Their target is the crowd. Their job is to plan and oversee our weekend seeker services, special worship emphases and events, and to provide music and worship resources to the rest of the church.

The Membership Team. This team is assigned the purpose of fellowship. Their target is the congregation. It is their business to care for the flock. They run our monthly class for prospective members (Class 101). They oversee all support groups, weddings, funerals, pastoral care, hospital visitation, and benevolence within the congregation, and they operate the counseling center. Finally, this team is responsible for all major fellowship events within our church family.

The Maturity Team. The maturity team is assigned the purpose of discipleship. Their target is the committed. Their goal is to lead our members to deeper spiritual commitment and help them develop to spiritual maturity. This team operates the monthly Class 201 and is responsible for the Life Development Institute, the midweek worship service, all Bible studies, growth groups in homes, and special church-wide spiritual growth campaigns. They also produce family devotional guides, Bible study curriculums, and other resources to help believers grow.

The Ministry Team. This team is assigned the purpose of ministry. Their target is the core. Their job is to turn members into ministers by helping members discover their SHAPE for ministry and guiding them to find either an existing place for ministry or a new ministry. This team operates the Ministry Development Center, and is responsible for all service groups as well as for the monthly Class 301 and SALT meetings. They also assist, train, and supervise the lay ministers of the church. The goal of this team is to help every member of the church find a meaningful place of service that best expresses his or her gifts and abilities.

7. *Preach on purpose*

To produce balanced, healthy believers, you need to plan a preaching schedule that includes a series on each of the five purposes over the course of a year. A four-week series related to each of the five purposes would require only twenty weeks.

There would still be more than half a year left to preach on other themes.

Planning your preaching around the five purposes of the church does not mean you must always be teaching about the church itself. Personalize the purposes! Talk about them in terms of God's five purposes for every Christian. For example, here are some titles of series I've preached in which I applied the purposes in a personalized way: "You Are Shaped for Significance" was a series to mobilize people for ministry; "The Six Stages of Faith" was a series on the circumstances God takes believers through to mature them; "Learning to Hear God's Voice" was a series on worship; "Answering Life's Toughest Questions" was a series based on Ecclesiastes to prepare people for evangelism; "Building Great Relationships" was a series based on 1 Corinthians 13, designed to deepen the fellowship of our church. When you use the five purposes of the church as a guide for planning your preaching schedule, you are preaching with a purpose.

8. Budget on purpose

We categorize every line item in our church budget by the purpose of the church that it supports or to which it relates. The quickest way to discover a church's priorities is to look at its budget and calendar. The way we spend our time and the way we spend our money show what is *really* important to us, regardless of what we claim to believe. If your church claims that evangelism is a priority, you need to be able to back up that claim with dollars allocated in your budget. Otherwise you're just blowing smoke.

9. Calendar on purpose

Designate two months of each year to give special emphasis to each purpose. Then give each purpose team (composed of staff or volunteers) the assignment of emphasizing that purpose church-wide during those months.

For example, January and June might each be Maturity months. During a month-long emphasis on spiritual maturity you might read through the New Testament as a congregation, memorize a Bible verse together each week, or hold a Bible conference or a church-wide Bible study.

February and July could each be Ministry months. During these months you could hold a ministry fair to recruit people for ministry. The pastor could preach a series on ministry. People could be encouraged to join a service group.

March and August might be Missions months, with activities like personal evangelism training, a missions conference, and special hands-on mission projects.

April and September could be Membership months. These months would be good months to put a special emphasis on recruiting attenders to become new members. You could plan a number of church-wide fellowship events like picnics, concerts, and festivals.

May and October could be Magnification months—two months that emphasize personal and corporate worship. By committing two months a year to each of the five purposes you will be left with two free months—in this example November and December, which are already busy with Thanksgiving and Christmas.

Don't fool yourself. If you don't schedule your purposes on your calendar, they won't get emphasized.

10. Evaluate on purpose

To remain effective as a church in an ever-changing world you need to continually evaluate what you do. Build review and revision into your process. Evaluate for excellence. In a purpose-driven church, your purposes are the standard by which you evaluate effectiveness.

Having a purpose without any practical way to review results would be like NASA planning a moon shot without a tracking system: You'll be unable to make midcourse corrections and will probably never hit your target. At Saddleback we've developed a tracking tool we call the "Saddleback Snapshot." Our pastoral staff reviews it each month. The Snapshot is a six-page overview of our disciple-development process. It identifies who is at each base of our Life Development Process (baseball diamond). Like the old Abbott and Costello routine, we want to know "Who's on first?" The Snapshot also shows how many people are currently in each Circle of Commitment, and measures a number of other key indicators of church health.

The Snapshot forces us to take an honest look each month at how well our church is fulfilling its purposes. Bottlenecks in the system become easy to spot. For instance, if worship attendance increases 35 percent in a year but membership and small group attendance only increases 20 percent, we know we've got to rectify some gap in the process. Statistics like this help us evaluate our assimilation process and determine where emphasis is needed. As I mentioned in an earlier chapter, we must be constantly asking, "What is our business?" and "How's business?"

Growing Stronger

As you seek to apply your purposes to every area of your church you will notice the church growing stronger and stronger. Instead of constantly looking for new programs each year to keep people excited and motivated, you will be able to focus on the essentials. You will be able to learn from each mistake and build on every success. If unchanging purposes guide your church, you will be able to work on fulfilling those purposes better each passing year. Momentum works in your favor. The more your members understand and commit to your purposes, the stronger your church will become.

Part Three

Reaching Out to Your Community

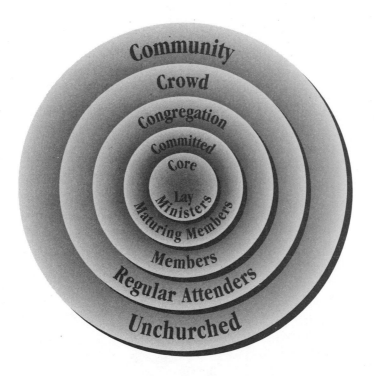

Community
Crowd
Congregation
Committed
Core
Lay
Ministers
Maturing Members
Members
Regular Attenders
Unchurched

9

Who Is Your Target?

Jesus: "I was sent only to the lost sheep of Israel."

Matthew 15:24

Paul: "I had been entrusted with the task of preaching the gospel to the Gentiles, just as Peter had been to the Jews."

Galatians 2:7

I once saw a *Peanuts* cartoon that described the evangelistic strategy of many churches. Charlie Brown was practicing archery in his backyard. Instead of aiming at a target, he would shoot an arrow at his fence and then walk over and draw a target around wherever the arrow stuck. Lucy walked up and said, "Why are you doing this, Charlie Brown?" He replied without embarrassment, "This way I never miss!"

Unfortunately the same logic is behind a lot of churches' evangelistic outreach efforts. We shoot arrows of good news into our community and if they happen to hit anyone we say, "That was our target all along!" There is little planning or strategizing behind our efforts—we don't aim at any specific target. We just draw a bull's-eye around whomever we reach and settle for that. This is an incredibly callous approach to evangelism. Bringing people to Christ is too important a task for us to have such a casual attitude toward it.

Too many congregations are naive in their thinking about evangelism. If you ask the members, "Who is your church try-

> No single church can possibly reach everyone. It takes all kinds of churches to reach all kinds of people.

ing to reach for Christ?" the response will likely be, "Everybody! We're trying to reach the entire world for Jesus Christ." Of course this is the goal of the Great Commission, and it should be the prayer of every church, but in practice there is not a local church anywhere that can reach everybody.

Because human beings are so different, no single church can possibly reach everyone. That's why we need all kinds of churches. Together we can accomplish what no single congregation, strategy, or style can accomplish by itself.

Sit in an airport terminal for half a day and it will become quite obvious that God loves diversity. He created an infinite variety of people with different interests, preferences, backgrounds, and personalities. To reach all of these people for Christ will require a variety of styles of evangelism. The message must stay the same, but the methods and style of communicating it will vary greatly.

I always refuse to debate which method of evangelism works best. It depends on who you are trying to reach! Different kinds of bait catch different kinds of fish. I'm in favor of any method that reaches at least one person for Christ—as long as it is ethical. I think it will be very embarrassing someday when

> Never criticize any method that God is blessing!

critics of a particular method of evangelism get to heaven and discover all the people who are there because of it! We should never criticize any method that God is blessing.

For your church to be most effective in evangelism you must decide on a target. Discover what types of people live in your area, decide which of those groups your church is best equipped to reach, and then discover which styles of evangelism best match your target. While your church may never be able to reach everyone, it is especially suited to reaching certain types of people. Knowing who you're trying to reach makes evangelism much easier.

Imagine what would happen to a commercial radio station if it tried to appeal to everyone's taste in music. A station that alternated its format between classical, heavy metal, country, rap, reggae, and southern gospel would end up alienating everyone. No one would listen to that station!

Successful radio stations select a target audience. They research their broadcast area, figure out which segments of the population are not being reached by other stations, and then choose a format that reaches their target.

Defining our evangelistic target has been the second most important factor behind Saddleback's growth. After figuring out who our church was best capable of reaching for Jesus Christ, we intentionally went after those people. When we plan an evangelistic effort we always have a specific target in mind. The Bible determines our message, but our target determines when, where, and how we communicate it.

> The Bible determines our message, but our target determines when, where, and how we communicate it.

It is imperative that you not even *think* about who your target may be until after you've clarified the purposes of your church. The biblical foundation must be laid first. I have watched some churches develop their evangelism strategy beginning with their target, without laying the foundation of God's eternal purposes. The result was an unstable and unbiblical church driven by market forces rather than the Word of God. The message must never be compromised.

Targeting for Evangelism Is Biblical

The practice of targeting specific kinds of people for evangelism is a biblical principle for ministry. It's as old as the New Testament. Jesus targeted his ministry. When a Canaanite woman asked Jesus to minister to her demon-possessed daughter, he publicly stated that the Father had told him to focus on "the lost sheep of Israel" (see Matt. 15:22–28). Although Jesus went ahead and healed the Canaanite woman's daughter because of her faith, he publicly identified his ministry target as the Jews. Was Jesus being unfair or prejudiced? Certainly not! Jesus targeted his ministry in order to be effective, not to be exclusive.

Earlier, Jesus had instructed the disciples to target their ministry also. Matthew 10:5–6 says, "These twelve Jesus sent out with the following instructions: 'Do not go among the Gentiles or enter any town of the Samaritans. Go rather to the lost sheep of Israel.'" Paul targeted his ministry to Gentiles, and Peter targeted his ministry to Jews (Gal. 2:7). Both ministries were needed. Both were important. Both were effective.

Even the gospels were written with specific target audiences in mind. Have you ever considered why God used four writers and four books to communicate the one life of Christ? After all, almost all of the stories and teaching in the gospel of Mark are covered in the gospel of Matthew. Why do we need both books? Because Matthew's gospel was targeted for the Hebrew

> Jesus targeted his ministry in order to be effective, not to be exclusive.

reader and Mark's was targeted for the Gentile reader. They had the same message, but because they wrote for different audiences, their style of communication differed. Targeting your audience for evangelism is a method God invented! He expects us to witness to people in their own terms.

The concept of evangelistic targeting is built into the Great Commission. We are to make disciples of "all nations." The Greek term *ta ethne,* from which we derive the word *ethnic,* refers literally to "all people groups." Each of these unique people groups needs an evangelistic strategy that communicates the Gospel in terms that their specific culture can understand.

In March of 1995, Billy Graham's Puerto Rico crusade was broadcast simultaneously in 116 languages to audiences around the world. The message was the same, but it was translated into each country's language, and culturally appropriate music and testimonies were dubbed into the broadcast. Over one billion people heard the Gospel in languages, music, and testimonies that matched their particular group. It was history's greatest example of targeted evangelism.

The practice of evangelistic targeting is especially important to small churches. In a small church with limited resources, it is vital that you make the most of what you've got. Focus your resources on reaching the people your church can best communicate with.

Small churches must also make choices on tough issues. For example, since it's impossible to appeal to everyone's taste in music style in a single service, and small churches can't offer multiple services, they must choose a target. Changing styles on alternate weeks will produce the same effect as a radio station with a mixed format. No one will be happy.

One of the advantages of being a large church is that you have the resources to go after multiple targets. The larger your church becomes, the more you'll be able to offer choices in programs, events, and even worship styles. When Saddleback began, we focused on only one target: young, unchurched, white-collar couples. We focused on them because they were the largest group in the Saddleback Valley, and because that was who I related to best. But as our church has grown, we've been able to add additional ministries and outreach programs to reach young adults, single adults, prisoners, the elderly, parents with ADD children, and Spanish-, Vietnamese-, and Korean-speaking people, as well as many other targets.

> Small churches become more effective when they specialize in what they do best.

How Do You Define Your Target?

Targeting for evangelism begins with finding out all you can about your community. Your church needs to define its target in four specific ways: geographically, demographically, culturally, and spiritually.

When I took hermeneutics and preaching classes in seminary, I was taught that to understand the message of the New Testament I had to first understand the geography, customs, culture, and religion of the people who lived at that time. I could then extract the timeless, eternal truth of God from that context. This process is called "exegesis." Every biblical preacher uses it.

Unfortunately, no class taught me that before I communicate that timeless truth to people today, I need to "exegete" my own community! I must pay as much attention to the geography, customs, culture, and religious background of my community as I do to those who lived in Bible times if I am to faithfully communicate God's Word.

Define your target geographically

Jesus had a plan to evangelize the world. In Acts 1:8 he identified four geographic targets for the disciples: "But you will receive power when the Holy Spirit comes on you; and you will be my witnesses in Jerusalem, and in all Judea and Samaria, and to the ends of the earth." Many Bible scholars point out that this is the exact pattern of growth described in the rest of the book of Acts. The message was taken first to the Jews in Jerusalem, then to Judea, then to Samaria, and eventually it spread across Europe.

In your ministry, geographic targeting simply means you identify where the people live that you want to reach. Get a map of your city or area and mark where your church is located. Estimate a fifteen- to twenty-minute drive in each direction from your church and mark those as borders of your primary ministry area. This is your "evangelistic fishing pond." Using the zip codes included in your boundaries, your county government can tell you exactly how many people live within a reasonable driving distance of your church.

When determining your geographic target, there are several factors to keep in mind. First, "reasonable driving distance" is a highly subjective term. The average trip time in a community varies greatly depending on what part of the country you are talking about. Rural residents are willing to drive farther than urban dwellers. People are more likely to travel farther on a freeway than through miles of city stoplights. My best guess is that most people will tolerate about a dozen stoplights at the most when driving to church.

Second, people choose churches today primarily on the basis of relationships and programs, not location. Just because your church is closest to someone doesn't mean you can automatically reach them. Your church may not *fit* them. On the other hand there are people who will drive past fifteen other churches to attend yours if it meets their needs.

Third, the larger your church grows, the farther its reach will extend. We have people who drive over an hour to attend Saddleback because we offer a program or support group they can't find anywhere closer to them. As a rule, people are willing to drive farther to attend a large church with a multifaceted ministry than a smaller church with a limited ministry.

Another way to map your ministry target area is to draw a circle around your church representing five miles. Then find out how many people live in that circle. This is your *initial* ministry area. Approximately 65 percent of America is unchurched, and that percentage is much higher in many areas, particularly in the West and Northeast and in urban areas. If you calculate the population of your ministry area and then figure what 65 percent of that number is, you'll see that truly "the fields are ready for harvest."

Once you've defined your geographic target, you'll know how many people are in your fishing pond. This is very important, since the population of your area is a major factor in determining what strategy you use to bring them in. In a large population center, it is possible to focus on only one segment and still grow a large church. In a smaller population area, you'd have to develop outreaches to several different segments to grow a large church.

It's foolish to ignore the role of population in predicting how large a church will grow. No matter how dedicated a church is, if the ministry area only has a thousand people in it, the church will never be large. It's not the pastor's fault, nor is it a lack of commitment on the part of the congregation. It's simple arithmetic.

I've visited some large churches in metropolitan areas that have chosen a highly specialized strategy that may only reach ½ percent of the population. But because 200,000 people live in the area, the church has 1,000 in attendance. You'd be mistaken and disappointed if you thought that by imitating their same strategy your small-town church would grow to the same size. To be realistic, you need to focus on the percentage of population being reached, not the actual numbers. A strategy that reaches 1,000 in a city of 200,000 is likely to reach 50 in a town of 1,000.

It is both unwise and unhelpful to compare attendance between churches. Every church has a unique fishing pond, and each pond is stocked with a different number and type of fish. It's like comparing tangerines and submarines: Two churches may sound a lot alike, but on a closer look, their differences will be obvious.

Define your target demographically

Not only do you need to find out how many people live in your area, you need to know what type of people live there. First, let me warn you: Don't overdo demographic research! You can waste a lot of time collecting facts and information about your community that won't make any real difference to your church. I've known some church planters who spent months preparing beautiful binders full of demographic information on their areas. All of it was interesting, but much of it was not that useful for their church's purposes.

There are only a handful of relevant demographic facts that you need to discover about the people in your community. I consider the most important factors in targeting a community for evangelism to be

- Age: How many are in each age group?
- Marital status: How many are single adults? How many are married couples?
- Income: What is both the median and the average household income?
- Education: What is the education level of the community?
- Occupation: What types of work are predominant?

Each of these factors will influence how you minister to people and how you communicate the Good News.

Young adults, for example, have different hopes and fears than retirees. A Gospel presentation that emphasizes the assurance of heaven as the benefit of salvation will probably be ineffective in ministering to a young adult who thinks he has his entire life in front of him. He's not interested in the afterlife. He's consumed with finding out if there is any meaning or purpose to *this* life. One national survey showed that less than 1 percent of Americans were interested in the answer to the question, "How can I get to heaven?"

A more effective way to witness to a young adult would be to show how we were made to have fellowship with God *now* through Christ. On the other hand, many elderly have a very great interest in being prepared for eternity because they know their time on earth may be up at any moment.

Married couples have different interests than single adults. The poor face different problems than the middle class. The wealthy have their own set of worries. College graduates tend to see the world differently than high school graduates. It is important to know the perspective of those you are seeking to win to Christ.

If you are serious about having your church make an impact, become an expert on your community. Pastors should know more about their communities than anyone else. As I explained in chapter 1, before moving to my community I spent three months studying census statistics and demographic studies so I could determine what kinds of people lived in the Saddleback Valley. Before I set foot there I knew how many people lived there, where they worked, how much they earned, their educational level, and much more.

Where can you get this kind of information? There are a number of resources including the U.S. Census Library, county or city planning departments, newspaper offices, the local

Chamber of Commerce, the United Way, local contractors, realtors, and utility companies. Most large denominations also maintain demographic databases you can access.

Define your target culturally

Understanding the demographics of your community is important, but understanding the culture of your community is even more important. This is something you won't find in census statistics. I use the word *culture* to refer to the lifestyle and mind-set of those who live around your church. The business world uses the term *psychographics,* which is just a fancy way of referring to people's values, interests, hurts, and fears. Long before businesses became enamored with psychographics, Christian missionaries were identifying the differences between cultures.

> One of the major barriers to church growth is "people blindness."

No missionary to a foreign land would try to evangelize and minister to people without first understanding their culture. It would be foolish to do so. In today's secular environment it is just as important for us to understand the culture we minister in. We don't have to agree with our culture, but we *must* understand it.

Within your community there are most likely many subcultures, or subgroups. To reach each of these groups you need to discover how they think. What are their interests? What do they value? Where do they hurt? What are they afraid of? What are the most prominent features of the way they live? What are their most popular radio stations? The more you know about these people, the easier it will be to reach them.

One of the major barriers to church growth is "people blindness"—being unaware of social and cultural differences between people. Are all white people alike? Of course they aren't. Are all black people alike? Of course not. Are all Hispanics or Asians alike? No. A trained eye will pick up on important distinctions between people who live in your area.

The best way to find out the culture, mind-set, and lifestyle of people is to talk to them personally. You don't need to hire a marketing firm, just go out and meet with the people in your community face-to-face. Take your own survey. Ask them what *they* feel are their greatest needs. Listen for their hurts, interests, and fears. No book or demographic report can replace actually talking with the people in your community. Statistics paint only a part of the picture. You must personally spend time with people, getting a feel for your community through one-on-one interaction. I believe there is no substitute for this.

> The best way to find out the culture, mind-set, and lifestyle of people is to talk to them!

Define your target spiritually

After you have defined your target area culturally, you need to discover the spiritual background of the people in your community. Determine what those in your target area already know about the Gospel. For instance, when I studied the Saddleback Valley, I discovered that 94 percent of Orange County residents believed in God or a universal spirit, 75 percent believed in the biblical definition of God, 70 percent believed in life after death, and 52 percent believed they were here on earth for a spiritual purpose. This was very helpful in knowing where to start with people when witnessing to them.

In order to determine a community's spiritual climate, you might interview other pastors in the area. Pastors who have served a dozen years in a community should be very aware of that area's local issues and spiritual trends.

Before I moved to California to start our church, I contacted each of the evangelical pastors in the Saddleback Valley to hear their assessment of the Valley's spiritual needs. The task was surprisingly simple. I went to the city library, found a Yellow Pages directory for Orange County, California, looked up "churches," and wrote down the names and addresses of all the evangelical congregations in the Saddleback Valley. Then I wrote a letter to each pastor explaining what I was doing, and I asked him to answer six questions on an enclosed stamped reply card. I got about thirty cards back. I gained some great insight and began some wonderful long-term friendships with many of those pastors.

A few years ago I read about a study done by New York University on the religious life of Americans. The study reported that 90 percent of all Americans claim some kind of religious affiliation. While that doesn't mean they are actively practicing their faith, it does mean that almost every American has had some kind of contact with a religious organization in the past.

The term *unchurched* doesn't refer to only people who have never been inside a church. It also includes those who have a church background but no personal relationship to Christ, and those who haven't been in a church for some time, usually years.

Twenty-six percent of Americans claim a Catholic background. If you live on the West Coast, your number-one prospect is probably a former Catholic. If you live in the South, your largest pool of prospects will definitely be those claiming a Baptist background (30 percent). In North Dakota, the odds are that the unchurched person you talk to has a Lutheran background (28 percent), and in Kansas or Iowa he or she is likely to have a Methodist background (13 percent). In Idaho, Wyoming, and Utah expect a Mormon background. You need to know your area!

Whenever I witness to someone who doesn't have a relationship to Christ, I try to discover any common ground we may have due to their religious background. For example, when I talk with a Catholic, I know they accept the Bible but have probably never read it, and that they accept the Trinity, the Virgin Birth, and Jesus Christ as the Son of God. We already have basic agreement on some major issues. My job then becomes communicating the difference between having a religion based on works and having a relationship to Christ based on grace.

> The unchurched in America are not all alike!

When I speak at pastors' conferences, I will often have pastors tell me that their church is "just like Saddleback." When I ask what they mean by that, they respond, "Well, we're focused on reaching the unchurched." I say, "That's wonderful! What *kind* of unchurched are you reaching?" After all, the unchurched are not all alike! To say that your target is the "unchurched" is an incomplete description. Unchurched intellectuals in Berkeley are very different from farmers in Fresno or unchurched immigrants in Los Angeles.

Defining your church's evangelistic target takes time and serious study. But once you've completed your research you'll understand why some evangelistic methods work in your area and why others don't. It can spare you from wasting valuable effort and money on evangelistic approaches that won't work.

In the early 1980s some churches tried using telemarketing as a tool for evangelism. Saddleback never jumped on the bandwagon. Why? Because in our targeting surveys we'd already discovered two things: First, we knew that the number-one personal annoyance of Orange County residents was "strangers who call to sell me something on the telephone." Second, we knew that more than half of our community had unlisted phone numbers! That settled that. It is amazing to me that churches often spend thousands of dollars on evangelistic projects without first asking the people they intend to reach if they think the program will work.

Personalize Your Target

Once you've collected all the information on your community, I encourage you to create a composite profile of the typical unchurched person your church wants to reach. Combining the characteristics of residents in your area into a single, mythical person will make it easier for members of your church to understand who your target is. If you've done a good job at collecting information, your members should recognize this mythical person as their next-door neighbor.

At Saddleback, we've named our composite profile "Saddleback Sam." Most of our members would have no problem describing Sam. We discuss him in detail in every membership class.

Saddleback Sam is the typical unchurched man who lives in our area. His age is late thirties or early forties. He has a college degree and may have an advanced degree. (The Saddleback Valley has one of the highest household education levels in America.) He is married to Saddleback Samantha, and they have two kids, Steve and Sally.

Surveys show that Sam likes his job, he likes where he lives, and he thinks he's enjoying life now more than he was five years ago. He's self-satisfied, even smug, about his station in life. He's either a professional, a manager, or a successful entrepreneur. Sam is among the most affluent of Americans, but he carries a lot of debt, especially due to the price of his home.

Health and fitness are high priorities for Sam and his family. You can usually see Sam jogging each morning, and Samantha attends an aerobics class three times a week at the Family Fit-

Our Target: Saddleback Sam

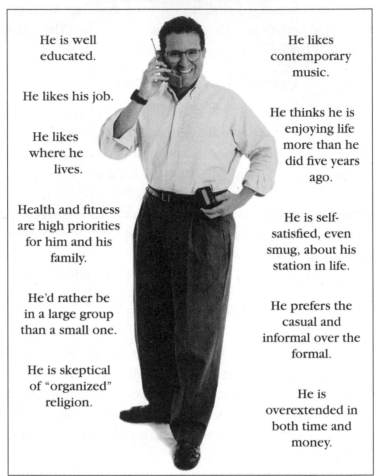

He is well educated.

He likes his job.

He likes where he lives.

Health and fitness are high priorities for him and his family.

He'd rather be in a large group than a small one.

He is skeptical of "organized" religion.

He likes contemporary music.

He thinks he is enjoying life more than he did five years ago.

He is self-satisfied, even smug, about his station in life.

He prefers the casual and informal over the formal.

He is overextended in both time and money.

ness Center. Both of them like to listen to contemporary pop and country music, especially when they are working out.

When it comes to socializing, Sam and his wife would rather be in a large group than a small one. Why? In a crowd, Sam can hide and maintain the anonymity and privacy that he jealously guards. Sam has an unlisted phone number and may live in a gated community. (This was the main reason we used direct mail advertising in the first years of Saddleback. It was the only way to contact many of the homes in our area.)

Another important characteristic of Sam's is that he's skeptical of what he calls "organized" religion. He's likely to say, "I believe in Jesus. I just don't like organized religion." We like to counter this by joking, "Then you will like Saddleback. We're *disorganized* religion!"

Sam, because he is a southern Californian, prefers casual, informal meetings over anything stiff and formal. He loves to dress down for the mild southern California climate. We take this into account when planning services to attract Sam. For example, I never wear a coat and tie when I speak at Saddleback services. I intentionally dress down to match the mind-set of those I'm trying to reach. I follow Paul's strategy given in 1 Corinthians 9:20: "To the Jews I became like a Jew, to win the Jews." In my situation I'm sure Paul would say, "When in southern California I became like a southern Californian in order to win southern Californians!" I don't think how people dressed mattered a lot to Jesus. We'd rather have a pagan come to church in tennis shoes and shorts than not come because he doesn't own a suit.

Saddleback Sam is also overextended in time and money. His credit card is used to the limit. He is very materialistic, and yet will honestly admit that his wealth has not brought him lasting happiness.

Why do we go to all this trouble defining the typical person we're trying to reach? Because the more you understand someone the easier it is to communicate with him.

If you were to create a profile of the typical resident in your area, what characteristics would you give him? What would you name him? It's worth thinking about. Once you've defined and named your church's evangelistic target, do me a favor: Send me a copy. I have a hobby of collecting church evangelistic profiles. I have a file filled with characters like *Dallas Doug*, *Memphis Mike*, and *Atlanta Al*.

Can you imagine a photographer shooting pictures without taking the time to focus? What deer hunter would stand on top of a hill and shoot randomly into the valley without taking aim at something? Without a target, our efforts at evangelism are often only wishful thinking. Of course it takes time to focus and aim, but it also pays off. The more your target is in focus, the more likely it is that you will be able to hit it.

10

Knowing Whom You Can Best Reach

The first thing Andrew did was to find his brother Simon and tell him, "We have found the Messiah."

John 1:41

While Jesus was having dinner at Matthew's house, many tax collectors and "sinners" came and ate with him and his disciples.

Matthew 9:10

Even a casual reading of the New Testament will show that the Gospel spread primarily through relationships. As soon as Andrew heard about Christ he went and told his brother, Simon Peter. Philip immediately contacted a friend, Nathaniel. Matthew, a tax collector, held an evangelistic dinner party for other tax collectors. The woman at the well told everyone in her village about Christ. The list goes on and on.

I believe that the most effective evangelistic strategy is to first try to reach those with whom you already have something in common. After you've discovered all the possible target groups in your community, which group should you focus on first? The answer is to go after those you are most likely to reach.

As we've already discussed, every church is best suited to reach certain types of people. Your church will have an easier

173

time reaching some kinds of people and more difficulty reaching other kinds of people. And there are some types of people your church will never reach, because they require a completely different style of ministry than you can provide.

Many factors cause people to be resistant to attending your church: theological barriers, relational barriers, emotional barriers, lifestyle barriers, and cultural barriers. Although the first four barriers are very real, in this chapter I would like to focus on the cultural barrier. The people your church is most likely to reach are those who match the existing culture of your church.

Who Already Attends Our Church?

How do you determine your church's culture? Ask yourself, "What kind of people already attend our church?" This may discourage some pastors, but it is the truth: Whatever type of people you already have in your congregation is the same type you are likely to attract more of. It is unlikely that your church will attract and *keep* many people who are very different from those who already attend.

When visitors walk into your church, the first question they ask isn't a religious question, but a cultural one. As their eyes scan the room full of strange faces they are unconsciously asking, "Is there anybody here like me?" A visiting retired couple looks to see if there are any other older folks present in the congregation. A serviceman looks for anyone else wearing a uniform or who has a military haircut. Young couples with infants immediately scan the crowd to see if there are other young couples with babies or small children. If visitors find other people in your church that seem similar to them, they are much more likely to come back again.

What is the likelihood of a church full of retirees reaching teenagers? Not likely. How about the likelihood of a church made up of military personnel reaching peace activists? Highly unlikely! Or what's the likelihood of a church composed primarily of blue-collar factory workers reaching white-collar executives? It's possible, but don't bet on it.

Of course, as believers we must want and welcome all people into our church family. After all, we are all the same in the eyes of God. But remember, the fact that a church may be unsuccessful in reaching certain types of people isn't a matter of right or wrong, but a matter of simply respecting the wonderful variety of people God has placed in the world.

What Kind of Leaders Do We Have?

The second question to ask when figuring out who your church can best reach is, "What is the cultural background and personality of our church's leadership?" The personal characteristics of your leadership, both paid staff and lay leaders, have enormous impact on your church's ministry. Leaders cast long shadows. Many studies have shown that the number one reason people choose a church is because they identify with the pastor. Don't misunderstand this: The pastor does not attract first-time visitors, but he *is* a

> The pastor does not attract first-time visitors, but he is a major reason visitors come back.

major reason visitors come back (or don't). When visitors identify with the pastor, they are far more likely to return.

If you are a pastor, you must honestly ask yourself, "What kind of person am I? What is my cultural background? What kind of people do I naturally relate to and what kind do I have a harder time understanding?" You need to do a frank analysis of who you are and the type of people to whom you relate best

While I was a college student, I served as an interim pastor in a small church made up almost entirely of truck drivers and mechanics. Since I have absolutely no background or ability with mechanical things, I had difficulty holding an intelligent conversation with many of the members. Even though I dearly loved those folks, I was a fish out of water and they knew it. They were very polite to this young preacher, but I wasn't at all what that church needed. They needed a leader that matched who they were.

On the other hand, I feel right at home with entrepreneurial businessmen, managers, and professionals. In fact, I've noticed that they are attracted to my ministry. It's nothing I planned, it's just the way God wired me.

I deeply believe that God has uniquely called and shaped each of us in different ways to reach different types of people. You can reach people that I will never be able to reach for Christ, and I can probably reach some whom you can't relate to. That is why we are all needed in the body of Christ.

If God has called you to ministry, then who and what you are must also be a part of that plan. You don't minister in spite of yourself, but through the personality God gave you. You were shaped by God for a purpose. If he has called you to be a pastor, that means there must be people somewhere in the world whom you can reach better than anyone else.

There are two principles to remember when seeking to discern God's direction for your ministry.

You'll best reach those you relate to. The easiest people for you to reach for Christ are those who are most like you. This is not to say you *can't* reach people unlike yourself. Of course you can. It's just harder. Some pastors relate best to highly educated intellectuals, and other pastors relate better to simple, common folk. Both groups need Christ, and both need a pastor who understands them and loves being with them. Your greatest contribution will occur when you match your target. Then you can have an impact by being yourself.

Second, *as a leader you'll attract who you are, not who you want.* When I started Saddleback Church I was twenty-six years old. No matter how hard I tried, I couldn't get anyone over forty-five to join our church; the congregation pretty much matched my age group. It wasn't until I added staff who were older than I was that we began to reach senior adults. Now, as I enter middle age, I'm having to add younger staff to relate to those younger than I am.

Sometimes because pastors want to reach a certain target group, they aren't realistic about who they are. I knew a pastor in his fifties with a farming background who decided to start a church to reach "baby-busters" because he'd seen another church do it and it looked exciting. The church failed miserably. He later con-

> **You will attract who you *are*, not who you want.**

fided, "I just couldn't connect on their wavelength."

An exception to these two principles occurs if you have been given what I call the "missionary gift." The ability to minister cross-culturally requires a special gift, an ability from the Holy Spirit to be able to communicate to people with backgrounds very different from your own.

The apostle Paul obviously had the missionary gift. His upbringing made him a "Hebrew of Hebrews" (see Phil. 3:5), yet God called him to plant Gentile churches. I know some pastors who were raised in rural areas but minister very effectively in the inner city. I've also seen some southern-born pastors who have been greatly used by God in northeastern cities. But these gifted pastors are the exception to the rule.

Explosive growth occurs when the type of people in the community match the type of people that are already in the church, and they both match the type of person the pastor is. But if the members and the pastor *don't* match, there will probably be just an explosion without the growth! Many church conflicts are caused by mismatched leaders. Placing the wrong type of leader in a church is like mismatching jumper cables on a car battery—sparks are guaranteed to fly.

There have been many times I've seen pastors who are having a hard time ministering to people in their communities because they don't match them culturally. The problem is not dedication, but background! A godly man in the wrong place will still produce only mediocre results.

Personally, I have no doubt that there are many parts of our country where I would completely fail as a pastor because I'd never match the culture. God made me to minister exactly where I am. The changed lives in our church family prove it.

Sometimes the wisest thing a pastor can do is to admit that he doesn't match the church or community and move somewhere else. A number of years ago Saddleback started a new church in nearby Irvine, California. A friend of mine moved from Atlanta to pastor it. He had started a church in Atlanta that had grown to over 200 in attendance, so I knew he had the gifts needed to be a church planter. After about eight months, the new church in Irvine had still not gotten off the ground.

I asked John what he thought the problem was. He said, "It's obvious I don't fit here. This area of Irvine is composed of wealthy, middle-aged couples with teenagers."

I then asked him, "Who do you think you could best reach?"

John replied, "I feel I can reach young couples with preschoolers and young single adults who are out on their own for the first time. I understand their problems."

"Then we need to move you to a section of Huntington Beach!" I said. We moved John to Huntington Beach, started over with a new church, and within a year his church was running over 200 in attendance.

I have another friend who pastors an African-American congregation in Long Beach, California. He came to see me one day very discouraged by the lack of growth in his church. I soon discovered that he didn't fit the educational level of his congregation. He had several advanced degrees and a very sophisticated vocabulary, but most of those in his church and community were barely high school graduates. His speaking style was turning people off. After discovering that there was an entire community of professional African-Americans living about four miles away, I suggested that he resign from his current pastorate and start a church in that part of Long Beach. He did exactly that and two years later reported back that the new church had over 300 attending each Sunday.

If you are a pastor struggling with a ministry "misfit," and you don't match your area, you know exactly what I've been describing. You've probably had a gut feeling about it all along. Don't feel bad. It's not a sin that you don't fit a particular area. Just move! If God has gifted you and called you into ministry, he has a place that's just right for you.

What If Our Church Doesn't Match Our Community?

Often communities change, but the makeup of a church doesn't. What do you do if you're serving in a church that doesn't match the community?

Build on your strengths

Don't try to be something you're not. If your church is primarily made up of elderly folks, decide to become the most effective ministry to senior citizens that you can possibly be. Don't try to become a baby-buster congregation. Strengthen what you are already doing and don't worry about what you can't do. Keep doing what you've been strong at, just do it better. Chances are that there's a pocket of people in your community that only your church can reach.

Reinvent your congregation

Reinventing the congregation is when you intentionally change the makeup of your church in order to match a new target. You completely replace all the old programs, structures, and worship styles with new ones.

I want this to be very clear: *I do not advise this!* It is a painful process and may take many years. People will leave the church due to the enormous, inevitable conflicts. If you lead this process, you will probably be vilified as Satan incarnate by older members unless you've been there longer than everyone else. I have seen this done successfully, but not without an enormous amount of persistence and willingness to absorb criticism. It takes a very loving, patient, and gifted pastor to lead a church in reinventing itself.

Don't even consider this option in a church with over one hundred attenders unless God tells you to. It is a road to martyrdom. However, if you are in a church of fifty people or less, this may be a viable option for you. One advantage for the small church is that it can be completely transformed by having just a few families leave and a few new families join. But the bigger a church gets, the less likely you'll be able to do this.

Start new congregations

This third option is the one I love to recommend. There are a couple of ways to start a new congregation to reach a new target in your community. First, you can add another worship service with a different worship style in order to reach people that are not being reached by the current style of your worship service. All across America, churches are beginning second and even third worship services in order to offer options and increase their outreach.

A second approach is to actually begin a mission, which you intend to become a self-supporting congregation. Starting new congregations is the fastest way to fulfill the Great Commission.

You may remember being taught in your high school biology class that the primary characteristic of biological maturity is the ability to reproduce. I believe the same is true for the church, which the Bible refers to as a "body." The mark of a truly mature church is that it has babies: It starts other churches.

You do not have to be a large church to start new congregations. Saddleback Church started our first daughter church when our church was just a year old. Each year since then we've started at least one new daughter church. As I mentioned in the last chapter, by our fifteenth anniversary we had started twenty-five other churches.

Recognizing Spiritual Receptivity
in Your Community

Jesus taught in the Parable of the Sower and the Soils (see Matt. 13:3–23) that spiritual receptivity varies widely. Like different kinds of soil, people respond differently to the Good News. Some people are very open to hearing the Gospel, and others are very closed. In the parable of the sower Jesus explained that there are hard hearts, shallow hearts, distracted hearts, and receptive hearts.

For evangelism to have maximum effectiveness, we need to plant our seed in the good soil—the soil that produces a hundredfold harvest. No farmer in his right mind would waste seed, a precious commodity, on infertile ground that won't produce a crop. In the same way, careless, unplanned broadcasting of the Gospel is poor stewardship. The message of Christ is too important to waste time, money, and energy on nonproductive methods and soil. We need to be strategic in reaching the world, focusing our efforts where they will make the greatest difference.

Even within your church's target group there will be various pockets of receptivity. Spiritual receptivity is something that comes and goes in people's lives like an ocean tide. At various times in life people tend to be more open to spiritual truth than at other times. God uses a variety of tools to soften hearts and prepare people to be saved.

Who are the most receptive people? I believe there are two broad categories: People in transition and people under tension. God uses both change and pain to get people's attention and make them receptive to the Gospel.

People in transition

Any time someone experiences major change, whether positive or negative, it seems to create a hunger for spiritual stability. Right now there is enormous interest in spiritual matters due to the massive changes in our world that are making people frightened and unsettled. Alvin Toffler says that people look for "islands of stability" when change becomes overwhelming. This is a wave the church needs to ride.

> God uses both change and pain to make people receptive to the gospel.

At Saddleback, we've found that people are more receptive to the Gospel when they face changes like a new marriage, a new baby, a new home, a new job, or a new school. This is why churches generally grow faster in new communities where residents are continually moving in than in stable, older communities where people have lived for forty years.

People under tension

God uses all kinds of emotional pain to get people's attention: the pain of divorce, death of a loved one, unemployment, financial problems, marriage and family difficulties, loneliness, resentment, guilt, and other stresses. Fearful or anxious people often begin looking for something greater than themselves to ease the pain and fill the void they feel.

I make no claim to immaculate perception, but based on fifteen years of pastoring I offer the following list of what I believe have been the ten most receptive groups of people that we've reached out to at Saddleback:

1. Second-time visitors to the church
2. Close friends and relatives of new converts
3. People going through a divorce
4. Those who feel their need for a recovery program (alcohol, drugs, sexual, and so forth)
5. First-time parents
6. The terminally ill and their families
7. Couples with major marriage problems
8. Parents with problem children
9. Recently unemployed or those with major financial problems
10. New residents in the community

A possible goal for your church might be to develop a specific program or outreach to each of the most receptive people groups in your community. Of course, if you begin to do this someone is likely to say, "Pastor, I think that before we try to reach all these new people we should try to reactivate all the old members that have stopped coming." This is a guaranteed strategy for church decline! It doesn't work. It usually takes about five times more energy to reactivate a disgruntled or carnal member than it does to win a receptive unbeliever.

I believe God has called pastors to catch fish and feed sheep, not to corral goats! Your inactive members probably need to join somewhere else for a number of reasons. If you want to grow, focus on reaching receptive people.

> Growing churches focus on reaching receptive people. Nongrowing churches focus on reenlisting inactive people.

Once you know who your target is, who you are most likely to reach, and who the most receptive people in your target group are, you are ready for the next step: establishing an evangelism strategy for your church.

11
Developing Your Strategy

Whatever a person is like, I try to find common ground with him so that he will let me tell him about Christ and let Christ save him.

1 Corinthians 9:22 (LB)

Jesus called out, "Come along with me and I will show you how to fish for the souls of men!"

Matthew 4:19 (LB)

My dad is the best fisherman I've ever met. If there is only one fish in a lake or stream he will catch it. This always amazed me growing up. Ten of us could be fishing the same lake and my dad would catch all the fish. How did he do it? Was it magic? Did God just like him better?

As I got older I realized his secret: My dad understood fish. He could "read" a lake and figure out exactly where the fish were; he knew what time of day they liked to eat; he knew what bait or lure to use depending on the type of fish; he knew when to change bait as the temperature changed; he even seemed to know exactly how deep to drop the line into the water. He made it as easy and attractive as possible for fish to swallow his hook—so they did! He caught fish on their terms.

In contrast, I never had a strategy when I went fishing. I'd cast out anywhere in the lake hoping something might bite. Fish rarely went for my hook because I fished with a take-it-or-leave-it attitude. I was always more interested in enjoying the outdoors than actually catching anything. While my dad would crawl through brush or get wet up to his waist in order to get to where the fish were, my fishing spots were usually determined by what was most comfortable to me. I had no strategy, and my results showed it.

Unfortunately, many churches have this same lackadaisical attitude toward fishing for men and women. They don't take the time to understand the people they want to reach, and they don't have a strategy. They want to win people to Christ as long as it can be done in a comfortable way.

The secret of effective evangelism is to not only share Christ's message but to follow Christ's methodology. I believe Jesus gave us not only what to say but also how to share it. He had a strategy. He modeled timeless principles of evangelism that still work today if we'll apply them.

Matthew 10 and Luke 10 are two revealing accounts of Jesus' strategy for targeted evangelism. Before Jesus sent out his disciples to evangelize, he gave them specific instructions about whom they were to spend their time with, whom they were to ignore, what they were to say, and how they were to share it. There isn't space in this chapter for a detailed exposition of all the instructions Jesus gave. Instead, I want to identify five fishing guidelines for evangelism found in Jesus' instructions to his disciples. We have built Saddleback's evangelism strategy around these five principles.

Know What You Are Fishing For

The kind of fish you want to catch will determine every part of your strategy. Fishing for bass, catfish, or salmon requires different equipment, bait, and timing. You don't catch marlin the same way you catch trout. There is no "one-size-fits-all" approach to fishing. Each demands a unique strategy. The same is true in fishing for men—it helps to know what you're fishing for!

When Jesus sent his disciples out on their first evangelistic campaign, he defined the target very specifically: They were to focus on their own countrymen. "These twelve Jesus sent out with the following instructions: 'Do not go among the Gentiles or enter any town of the Samaritans. Go rather to the lost sheep of Israel'" (Matt. 10:5–6).

There may have been several reasons Jesus narrowed the target, but one thing is certain: He targeted the kind of people the disciples were most likely to reach—people

> There is no "one-size-fits-all" approach to fishing. You must know what you are fishing for!

like themselves. Jesus was not being prejudiced, he was being strategic. As I mentioned in chapter 9, Jesus defined the disciples' target so they'd be effective, not in order to be exclusive.

Go Where the Fish Are Biting

It is a waste of time to fish in a spot where the fish aren't biting. Wise fishermen move on. They understand that fish feed in different spots at different times of the day. Nor are they hungry all the time.

This is the principle of receptivity that I explained in the last chapter. At certain times, unbelievers are more responsive to spiritual truth than at other times. This receptivity often lasts only briefly, which is why Jesus said to go where people would listen. Take advantage of the responsive hearts that the Holy Spirit prepares.

Notice Jesus' instructions in Matthew 10:14 (NCV): "If a home or town refuses to welcome you or listen to you, *leave that place* and shake its dust off your feet" (italics added). This is a very significant statement that we shouldn't ignore. Jesus told the disciples they were not supposed to stay around unresponsive people. We aren't supposed to pick the green fruit, but to find the ripe fruit and harvest it.

Before starting Saddleback, I led evangelistic crusades and revivals in many churches. Often the local pastor and I would spend the afternoons making evangelistic house calls. Many times the pastor would take me to the same stubborn case that previous evangelists had failed to win. It was a waste of time.

Is it good stewardship to continue badgering someone who has rejected Christ a dozen times when there is a whole community of receptive people waiting to hear the Gospel for the first time? I believe the Holy Spirit wants to direct us to the people he's already prepared to respond. Jesus told us not to worry about the unresponsive. Shake the dust off your feet and move on.

The apostle Paul's strategy was to go through open doors and not waste time banging on closed ones. Likewise, we should not focus our efforts on those who aren't ready to listen. There are far more people in the world who are ready to receive Christ than there are believers ready to witness to them.

Learn to Think Like a Fish

In order to catch fish it helps to understand their habits, preferences, and feeding patterns. Certain fish like smooth, still water, and others like to swim in rushing rivers. Some fish are bottom crawlers, and others like to hide under rocks. Successful fishing requires the ability to think like a fish.

Jesus often knew what unbelievers were thinking (see Matt. 9:4; 12:25; Mark 2:8; Luke 5:22; 9:47; 11:17). He was effective in dealing with people because he understood and was able to defuse the mental barriers they held.

Colossians 4:5 (NCV) says, "Be wise in the way you act with people who are not believers, making the most of every opportunity." We must learn to think like unbelievers in order to win them.

The problem is, the longer you are a believer, the less you think like an unbeliever. Your interests and values change. Because I've been a Christian for most of my life, I think like a Christian. I don't normally think like an unbeliever. Worse than that, I tend to think like a *pastor,* and that's even further removed from an unbeliever's mind-set. I must intentionally change mental gears when seeking to relate to non-Christians.

> ## The longer you are a believer, the less you think like an unbeliever.

If you look at most church advertising, it's obvious that it was written from a believer's viewpoint, not from the mind-set of an unchurched person. Take a church ad that announces "Preaching the inerrant Word of God!" Such a statement certainly doesn't appeal to unbelievers. Personally, I consider the inerrancy of Scripture as a nonnegotiable belief, but the unchurched don't even understand the term. The spiritual terminology that Christians are familiar with is just gibberish to unbelievers. If you want to advertise your church to the unchurched you must learn to think and speak like they do.

I've often heard pastors complain that unbelievers are more resistant to the Gospel today than in the past. I don't think that is true at all. More often than not, resistance is just poor communication. The message just isn't getting through. Churches need to stop saying people are closed to the Gospel and start finding out how to communicate on the unbeliever's wavelength. No matter how life-changing our message is, it won't do any good if we're broadcasting on a different channel from the unchurched.

How do you learn to think like unbelievers? Talk to them! One of the greatest barriers to evangelism is that most believers spend all their time with other Christians. They don't have any non-believing friends. If you don't spend any time with unbelievers, you won't understand what they're thinking.

As I shared in chapter 1, I began Saddleback by going door-to-door for twelve weeks and surveying the unchurched in my area. Six years earlier I had read Robert Schuller's book *Your Church Has Real Possibilities*, which told how he had gone door-to-door in 1955 and asked hundreds of people, "Why don't you go to church?" and "What do you want in a church?" I thought this was a great idea but felt the questions needed to be rephrased for the more skeptical 1980s. I wrote down in my notebook five questions I would use to start Saddleback:

1. *What do you think is the greatest need in this area?* This question simply got people talking to me.

2. *Are you actively attending any church?* If they said yes, I thanked them and moved on to the next home. I didn't bother asking the other three questions because I didn't want to color the survey with believers' opinions. Notice that I didn't ask, "Are you a *member?*" Many people who haven't been inside a church for twenty years still claim membership in some church.

3. *Why do you think most people don't attend church?* This seemed to be a less threatening and offensive wording than "Why don't *you* attend church?" Today many people would answer that question with "It's none of your business why I don't go!" But when I asked why they thought *other people* didn't attend, they usually gave me their personal reasons anyway.

4. *If you were to look for a church to attend, what kind of things would you look for?* This single question taught me more about thinking like an unbeliever than my entire seminary training. I discovered that most churches

were offering programs that the unchurched were not interested in.

5. *What could I do for you? What advice can you give to a minister who really wants to be helpful to people?* This is the most basic question the church must ask its community. Study the gospels and notice how many times Jesus asked someone, "What do you want me to do for you?" He began with people's needs.

When I took the survey, I introduced it by saying: "Hi, my name is Rick Warren. I'm taking an opinion poll of our community. I'm not here to sell you anything or sign you up for anything. I'd just like to ask you five questions. There are no right or wrong answers, and it will only take about two minutes."

Several thousand churches have now used these five survey questions in their own communities. One denomination that I consulted with used these questions to start 102 new churches on a single day! If you have never surveyed the unchurched in your area, I strongly recommend that you do.

Four basic complaints

We discovered four common complaints about churches from our survey in the Saddleback Valley.

"Church is boring, especially the sermons. The messages don't relate to my life." This is the complaint I heard the most. It is amazing how churches are able to take the most exciting book in the world and bore people to tears with it. Miraculously they are able to turn bread into stones!

The problem with boring preachers is that it causes people to think God is boring. From this complaint, I determined to learn how to communicate God's Word in a practical, interesting way. A sermon does not have to be boring to be biblical, and it doesn't have to be dry to be doctrinal. The unchurched aren't asking for watered-down messages, just practical ones. They want to hear something on Sunday that they can apply on Monday.

"Church members are unfriendly to visitors. If I go to church I want to feel welcomed without being embarrassed." Many unchurched people told me that they felt like the church was a clique. When they didn't know the "inside" terminology, songs, or rituals, they felt foolish and felt the members were watching them in judgment. The greatest emotion the unchurched feel when they visit a service is *fear.* As a result, we determined that at Saddleback we would do whatever it took to make visitors feel welcomed and wanted without feeling watched.

"The church is more interested in my money than in me." Due to the highly visible fund-raising efforts of televangelists and other Christian organizations, the unchurched are incredibly sensitive to appeals for money. Bill Hybels found this to be the greatest complaint in his area when he took a similar survey. Many believe that pastors are "in it just for the money," and opulent church buildings have only added fuel to the fire. We decided to counteract this complaint by giving a disclaimer when we take an offering. We explain that the offering is only for those who are a part of our church family. Visitors are not expected to give.

"We worry about the quality of the church's child care." The Saddleback Valley is filled with young couples, so we were not surprised to discover this complaint. The church must earn the trust of parents. Saddleback has adopted and published a set of stringent guidelines for our children's ministry to insure safety and quality. If you want to reach young couples, you must have an excellent program for their children.

Jesus told the disciples to be strategic in their evangelism. "I am sending you out like sheep among wolves. Therefore be as shrewd as snakes and as innocent as doves" (Matt. 10:16). In football, successful teams know how to "read the defense." When the offensive team lines up for each play, the quarterback looks out at the opposing team to see how they are lined up. He tries to figure out in advance how the defense will respond and what barriers might prevent the execution of the play. If the quarterback doesn't do this, he usually gets sacked!

In evangelism, "reading the defense" means understanding and anticipating the objections unbelievers will have before they voice them. It means learning to think like an unbeliever.

What seemed most interesting to me about our survey was that none of the complaints from the unchurched in our area were theological. I didn't meet a single person who said, "I don't go to church because I don't believe in God." However I *did* meet a lot of people who said, "I believe in God, but I don't feel church has anything I need." Most of the unchurched aren't atheists: They are misinformed, turned off, or too busy.

Using the information we gathered through the survey, we mailed an open letter to the community addressing the major concerns of the unchurched and announcing a church service designed to counteract the most common excuses they gave.

I wrote this letter totally on faith. When we sent it out, we hadn't even held a service yet. In faith, we announced in advance the kind of church we were determined to be.

I defined our target in the first sentence of the letter by positioning Saddleback as "a church for the unchurched." The entire tone of the letter was written to appeal to what the unchurched were looking for, not to attract Christians from other churches. In fact, all of the critical and angry letters I received in response to this first letter came from Christians who questioned why I had not mentioned Jesus or the Bible. Some even expressed doubt over my own salvation! They just didn't understand what we were trying to do.

Because of the letter, 205 people attended the first service of Saddleback, and within the next ten weeks eighty-two of them gave their lives to Christ. The results were worth being misunderstood by some Christians. You have to decide who you want to impress.

March 20, 1980

Hi Neighbor!

AT LAST!

A new church designed for those who've given up on traditional church services! Let's face it. Many people aren't active in church these days.

WHY?

Too often . . .

- The sermons are boring and don't relate to daily living
- Many churches seem more interested in your wallet than you
- Members are unfriendly to visitors
- You wonder about the quality of the nursery care for your children

Do you think attending church should be enjoyable?

WE'VE GOT GOOD NEWS FOR YOU!

SADDLEBACK VALLEY COMMUNITY CHURCH is a new church designed to meet your needs in the 1980s. We're a group of friendly, happy people who have discovered the joy of the Christian lifestyle. At Saddleback Valley Community Church you

- Meet new friends and get to know your neighbors
- Enjoy upbeat music with a contemporary flavor
- Hear positive, practical messages which encourage you each week
- Trust your children to the care of dedicated nursery workers

WHY NOT GET A LIFT THIS SUNDAY?

I invite you to be my special guest at our first public celebration service EASTER SUNDAY, April 6 at 11:00 A.M. We are currently meeting in the Laguna Hills High School Theater. If you don't have a church home, give us a try!

DISCOVER THE DIFFERENCE!

Sincerely,
Rick Warren, Pastor

Catch Fish on Their Terms

This is the heart of Saddleback's evangelism strategy: We must be willing to catch fish on their own terms. As I pointed out in the illustration of my dad, successful fishing often requires doing things that are uncomfortable in order to get to the fish. Did you know that the average fisherman never ventures farther than a half mile from a paved road? *Serious* fishermen, however, will go to any length to catch fish. How serious are you about the Great Commission? How serious is your church? Are you willing to go to any length and be uncomfortable in order to win people to Christ?

Understanding and adapting to their culture

Jesus told the disciples, "When you enter a town and are welcomed, *eat what is set before you*" (Luke 10:8, italics added). In saying this, Jesus was giving more than dietary advice, he was commanding them to be sensitive to local culture. He was telling them to fit in with those they wanted to reach. They were to adapt to local customs and culture when it didn't violate a biblical principle.

When I served as a student missionary to Japan I had to learn to eat what was set before me. I didn't like everything I tasted, but I loved the Japanese I wanted to win to Christ, so I adapted to their ways.

Too often we let cultural differences between believers and unbelievers become barriers to getting the message out. For some Christians, any talk of "adapting to their culture" sounds like theological liberalism. This is not a new fear. In fact, it was the reason the apostles held the Jerusalem conference in Acts 15. In those days the issue was, "Do Gentile believers have to follow Jewish customs and culture to be considered true Christians?" The apostles and elders answered with a clear "No way!" From that point on, Christianity began to adapt to each new culture as it spread around the world.

The Gospel is always communicated in the terms of some culture. The only question is, which one? No church can be culturally neutral. It will express some culture because it is composed of human beings.

For 2,000 years Christianity has adapted itself to one culture after another. If it hadn't adapted, we'd still be a sect within Judaism! We are ignoring 2,000 years of church history when we insist that our own cultural expression of the faith is better or more biblical than any other.

I've noticed that whenever I go fishing the fish don't automatically jump into my boat or throw themselves up onto the shore for me. Their culture (under water) is very different from mine (air). It takes intentional effort on my part to make contact with fish. Somehow I must figure out how to get the bait right in front of their nose in their culture.

Churches that expect the unchurched to show up simply because they build a building and hang out a "We're Open" sign are deluding themselves. People don't voluntarily jump into your boat. You must penetrate their culture.

To penetrate any culture you must be willing to make small concessions in matters of style in order to gain a hearing. For example, our church has adopted the casual, informal style and dress of the southern California community we minister in. Since the beach is just a few miles away and the weather is sunny and mild most of the year, people don't dress up as much as in other parts of the country. So we designed our services to reflect that same informal style. If you see men in suits and ties at Saddleback, they're likely to be out-of-town visitors.

Letting your target determine your approach

Catching fish on their terms means letting your target determine your approach. When you go fishing, do you use the same kind of bait for every kind of fish? Of course not. Do you use the same size of hook for every kind of fish? No. You must use the bait and hook that best matches the fish you want to catch.

Paul always allowed his target to determine his approach. He describes his strategy in 1 Corinthians 9:19–22:

> Though I am free and belong to no man, I make myself a slave to everyone, to win as many as possible. To the Jews I became like a Jew, to win the Jews. To those under the law I became like one under the law (though I myself am not under the law), so as to win those under the law. To those not having the law I became like one not having the law . . ., so as to win those not having the law. To the weak I became weak, to win the weak. I have become all things to all men so that by all possible means I might save some.

Some critics might say Paul was being a chameleon, that by acting differently with different groups he was hypocritical in his ministry. Not so. Paul was being strategic. His motivation was his desire to see all people saved. I love the Living Bible paraphrase of 1 Corinthians 9:22–23: "Yes, whatever a person is like, I try to find common ground with him so that he will let me tell him about Christ and let Christ save him. I do this to get the Gospel to them and also for the blessing I myself receive when I see them come to Christ."

I once read through the gospels in order to discover the standard approach Jesus used in evangelism. What I learned was that he didn't have one! He had no standard approach in witnessing. He simply started wherever people were. When he was with the woman at the well, he talked about living waters; when he was with fishermen, he talked about catching fish; when he was with farmers, he talked about sowing seed.

Beginning with the felt needs of the unchurched

Whenever Jesus encountered a person he'd begin with *their* hurts, needs, and interests. When he sent his disciples out he told them to do the same: "Heal the sick, raise the dead, cleanse those who have leprosy, drive out demons. Freely you have received, freely give" (Matt. 10:8).

Notice the total emphasis on felt needs and hurts. When you are in pain, either physically or emotionally, you aren't interested in the meaning of Greek and Hebrew words. You just want to get well. Jesus always ministered to people's needs and hurts. When a leper came to Jesus, Jesus didn't launch into a long discourse on the cleansing laws of Leviticus. He just healed the man! When he encountered the sick, the demon-possessed, or the disturbed, he dealt with them at their point of pain. He didn't say, "I'm sorry, that doesn't fit my preaching schedule. Today we're continuing our series through the book of Deuteronomy."

If your church is serious about reaching the unchurched, you must be willing to put up with people who have a lot of problems. Fishing is often messy and smelly. Many churches want the fish they catch to be already scaled, gutted, cleaned, and cooked. That is why they never reach anyone.

Understanding and responding to the hang-ups of the unchurched

At Saddleback we take the hang-ups of the unchurched very seriously, even when they are based on ignorance. Unbelievers have hang-ups about churches asking them for money, about churches that use guilt or fear to motivate, about churches that expect them to attend every meeting the church holds, and about churches that make visitors stand up and introduce themselves.

Our strategy is to counteract these hang-ups as quickly as possible. For instance, in our surveys of the unchurched we found that denominational labels carried a lot of negative baggage for many of the unchurched in southern California. This caused us to choose the neutral name "Saddleback Church."

I am not ashamed of my Southern Baptist heritage, and we clearly explain in our membership class that Saddleback is affiliated both doctrinally and financially with the Southern Baptist Convention. But when we asked unchurched southern Californians, "What does the term *Southern Baptist* mean to you?" I was amazed at the widespread misperceptions. Many unbelievers, particularly those with Catholic backgrounds, told me they would never even consider visiting a Southern Baptist congregation.

This left me with two options: I could spend years educating the community about what the SBC really stood for *before* I got them to visit our church, or I could clear up the misconceptions *after* they accepted Christ. We chose the second option.

Did I get criticized for my choice? What do you think? Some well-meaning folks accused me of all sorts of theological heresy and lapses of integrity, but they weren't my target anyway. I wasn't trying to attract Christians or target other Baptists. Some of these people became my friends once they understood who we were trying to reach. Choosing a neutral name was an evangelism strategy, not a theological compromise.

In 1988, a Gallup poll revealed that 33 percent of all Protestants had changed denominational affiliations during their lifetime. I'm sure that number is even greater now. Given the increasing popularity of generic products, it's obvious that today's generation has very little "brand" loyalty. For most people, value is a greater draw. Few people choose a church on the basis of the denominational label. They choose the church that best ministers to their needs.

Change methods whenever necessary

If you've ever fished for an entire day, you know that sometimes you have to change bait as the day wears on. What the fish were biting on in the morning they seem to ignore in the late afternoon. The problem with many churches today is that they are still trying to use bait and hooks from the 1950s in the 1990s—and the fish are no longer biting. The greatest enemy to our success in the future is often the success of our past.

Use More Than One Hook

Where I grew up, using more than one hook was called "trotline fishing." It consisted of attaching multiple hooks to a single fishing line. The concept was that the more hooks you have in the water, the more fish you're likely to catch.

Due to advances in technology, people in America are offered more options than ever before. While there used to be three television networks, I can now get over fifty stations on my television, and with fiber optic cable that may soon grow to three times that. There used to be one kind of Coke®; now there is Diet Coke®, Cherry Coke®, Classic Coke®, Diet Cherry Coke®, Caffeine-Free Diet Coke®, and so forth.

Last year I saw a televised report on the choices now available to consumers. The documentary estimated that each week about 200 new grocery items enter the market, and each year nearly 300 new magazines are published. The Levi corporation alone has 70,000 products of different sizes, shapes, types, and materials. We live in a world of multiple choices.

These changes have produced a generation that expects to be offered options in every area. Unfortunately, when it comes to worship services most churches offer only two options: Take it or leave it! If you can't attend at 11 A.M., you're out of luck.

It is not pandering to consumerism to offer multiple services or even multiple styles of worship. It is strategic and unselfish, and it says we will do whatever it takes to reach more people for Christ. The goal is not to make it as difficult as possible but to make it as easy as possible for the unchurched to hear about Christ.

Growing churches offer multiple programs, multiple services, and sometimes even multiple locations. They realize it takes all kinds of approaches to reach all kinds of people. Jerry Falwell calls it "saturation evangelism": using every available means to reach every available person at every available time.

Why do we normally fish with only one hook? Why do most churches have few or no outreach programs? I believe it is because we ask the wrong question. Too often, the first question asked is, "How much will it cost?" The *right* question is, "Who will it reach?" How much is a soul worth? Isn't it worth it to spend five hundred dollars on a newspaper ad if it will reach one unbeliever for Christ?

It Costs to Reach Your Community

If your church is serious about developing a comprehensive evangelism strategy, it will cost money. With this in mind, let me conclude this chapter with some thoughts about financing your strategy.

First, money spent on evangelism is never an expense, it's always an investment. The people you reach will more than repay the cost you invested to reach them. Before we held the first service of Saddleback, the people in our small home Bible study went about $6,500 in debt preparing for that service. Where did we get the money? We used our personal credit cards! We believed the offerings of the people we reached for Christ would eventually enable everyone to be paid back.

One of the miracles of our dress rehearsal service was that a man who had not attended our home Bible study came to that service and gave a check for a thousand dollars when we took the offering. After it was over, the woman in charge of counting the offering came up and showed me the check. I said, "This is going to work!" Sure enough, we paid everyone back within four months. Please note: I'm *not* advocating that your church use credit cards to finance it. I'm just trying to illustrate how willing we were to pay the cost of reaching people for Christ.

When finances get tight in a church, often the first thing cut is the evangelism and advertising budget. That is the *last thing* you should cut. It is the source of new blood and life for your church.

The second thing to realize when thinking about church finances is that people give to *vision*, not to need. If need motivated people to give, every church would have plenty of money. It is not the neediest institutions that attract contributions but those with the greatest vision. Churches that are making the most of what they've got are the churches that attract more gifts. That's why Jesus said, "It is always true that those who have, get more, and those who have little, soon lose even that" (Luke 19:26 LB).

If your church is constantly short on cash, check out your vision. Is it clear? Is it being communicated effectively? Money flows to God-given, Holy Spirit-inspired ideas. Churches with money problems often actually have a vision problem.

Third, when you spend nickels and dimes on evangelism, you get nickel and dime results. In Matthew 17, Jesus told Peter to go find money in a fish's mouth in order to pay the Roman taxes. Verse 27 says that Jesus told Peter: "Go to the lake and throw out your line. Take the first fish you catch; open its mouth and you will find a four-drachma coin." I believe there is an important lesson in that story: The coins are always in the mouths of the fish. If you'll focus on fishing (evangelism), God will pay your bills.

Finally, remember the famous motto of the great missionary strategist Hudson Taylor: "God's work done God's way will not lack God's support."

Fishing Is Serious Business

I've always loved Jesus' analogy of evangelism as "fishing," but I've had one hesitation about it: Fishing is just a hobby for most people, something they do in their spare time. No one sees fishing as a responsibility. Yet fishing for men is serious business. It's not a hobby for Christians; it is to be our lifestyle!

Part Four

Bringing In a Crowd

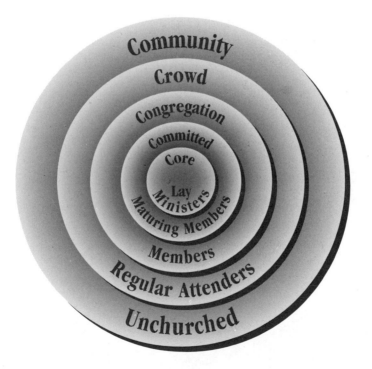

Community

Crowd

Congregation

Committed

Core

Lay
Ministers

Maturing Members

Members

Regular Attenders

Unchurched

12

How Jesus Attracted Crowds

Enormous crowds followed him wherever he went.

Matthew 4:25 (LB)

The large crowd listened to him with delight.

Mark 12:37

One of the impressive characteristics of Jesus' ministry was that it attracted crowds. Large crowds. *Enormous* crowds. The King James Version calls them "multitudes." The crowds Jesus attracted were so huge that one time he was almost crushed by one (Luke 8:42). Seekers loved to listen to him and thronged to wherever he was, even if it meant traveling a long distance. When Jesus fed the 5,000, that number counted only the men (Matt. 14:21). When you add in the women and children who must have been there too, there may have been more than 15,000 in attendance at that service! Jesus' ministry had a magnetic quality about it.

A Christlike ministry still attracts crowds. You don't have to use gimmicks or compromise your convictions to gather a crowd. You don't have to water down your message. I've even found that you don't need a church building to draw a crowd! But you do have to minister to people the way Jesus did.

What attracted large crowds to Jesus' ministry? Jesus did three things with crowds: He loved them (Matt. 9:36, et al.), he met their needs (Matt. 15:30; Luke 6:17–18; John 6:2, et al.), and he taught them in interesting and practical ways (Matt. 13:34; Mark 10:1; 12:37, et al.). These same three ingredients will attract crowds today.

Jesus Attracted Crowds by Loving Unbelievers

Jesus loved lost people and loved spending time with them. From the gospels, it is obvious that Jesus enjoyed being with seekers far more than being with religious leaders. He went to their parties and was called the "friend of sinners" (Luke 7:34). How many people would call you that?

People could feel that Jesus loved being with them. Even little children wanted to be around him, which speaks volumes about what kind of person he was. Children instinctively seem to gravitate toward loving, accepting people.

Loving unbelievers like Jesus did

Loving unbelievers the way Jesus did is the most overlooked key to growing a church. Without his passion for the lost, we will be unwilling to make the sacrifices necessary to reach them.

The command to love is the most repeated command in the New Testament, appearing at least fifty-five times. If we don't love people, nothing else matters. "Whoever does not love does not know God, because God is love" (1 John 4:8). When I've asked the new converts I baptize what attracted them to our church family, I've never had anyone say, "It was because of the Reformation theology you believe" or "It was your beautiful buildings" or "It was your full calendar of activities." Instead, the most common response was, "I felt an incredible spirit of love *toward me* that drew me in."

Notice the focus of that statement. Our members' love is focused toward newcomers, not just toward each other. I know of many churches where the members love *each other,* and they have great fellowship, but the churches are still dying because all the love is focused inwardly. The fellowship in these churches has become so tight that newcomers are unable to break into it. They don't attract unbelievers because they don't love unbelievers.

Of course, every congregation *thinks* their church is loving. That's because the people who think it is unloving aren't there! Ask typical members, and they will say, "Our church is very friendly and loving." What they usually mean is, "We love each other. We are friendly and loving to the people *already here.*" They love the people they feel comfortable with, but that warm fellowship doesn't automatically translate into love for unbelievers and visitors.

Some churches point to their lack of a crowd as proof that they are biblical, orthodox, or Spirit-filled. They maintain that their small size is proof that they are a pure church, that they haven't compromised their beliefs. It may actually mean they don't love lost people enough to reach out to them. The honest reason many churches do not have a crowd is because they don't want one! They don't like having to relate to unbelievers and feel that attracting a crowd would disturb their comfortable routine. This kind of selfishness keeps a lot of churches from growing.

> The most overlooked key to growing a church: We must love unbelievers the way Jesus did.

Years ago Dean Kelly published research that showed churches grow because they are conservative in doctrine; they know what they believe and are not ashamed of it. I believe Kelly was only half right. There are many Bible-believing churches that are dying on the vine. Churches that grow are those who hold conservative beliefs *and* are loving to outsiders. Win Arn has done an exhaustive study that confirms this fact: Great churches are built on love—for God, for each other, and for unbelievers.

One of the primary reasons for Saddleback's growth is that we love new people. We love visitors. We love the lost. For fifteen years I've watched our members express that love in practical ways: setting up and taking down chairs and Sunday school equipment each weekend in temporary facilities, being willing to use seventy-nine different locations so the church could keep growing and reaching more people, parking off campus so visitors could have their parking spots, standing through packed-out services so visitors could have their seats, and even offering their coats to visitors on cold days in our tent.

> Love draws people in like a powerful magnet. A lack of love drives people away.

It is a myth that large churches are always cold and impersonal, and that small churches are automatically warm and loving. Size has nothing to do with love or friendliness. The reason some churches remain small is because they *aren't* loving. Love draws people in like a powerful magnet. A lack of love drives people away.

Creating an atmosphere of acceptance

Plants need the right climate to grow and so do churches. The right climate for church growth is an atmosphere of acceptance and love. Growing churches love; loving churches grow. It seems obvious, but it is often overlooked: For your church to grow you must be *nice* to people when they show up!

In the survey of the unchurched that I took prior to beginning Saddleback, the second most common complaint I discovered was "Church members are unfriendly to visitors. We feel we don't fit." Long before the pastor preaches, the visitors are already deciding whether or not they will come back. They are asking themselves, "Do I feel welcome here?"

At Saddleback we make every effort to counteract this complaint. We have thought through a strategy for creating a climate of love and acceptance that visitors can feel. We monitor our effectiveness on a weekly basis by asking first-time visitors to give us their frank, anonymous, first impressions of our church.

When we mail each first-time visitor a "Thanks for being our guest" letter, we enclose a postage-paid "My First Impression" postcard.

> Long before the pastor preaches, the visitors are already deciding if they will come back.

The card says, "Our church wants to serve you better, so would you please give us your opinion?" There are only three questions on the card: "What did you notice first?" "What did you like best?" "What did you like least?" We've now received thousands of these cards, and nearly 90 percent answer the first question with some variation of this sentence: "I noticed the warmth and friendliness of the people." That response is not an accident. It is the result of an intentional strategy to express love to visitors in a manner that they can comprehend.

To make an impact on a visitor, love must be expressed in a practical way. Even if a church genuinely feels compassion for the unchurched, that compassion might not be being expressed in ways the unchurched understand. We must intentionally act in ways that demonstrate our love for visitors and for those who don't know Christ. Love is more than a feeling; it is a behavior.

It means being sensitive to someone else's needs and putting them ahead of our own. In the next chapter I'll suggest a number of practical ways we've done this at Saddleback.

The pastor must be loving

The pastor of a church sets the tone and atmosphere of the congregation. If you are a pastor and you want to know the warmth of your church, put the thermometer in your own mouth. I've visited some churches where the pastor's lack of love is the main reason the church isn't growing. Some pastors, by their cold demeanor and lack of personal warmth, virtually guarantee that visitors won't come back. And in some larger churches, I've gotten the impression that the pastor loves audiences but doesn't like people.

I often hear pastors enthusiastically admit, "I *love* to preach!" That never impresses me. It may just mean they enjoy the attention or adrenaline rush they feel from being in front of people. What I want to ask those pastors is this: Do you love *the people* you preach to? That is a far more important issue. The Bible says, "If I speak in the tongues of men and of angels, but have not love, I am only a resounding gong or a clanging cymbal" (1 Cor. 13:1). In God's view, great preaching without love is just noise.

Every time I speak to the crowd service at Saddleback I repeat a simple reminder to myself. I never preach or teach without thinking this:

> Father, I love you and you love me. I love these people and you love these people. Love these people through me.
>
> This is not an audience to be feared, but a family to be loved.
>
> There is no fear in love; perfect love casts out all fear.

Roger Ailes, communications consultant to Presidents Reagan and Bush, believes the most influential factor in public speaking is "likability." If people like you, they'll listen to you. If they don't like you, they will ignore you or discount your message. How do you become likable? It's simple: *Love people.* When people know you love them, they listen to you.

Let me suggest some practical ways that pastors can demonstrate love to the crowd.

Memorize names. Remembering names shows that you're interested in people. Nothing sounds sweeter to a second-time visitor than hearing you use his or her name. While I don't have a particularly good memory, I work hard at remembering names. In the early years of Saddleback, I took pictures of people and made flash cards to help me remember their names. I knew every person's name in our church up to about 3,000 in attendance. After that my brain fried! I ask new members in the membership class to tell me their names on three different occasions to help me remember them. When you work hard at remembering people's names, it pays great relational dividends.

Personally greet people before and after services. Be approachable. Don't hide out in your study. For the first three years of our church, we met in a fenced-in high school where everyone had to exit through the same gate. Each week, I personally greeted every person who came to our church. They couldn't get out without passing by me!

One of the best ways to warm up a crowd is to meet as many people as you can before you speak to them. Get out among the crowd and talk to people. It shows you are interested in them personally.

Many pastors like to gather their staff or key leaders in a private room before the service and pray while the people are coming in. I believe you ought to pray for your service at some other time. Don't miss an opportunity to be with people when you have the chance.

I have a prayer team of lay people that prays for me during each of our four services, and I spend extended time each week praying for our services. Our staff also prays together. But we do not have "Holy Huddles" before our services. We get only one shot a week to have contact with many of the people in our crowd, so when they come I want every staff member and every key lay leader interacting with people.

Touch people. Study the ministry of Jesus and you will see the powerful effect of giving people a look, a word, and a touch. At Saddleback we believe in a "high-touch" ministry. We give a lot of hugs and handshakes and pats on the back. Our world is filled with lonely people who are starving for the affirmation of a loving touch. Many individuals live by themselves and have told me the only loving physical contact they ever get is at church. When I hug somebody on Sunday morning I often wonder how long that hug will have to last them.

> Our world is filled with lonely people who are starving for the affirmation of a loving touch.

I recently got this note on a registration card: "Pastor Rick, I can't tell you what it meant to me when you put your arm around me in comfort today. I felt as though Jesus was hugging me in such compassion and tenderness. I now know I will make it through this scary time, and I know he sent you to help me. It's wonderful that there's such caring and love in this church. Thank you." I had no idea when I hugged her she was going in for breast cancer surgery the next day.

Another note from the same week said, "I have been asking God for a positive sign that he is with me. Before the service, Pastor Glen, whom I've never met, walked by my seat, and without saying a word, put his hand on my shoulder. I know now that the Lord has not forgotten me." The man's wife had left him that week.

On weekends when someone else on our preaching team is speaking, I usually spend the entire time giving a look, a word, and a touch to hundreds of people. You never know how a tender word and a caring touch will make all the difference in the world to someone. Behind every smile is a hidden hurt that a simple expression of love may heal.

Use a warm, personal style in writing to visitors. We have a series of letters I've written to first-time, second-time, and third-time visitors, telling them how glad we are to see them. I don't sign them "Dr. Warren" or even "Pastor Warren," I simply sign them "Rick." I want visitors to feel they can relate to me on a first-name basis.

If you send a letter to visitors, write it just as you talk to people, not in stilted, formal language. I received a visitor letter once that said, "Our church would like to acknowledge your presence with us last Sunday and extend to you a cordial invitation to return on the next Lord's Day." Does anyone really talk like that? Instead say, "It was really great to have you. Hope you can come back." Don't write like you're drafting correspondence for British royalty.

One of the most important decisions each pastor must make is whether to *impress* people or *influence* them. You can impress people from a distance, but you have to get up close to people to love and influence them. Proximity determines impact. I think the reason some pastors stay distant from their people is because they aren't impressive up close.

If a church wants to attract a crowd, both the pastor and the members must act in loving ways toward

> Every pastor must decide whether he wants to *impress* people or *influence* them.

outsiders. You must demonstrate the attitude, "If you come here, we're going to love you. No matter who you are or what you look like or what you've done, you're going to be loved in this place."

Accepting without approving

In order to love unbelievers unconditionally, people must understand the difference between acceptance and approval. As Christians, we are all called to accept and love unbelievers without approving of sinful lifestyles. Jesus did this when he showed acceptance and love to the Samaritan woman at the well without approving of her licentious lifestyle. He also ate with Zacchaeus without approving of his dishonesty. And he publicly defended the dignity of the woman caught in adultery without minimizing her sin.

Any good fisherman knows that sometimes in order to reel a fish in, particularly a feisty one, you have to cut it a little slack in the line. If you pull hard and straight in the fish will probably snap your line and maybe your pole. You have to work with the fish, letting him have his way sometimes. The same is true in fishing for people: Sometimes you need to give unbelievers some slack in order to reel them in. Don't hit them over the head with everything they're doing wrong. A lot of their sins will be dealt with after they come to Christ.

> We cannot expect unbelievers to act like believers until they are believers.

We cannot expect unbelievers to act like believers until they are believers. The book of Romans teaches that it is impossible for unbelievers to act like believers because they don't have the power of the Holy Spirit within them.

The crowds that Jesus drew were a mixture of believers and unbelievers. Some were dedicated followers, some were sincere seekers, and some were insincere skeptics. This didn't bother Jesus. He loved them all.

At Saddleback, we know that many who attend our crowd services have questionable lifestyles, sinful habits, and even notorious reputations. That doesn't bother us. We make a distinction between the crowd (uncommitted attenders) and the congregation (our membership). The congregation, not the crowd, is the church. The crowd service is just a place where members can bring unbelieving friends to whom they've been personally witnessing.

We apply different standards of conduct to members and attenders. Members of our church are expected to abide by the lifestyle guidelines of our membership covenant. Those who engage in immoral activities are subject to church discipline. Unbelievers in the crowd are not subject to church discipline because they are not actually a part of our church family. Paul made this distinction clear in 1 Corinthians 5:9–12 (italics added):

> I have written you in my letter not to associate with sexually immoral people—*not at all meaning the people of this world* who are immoral, or the greedy and swindlers, or idolaters. In that case you would have to leave this world. But now I am writing you that you must not associate with anyone *who calls himself a brother* but is sexually immoral or greedy, an idolater or a slanderer, a drunkard or a swindler. With such a man do not even eat. *What business is it of mine to judge those outside the church?* Are you not to judge those inside?

We do not expect unbelieving attenders to get rid of their sinful habits or change their lifestyle in order to attend a service. Instead, they're encouraged to come "just as they are." The church is a hospital for sinners. We'd rather have a southern California pagan attend our crowd service in shorts and a

Budweiser® T-shirt than stay home or go to the beach. If we can get them to hear the Good News and witness some changed lives, we believe it will be just a matter of time until many open their hearts to Christ.

Jesus did not say, "Clean up your act and then I'll save you." He loved you even *before* you changed. And he expects you to do the same with other people. I can't count the large number of couples who started attending Saddleback while living together and, once they were saved, asked to be married. Some time ago I married a couple of new converts who'd been living together for seventeen years. As soon as they came to Christ they said, "I guess we need to be married." And I said, "You certainly do!" Sanctification comes *after* salvation.

> There is no method, program, or technology that can make up for a lack of love for unbelievers.

There is no method, no program, and no technology that can make up for a lack of love for unbelievers. Our love for God and our love for lost people is what motivates Saddleback to keep growing. It is what has motivated me to preach four services each weekend for years even though it is incredibly draining. Believe me, once you've delivered a message to a crowd of several thousand, there is no additional personal benefit in repeating it three more times. You do it because people need the Lord. Love is the motivating factor. Love leaves no choice.

Whenever I feel my heart growing cold toward people who don't know Christ, I remind myself of the cross. That's how much God loves lost people. It was love, not nails, that kept Jesus on the cross. He stretched out his arms and said, "I love lost people this much!" When Christians love people that much, their churches will attract crowds.

Jesus Attracted Crowds by Meeting People's Needs

People crowded around Jesus because he met their needs—physical, emotional, spiritual, relational, and financial. He did not judge some needs as being "more legitimate" than others, and he certainly did not make people feel guilty for their needs. He treated each person with dignity and respect.

Jesus often met a felt need in order to establish a beachhead for evangelism in a person's life. I pointed out earlier that Jesus frequently asked people, "What do you want me to do for you?" God uses all kinds of human needs to get people's attention. Who are we to judge whether a person's interest in Christ is for the right reason or the wrong reason? It doesn't matter *why* people initially come to Jesus, what matters is *that* they come. He can work on their motives, values, and priorities once they enter his presence.

> Jesus often established a beachhead for evangelism in a person's life by meeting a felt need.

I doubt that any of us had absolutely unselfish, unmixed motivations when we asked Christ to save us. We came when we sensed a need that he could meet. We should not expect unbelievers to have Christlike motives and values.

It is my deep conviction that anybody can be won to Christ if you discover the key to his or her heart. That key to each person's heart is unique so it is sometimes difficult to discover. It may take some time to identify it. But the most likely place to start is with the person's felt needs. As I pointed out earlier, this was the approach Jesus used.

Getting people's attention

Before you can share the Good News of salvation with someone, you have to get his or her attention. As I drive the

ߏߏߏߏ

---

freeways of southern California I often find myself praying, *Lord, how can I get all these people to slow down long enough to hear the Good News? How can I get their attention?* In the earlier part of this century, getting people's attention wasn't as much of a problem for churches. The church was usually the biggest building in town, the pastor was often the most educated and prominent person in town, and the church program was the social calendar of the community.

> Anybody can be won to Christ if you discover the key to his or her heart.

None of this is true anymore. A church can sit right next to a freeway with 100,000 cars driving by daily, and it will still be ignored. Pastors are often portrayed on television shows as either con men, wimps, or crazed perverts. And church programs must compete with everything else in our entertainment-obsessed culture. The only way a church can capture the attention of the unchurched today is by offering them something they cannot get anywhere else.

At Saddleback, we take seriously the task of meeting needs in Christ's name. That's what "ministry" is all about: meeting needs in Jesus' name. The first line of Saddleback's vision statement says, "It is the dream of a place where the hurting, the hopeless, the discouraged, the depressed, the frustrated, and the confused can find love, acceptance, guidance, and encouragement."

Written into the bylaws of Saddleback Church is this sentence: "This church exists to benefit the residents of the Saddleback Valley by providing for their spiritual, physical, emotional, intellectual, and social needs." Our objective is to minister to the total person. We do not limit our ministry to only the so-called "spiritual" needs. We believe God cares about every part of a person's life. People cannot be compartmentalized. Their needs spill over onto each other.

James gave a strong rebuke to Christians who think the answer to every need is a sermon or a Bible verse: "Suppose a brother or sister is without clothes and daily food. If one of you says to him, 'Go, I wish you well; keep warm and well fed,' but does nothing about his physical needs, *what good is it?*" (James 2:15–16, italics added). Meeting human needs, regardless of what they are, is being a "doer of the Word."

> # A church will never grow beyond its capacity to meet needs.

Look beyond the hype of every growing church and you will find a common denominator: They have figured out a way to meet the real needs of people. A church will never grow beyond its capacity to meet needs. If your church is genuinely meeting needs, then attendance will be the least of your problems—you'll have to lock the doors to keep people out.

What are the needs of the unchurched in your community? I can't answer that question for you. You need to survey your own community because every area has its own unique needs. I know of a church that discovered through a survey that the number one felt need in their community was potty training for preschoolers! The area was filled with young couples who wanted help with potty training. Rather than ignore this need as "unspiritual," the church used it as an opportunity for evangelism. The church held a "Parenting Preschoolers" conference which, among other things, taught this vital skill. Later the pastor joked that their biblical basis was Proverbs 22:6: "Train a child in the way he should *go!*" The idea is funny, but the results were serious. Dozens of couples were reached for Christ through that initial contact.

When it comes to using felt needs as an open door for evangelism, the possibilities are limitless. Saddleback has over seventy targeted ministries to the crowd and community, each built around a specific need. We have a support group called "Empty Arms" for couples dealing with miscarriage and stillbirths. "Peacemakers" is an outreach to meet the needs of people in law enforcement. "Hope for the Separated" ministers to people who are trying to save their marriage after a partner has walked out. "Lifelines" seeks to meet the needs of troubled teenagers. "Celebrate Recovery" ministers to over 500 people struggling with alcoholism, drug dependency, and other abuses. The list goes on and on.

> Changed lives are a church's greatest advertisement.

Are there any universal needs that exist among the unchurched? I believe there are. Regardless of where I've traveled, I've found that people feel the same emotional and relational needs. These include the need for love, acceptance, forgiveness, meaning, self-expression, and a purpose for living. People are also looking for freedom from fear, guilt, worry, resentment, discouragement, and loneliness. If your church is meeting these kinds of needs, you won't have to worry about advertising your services. Changed lives are a church's greatest advertisement.

Wherever needs are being met and lives are being changed the word quickly gets out into a community. Just today I heard of someone who visited a Saddleback service last weekend because "a hair stylist told a client who told my boss who told me that this is the place to go when you really need help."

Each time your church meets someone's need, a good rumor about the church begins traveling the interpersonal network of your community. When enough of those good rumors get spread around, your church will begin attracting people no visitation program could possibly have reached.

Jesus Attracted Crowds by Teaching in a Practical, Interesting Way

The Bible tells us that it was the custom of Jesus to teach the crowds (Mark 10:1). It also tells us the reactions of the crowd to his teaching. We learn that

- "the crowds were *amazed* at his teaching" (Matt. 7:28)
- "the crowds were *profoundly impressed*" (Matt. 22:33 LB)
- "the people were so *enthusiastic* about Jesus' teaching" (Mark 11:18 LB)
- "the great crowd *enjoyed* listening to him" (Mark 12:37 NASB)

The crowds had never heard anyone speak to them the way Jesus did. They were "*spellbound* by his teaching" (Mark 11:18 NRSV, italics added). There has never been a greater communicator than Jesus Christ.

To capture the attention of unbelievers like Jesus did, we must communicate spiritual truth the *way* he did. Jesus, not anyone else, must be our model for preaching. Unfortunately, some homiletics books pay more attention to Aristotle's methods and Greek rhetoric than how Jesus taught.

In John 12:49 Jesus admitted, "The Father who sent me commanded me *what to say* and *how to say it*" (italics added). Notice that both the content *and* the delivery style of Jesus' teaching were directed by the Father.

There's so much we can learn from Jesus' style of communication. However, in this chapter I want to only briefly identify three attributes of Jesus' teaching to the crowd.

Jesus began with people's needs, hurts, and interests

Jesus usually taught in response to a question or a pressing problem from someone in the crowd. He scratched where people itched. His preaching had an immediacy about it. He was always relevant and always on target for that moment.

When Jesus preached his first sermon at Nazareth, he read from Isaiah to announce what the preaching agenda of his ministry would be: "The Lord has put his Spirit in me, because he appointed me to tell the Good News to the poor. He has sent me to tell the captives they are free and to tell the blind that they can see again. God sent me to free those who have been treated unfairly and to announce the time when the Lord will show his kindness" (see Luke 4:18–19 NCV).

Notice the complete emphasis on meeting needs and healing hurts. Jesus had good news to share so people wanted to hear it. His message offered practical benefits to those who listened to him. His truth would "set people free" and bring all sorts of blessings to their lives.

We do not have to make the Bible relevant—it already is! But just as Jesus did, we have to *show* the Bible's relevance by applying its message personally to people's lives.

We must learn to share the Gospel in ways that show it is both "good" and "news." If it isn't good news, it isn't the Gospel. The Gospel is about what God has done for us and what we can become in Christ; it's about a personal relationship with Christ being the answer to our deepest needs. The Good News offers lost people what they are frantically searching for: forgiveness, freedom, security, purpose, love, acceptance, and strength. It settles

> We do not have to *make* the Bible relevant—it already is! But we do have to *show* its relevance.

our past, assures our future, and gives meaning to today. It is the best news in the world.

Crowds always flock to hear good news. There is enough bad news in the world that the last thing people need is to hear *more* bad news when they come to church. They are looking for anyone who can give them hope and help and encouragement. Jesus understood this and felt compassion for the crowds. He knew that they were "harassed and helpless, like sheep without a shepherd" (Matt. 9:36).

By beginning with people's needs when you preach or teach, you immediately gain the attention of your audience. Every good communicator understands and uses this principle. A good teacher knows to start with the students' interests and move them toward the lesson to be studied. A good salesman knows you always start with the customer's needs, not the product. A wise manager knows to begin with the employee's complaint, not her own agenda. You start where people are and move them to where you want them to be.

> The Good News offers lost people what they are frantically searching for.

Pick up any textbook on the brain and you'll learn that at the base of your brain stem is a filter called the "reticular activating system." God graciously put this filter in your mind so that you don't have to consciously respond to the millions of stimuli you are bombarded with on a daily basis. If you had to consciously respond to everything your senses pick up you'd go insane. But your reticular activating system continuously sifts and sorts the things you see, hear, and smell, forwarding only a few of those stimuli on to your consciousness. This way you are not overloaded and overwhelmed.

What *does* get your attention? Three things always make it past the reticular activating system: things you *value*; things that are *unique*; and things that *threaten* you. This fact has profound implications for those who preach and teach. If you want to capture the attention of an uninterested crowd you must tie your message to one of these three attention-getters.

While sharing the Good News in a unique or threatening way can get attention of the unchurched, I believe that showing its *value* to people is most consistent with how Christ taught. Jesus taught in a way that people understood the value and benefit of what he was saying. He didn't try to threaten the unchurched into the kingdom of God. In fact, his only threats were to religious people! He comforted the afflicted and afflicted the comfortable.

Because preachers are called to communicate truth, we often mistakenly assume that unbelievers are eager to hear it. But unbelievers aren't that interested in truth these days. In fact, surveys show that the majority of Americans reject the idea of absolute truth.

Moral relativism is the root of what is wrong in our society. People worry and complain about the rising crime rate, the breakup of the family, and the general decline of our culture, but they don't realize the cause of it all is that they don't value truth. Today tolerance is valued more than truth so it is a big mistake for us to think that unbelievers will race to church if we just proclaim, "We have the truth!" Their reaction will be, "Yeah, so does everybody else." Proclaimers of truth don't get much attention in a society that devalues truth. To overcome this, some preachers try to "yell it like it is." But preaching louder isn't the solution.

While most unbelievers aren't looking for truth, they *are* looking for relief. This gives us the opportunity to interest them in truth. I've found that when I teach a truth that relieves their pain or solves their problem, unbelievers say, "Thanks! What else is true in that book?" Sharing biblical principles that meet a need creates a hunger for more truth.

Very few of the people who came to Jesus were looking for truth; they were looking for relief. So Jesus would meet their felt need, whether it was leprosy, blindness, or a bent back. After their felt needs were met, they were always anxious to know the truth about this man who had helped them with a problem they couldn't solve.

Ephesians 4:29 says, "[Speak] *only* what is helpful for building others up according to their needs, that it may benefit those who listen" (italics added). Notice that what we say should be determined by the needs of the people to whom we are speaking. We are to speak only what benefits them. It stands to reason that

> **Most unbelievers are looking for *relief*, not truth.**

if this is God's will for our conversations, it must also be God's will for our sermons. Unfortunately, many pastors determine the content of their messages by what they feel they need to say rather than what the people need to hear.

One reason sermon study is so difficult for many pastors is because they ask the wrong question. Instead of asking, "What shall I preach on this Sunday?" they should be asking, "To whom will I be preaching?" Simply thinking through the needs of the audience will help determine God's will for the message.

Since God, in his foreknowledge, already knows who will be attending your services next Sunday, why would he give you a message totally irrelevant to the needs of those he is intending to bring? Why would he have you preach on something unhelpful to those he's planned to hear it? People's immediate needs are a key to where God would have you begin speaking on that particular occasion.

The crowd does not determine whether or not you speak the truth: The truth is not optional. But your audience does determine *which* truths you choose to speak about. And some truths are more relevant than others to unbelievers.

Can something be both true and irrelevant? Certainly! If you had been in a car accident and were bleeding to death in the emergency room, how would you feel if the doctor came in and wanted to talk about the Greek word for *hospital* or the history of the stethoscope? His information could be true, but it would be irrelevant because it doesn't stop your hurt. You would want the doctor to begin with your pain.

Your audience also determines how you *start* your message. If you are speaking to the unchurched and you spend the first part of the message on the historical background of the text, by the time you get to the personal application you will have already lost them. When speaking to the unchurched you need to *begin* where your sermons normally end up.

Jesus related truth to life

I love the practicality and simplicity of Jesus' teaching. It was clear, relevant, and applicable. He aimed for application because his goal was to *transform* people, not merely to inform them. Consider the Sermon on the Mount, the greatest sermon ever preached.

Jesus began the Sermon on the Mount by sharing eight secrets of genuine happiness. Then he talked about living an exemplary lifestyle, controlling anger, restoring relationships, and avoiding adultery and divorce. Next, he spoke of keeping promises and returning good for evil. After that, he moved on to other practical life issues like how to give with the right attitude, how to pray, how to store up treasure in heaven, and how to overcome worry. He wrapped up his message by telling us to not judge others, to be persistent when asking God to meet our needs, and to be wary of false teachers. He then concluded with a simple story that emphasized the importance of acting on what he had taught.

This is the kind of preaching we need in churches today — preaching that not only attracts crowds — it changes lives! It is not enough for us to simply proclaim that "Christ is the answer"; we must show the unchurched *how* Christ is the answer. Sermons that exhort people to change without sharing the practical steps of how to do it end up just producing more guilt and frustration.

A lot of preaching is what I call "Ain't it awful!" preaching. It just complains about our society and makes

> **People need fewer "ought-to" sermons and more "how-to" sermons.**

judgments about people in general. It is long on diagnosis and short on remedy. This kind of preaching may make Christians feel superior to "those out there," but it rarely changes anything. Instead of lighting a candle, it just curses the darkness.

When I go to a doctor, I don't want to just hear what's wrong with me; I want him or her to give me some specific steps to getting better. What people need today are fewer "ought-to" sermons and more "how-to" sermons.

Some pastors criticize "life-application" preaching as shallow, simplistic, and inferior. To them, the only real preaching is didactic, doctrinal preaching. This attitude implies that Paul was more profound than Jesus, that Romans is "deeper" material than the Sermon on the Mount or the parables. I call that heresy! The deepest kind of teaching is that which makes a difference in people's day-to-day lives. As D. L. Moody once said, "The Bible was not given to increase our knowledge but to change our lives." Our goal is Christlike character.

Jesus said, "I have come that you might have life" (John 10:10). He didn't say, "I've come that you might have *religion*."

Christianity is a life, not a religion, and Jesus was a life-application preacher. When he finished his teaching to the crowd, he always wanted them to "go and do likewise."

Christlike preaching is life-related and produces a changed lifestyle. It doesn't just inform, it transforms. It changes people because the Word is applied to where people actually live. Sermons that teach people how to live will never lack an audience.

> The deepest kind of teaching is that which makes a difference in people's day-to-day lives.

Please understand: The unchurched are not asking that we change the message or even dilute it, only that we show its relevance. Their big question is, "So what?" They want to know what difference our message makes. I've found that the unchurched in America are very interested in Bible doctrine when it is applied in practical and relevant ways to their lives.

For me, it is challenging and enjoyable to teach theology to the unchurched without telling them it is theology and without using theological terms. I've preached sermon series to the crowd on the incarnation, justification, and sanctification without ever using the terms. I've also preached sermon series to the unchurched crowd on the work of the Holy Spirit, the moral attributes of God, stewardship, and even the seven deadly sins.

It is a myth that you must compromise the message to draw a crowd. Jesus certainly didn't. You don't have to *transform* the message of the Bible but you do have to *translate* it into terms the unchurched will understand.

Jesus spoke to the crowd with an interesting style

The crowd loved to listen to Jesus. Mark 12:37 (NCV) says, "The large crowd listened to Jesus *with pleasure*" (italics added). The New International Version says they "listened . . . with delight." Do people "delight" in your messages?

Some pastors actually think they have failed in their preaching if people enjoy a message. I've heard pastors proudly say, "We're not here to entertain." Obviously they're doing a good job at it. A Gallup poll a few years ago stated that, according to the unchurched, the church is the most boring place to be.

If you look up the word *entertain* in a dictionary, you'll find this definition: "capturing and holding the attention for an extended period of time." I don't know any preacher who doesn't want to do that. We should not be afraid of being interesting. A sermon does not have to be dry to be spiritual.

To the unchurched, dull preaching is unforgivable. Truth poorly delivered is ignored. On the other hand, the unchurched will listen to absolute foolishness if it is interesting. To prove this, just turn on your television late at night and you will see the assortment of psychics, wackos, and weirdos that dominate the airwaves.

I mentioned in the last chapter that I am amazed at how some Bible teachers are able to take the most exciting book in the world and bore people to tears with it. I believe it is a *sin* to bore people with the Bible. When

> When God's Word is taught in an uninteresting way, people don't just think the pastor is boring, they think *God* is boring!

God's Word is taught in an uninteresting way, people don't just think the pastor is boring, they think *God* is boring! We slander God's character if we preach with an uninspiring style or tone. The message is too important to share it with a "take-it-or-leave-it" attitude.

Jesus captured the interest of large crowds with techniques that you and I can use. First, he told stories to make a point. Jesus was a master storyteller. He would say, "Hey, did you hear the one about . . ." and then tell a parable in order to teach a truth. In fact, the Bible shows that storytelling was Jesus' favorite technique when speaking to the crowd. "Jesus spoke all these things to the crowd in parables; he did not say anything to them without using a parable" (Matt. 13:34). Somehow preachers forget that the Bible is essentially a book of stories. That is how God has chosen to communicate his Word to human beings.

There are many benefits to using stories to communicate spiritual truth:

- *Stories hold our attention*. The reason television is so popular is because it is essentially a storytelling device. Comedies, dramas, the news, talk shows—even commercials—are stories.
- *Stories stir our emotions*. They impact us in ways that precepts and propositions never do. If you want to change lives, you must craft the message for impact, not for information.
- *Stories help us remember.* Long after a pastor's clever outline is forgotten, people will remember the stories from the sermon. It is fascinating, and sometimes comical, to watch how quickly a crowd tunes in when a speaker begins telling a story and how quickly that attention vanishes as soon as the story is finished.

Second, Jesus used simple language, not technical or theological jargon. He spoke in terms that normal people could understand. We need to remember that Jesus did not use the classical Greek language of the scholar. He spoke in Aramaic, the street language of that day. He talked of birds, flowers, lost coins, and other everyday objects that anyone could relate to.

While Jesus taught profound truths in simple ways, many pastors do the exact opposite; they teach simple truths in profound ways. They take straightforward texts and make them complicated. They think they are being "deep" when actually they are just being "muddy!" It is more important to be clear than clever in teaching and preaching.

Some pastors like to show off their knowledge by using Greek words and academic terms in their preaching. Every Sunday they speak in an unknown tongue without being charismatic! Pastors need to realize that no one cares as much about the Greek as they do. Chuck Swindoll once told me that he believes an overuse of Greek and Hebrew word studies in preaching discourages confidence in the English text. I agree.

> Jesus taught profound truths in simple ways. Today we teach simple truths in profound ways.

Jack Hayford, Chuck Smith, Chuck Swindoll, and I once taught a seminary doctoral course on how we each prepare and deliver sermons. At the end of the course the students mentioned that all four of us had, without collaboration, emphasized the same thing: *Keep it simple!*

It's easy to complicate the Gospel, and of course, Satan would love for us to do just that. The apostle Paul worried that "your minds [w]ould be led astray from the *simplicity* and purity *of devotion* to Christ" (2 Cor. 11:3 NASB, italics added). It takes a lot of thought and preparation to communicate profound truths in simple ways. Einstein once said, "You don't really understand something unless you can communicate it in a simple way." You can be brilliant, but if you can't share your thoughts in a simple way, your insights aren't worth much.

The Saddleback Valley is one of the most highly educated communities in America. Yet I find that the simpler I make the message, the more God blesses it. Simple does not mean *shallow* or *simplistic*; it means being clear and understandable. For instance, "This is the day the Lord has made" is simple, while "Have a nice day!" is simplistic.

Simple sermon outlines are always the strongest outlines. I consider it a compliment to be called a "simple" preacher. I'm interested in seeing lives changed, not impressing people with my vocabulary.

Most people communicate with a vocabulary of less than 2,000 words and rely on only about 900 words in daily use. If you want to communicate with most people you need to keep it simple. Never allow yourself to be intimidated by people who think they are intellectuals. It's been my observation that people who have to use big words are sometimes hiding bigger insecurities.

Ministry to Crowds Is Controversial

I realize that there are some Christians who will disagree with the thesis of this chapter. The controversy over attracting a crowd boils down to two issues. The first has to do with the legitimacy of what is called "attraction evangelism," and the other has to do with how the church should relate to the culture it seeks to evangelize.

"Go and tell" or "Come and see"?

Some church leaders deny that attraction is a legitimate method of evangelism. I've heard preachers say, "The Bible does not tell the world to come to church. It tells the church to go to the world." This is an inaccurate statement because it is only half true.

Of course the Bible commands Christians to "go and tell." That's what the Great Commission is all about! Christians are not to wait for the world to come and ask us about Christ. We are to take the initiative in sharing the Good News. To believers, Jesus says, "Go!"

But to the lost world, Jesus says, "Come!" When a couple of inquirers wanted to know about Jesus, he replied, "Come, and you will see!" (John 1:39). In Matthew 11:28 Jesus said to seekers, "Come to me, all you who are weary and burdened, and I will give you rest." And on the last day of the great Feast, "Jesus stood and said in a loud voice, 'If anyone is thirsty, let him come to me and drink'" (John 7:37).

> To believers, Jesus says, "Go!" But to the lost world, Jesus says, "Come!"

Both "Go and tell" and "Come and see" are found in the New Testament. In Luke 14, where Jesus compared the kingdom of God to a great banquet, the Master's servants are to *go out* and invite the hungry to *come in* and eat, "so that my house may be full."

We do not need to choose between "go" and "come"; both are valid forms of evangelism. Some people will be reached by attraction, while others will be reached by confrontation. A balanced, healthy church should provide opportunities and programs for both. At Saddleback, we use both approaches. We say "Come and see!" to our community, but to our core we say, "Go and tell!"

Responding to culture: imitation, isolation, or infiltration?

Another ongoing debate that affects evangelism has to do with how the church should respond to culture. There are two extreme positions: imitation and isolation. Those in the "imitation" camp argue that the church must become just like our culture in order to minister to it. Churches in this group sacrifice the biblical message and mission of the church in order to *blend in* with the culture. They are likely to endorse current cultural values such as the worship of success and wealth, radical individualism, radical feminism, liberal sexual standards, and even homosexuality. In their attempt to be relevant, these churches sacrifice biblical theology, doctrinal distinctives, and the Gospel of Christ. The call for repentance and commitment is compromised in order to attract a crowd. Syncretism destroys this kind of church.

At the other extreme is the "isolation" camp. This group insists we must avoid *any* adaptation to culture in order to preserve the purity of the church. They fail to see the distinction between the sinful values of our culture and the nonsinful customs, styles, and preferences that each generation develops. They reject new translations of Scripture, current musical styles, and any attempt to modify man-made traditions, such as the time and order of the worship service that they are accustomed to. Isolationists sometimes have a dress code, and a list of what is permissible and what isn't regarding issues that the Bible is silent on. (It is human nature to erect theological walls to defend personal preferences.)

Churches in this group confuse *their* cultural traditions with orthodoxy. They do not realize that the customs, styles, and methods they feel comfortable with were undoubtedly labeled as "modern, worldly, and heretical" by a previous generation of believers.

Must we choose between liberalism and legalism? Is there a third alternative to imitation and isolation? I'm convinced there is. The strategy of Jesus is the antidote to both extremes: *infiltration!*

Just as saltwater fish exist their entire lives in an ocean without becoming saturated with salt, Jesus ministered *in* the world without being *of* the world. He "made his dwelling among us" (John 1:14), and was even tempted in every way we are, "yet was without sin" (Heb. 4:15). He walked among people, spoke *their* language, observed *their* customs, sang *their* songs, attended their parties, and used their current events (see Luke 13:1-5) to capture attention when he taught. But he did all these things without compromising his mission.

Jesus' *sinner-sensitive* ministry made the religious establishment nervous, and they criticized him ruthlessly. They even attributed his ministry to Satan (Mark 3:22)! The Pharisees especially hated the way Jesus made unbelievers feel comfortable in his presence and the way he placed sinners' needs above religious traditions. They scorned Jesus' reputation as a "friend of tax collectors and sinners" — to them, such a title was the ultimate putdown, but Jesus wore it as a badge of honor. His response was, "It is not the healthy who need a doctor, but the sick. I have not come to call the righteous, but sinners" (Mark 2:17).

In Jesus' day, the Pharisees used the excuse of "purity" to avoid all contact with unbelievers. We still have Pharisees in the church today, who are more concerned about purity than people. If your church is serious about the Great Commission, you will never have a completely *pure* church because you will always be attracting unbelievers with their questionable lifestyles to your crowd services. Evangelism is sometimes messy. Even after people become believers, you still have to deal with their immaturity and carnality, so there will never be a completely pure church.

Are there unrepentant pagans mixed into Saddleback's crowd of 10,000? Without a doubt! When you fish with a big net you catch all kinds of fish. That's okay. Jesus said in one parable, "Don't worry about the *tares* mixed in among the wheat. One day I'll separate them." (See Matt. 13:29-30, italics added). We are to leave the weeding to Jesus because he knows who the real tares are.

Jesus reserved his most severe words for the rigid, religious traditionalists. When the Pharisees asked, "Why do your disciples break the tradition of the elders?" Jesus replied, "Why do you break the command of God for the sake of your tradition?" (Matt. 15:2–3). Fulfilling God's purpose must always take priority over preserving tradition.

If you are serious about ministering to people the way Jesus did, don't be surprised if some of today's religious establishment accuse you of selling out to culture and breaking traditions. You *will* be criticized! Sadly, some isolationists have been extremely judgmental of seeker-sensitive churches in books and articles. Most of these criticisms are unfair characterizations made out of ignorance and do not represent what actually happens in seeker-sensitive churches.

Trailblazers always get arrows shot at them. Translating the truth into contemporary terms is dangerous business. Remember, they burned Wycliffe at the stake for doing it. But criticism by other Christians should never keep you from ministering the way Christ did. Jesus should be our ultimate model for ministry, not anyone else.

13

Worship Can Be a Witness

God is spirit, and his worshipers must worship in spirit and in truth.

John 4:24

This weekend, millions of people will attend an evangelical worship service. The amazing thing is that most of those people could not articulate the purpose of the service they attend if they were asked. They might have a vague idea but it would be difficult for them to put into words.

In chapters 14 to 16, I will explain how we've designed a service format that has reached thousands of unbelievers for Christ. But first, I feel it is necessary to clarify the theological and practical reasons behind Saddleback's seeker service. Everything that we do in our weekend services is based on twelve deeply held convictions.

Twelve Convictions About Worship

1. Only believers can truly worship God. The direction of worship is from believers to God. We magnify God's name in worship by expressing our love and commitment to him. Unbelievers simply cannot do this. At Saddleback, our definition of worship is "Worship is expressing our love to God for who he is, what he's said, and what he's doing."

We believe there are many appropriate ways to express our love to God. These include praying, singing, thanking, listening, giving, testifying, trusting, obeying his Word, among many others. God, not man, is the focus and center of our worship.

2. You don't need a building to worship God. Acts 17:24 says, "The God who made the world and everything in it is the Lord of heaven and earth and does not live in temples built by hands." You'd probably expect this emphasis from a church that existed fifteen years and grew to over 10,000 in attendance without a building. I think we made our point.

Unfortunately many churches are obsessed with the edifice complex. No building (or lack of one) should ever be allowed to control, limit, or distract people from worshiping God. There's nothing wrong with buildings, unless you worship them instead of the creator. Jesus said, "For where two or three come together in my name, there am I with them" (Matt. 18:20).

3. There is no correct "style" of worship. Jesus only gave two requirements for legitimate worship: "God is spirit, and his worshipers must worship in spirit and in truth" (John 4:24). I don't

> Your preferred style of worship says more about your cultural background than your theology.

think God is offended or even bothered by different styles of worship as long as it is done "in spirit" and "in truth." In fact, I'm certain that God enjoys the variety! Remember, it was his idea to make us all different.

The style of worship that you feel comfortable with says far more about your cultural background than it does about your theology. Debates over worship style are almost always sociological and personality debates couched in theological terms.

Every church likes to believe its worship style is the most biblical. The truth is, there isn't a biblical style of worship. Each Sunday true believers around the world give glory to Jesus Christ using a thousand equally valid expressions and styles.

Regardless of style, true worship employs both your right brain and your left brain. It engages both emotion and intellect, your heart and your mind. We must worship in spirit and in truth.

4. Unbelievers can watch believers worship. Unbelievers can observe the joy that we feel. They can see how we value God's Word, how we respond to it, and how the Bible answers the problems and questions of life. They can notice how worship encourages, strengthens, and changes us. It is even possible for them to sense when God is supernaturally moving in a service, although they won't be able to explain it.

5. Worship is a powerful witness to unbelievers if God's presence is felt and if the message is understandable. In Acts 2, on the day of Pentecost, God's presence was so evident in the disciples' worship service that it attracted the attention of unbelievers throughout the entire city. Acts 2:6 says ". . . a crowd came together." We know it must have been a big crowd because 3,000 people were saved that day.

Why were those 3,000 people converted? Because they felt God's presence, and they understood the message. Both of these elements are essential in order for worship to be a witness. First, God's presence must be sensed in the service. More people are won to Christ by feeling God's presence than by all of our apologetic arguments combined. Few people, if any, are converted to

Christ on purely intellectual grounds. It is the sense of God's presence that melts hearts and explodes mental barriers.

At the same time, the worship and the message need to be understandable. At Pentecost, the Holy Spirit miraculously translated the message into words each person understood. The crowd of unbelievers said, "We hear them telling *in our own languages* about the great things God has done!" (Acts 2:11 NCV, italics added). This ability to understand caused them to be converted. Even though God's presence was evident in the service, they wouldn't have known what to do if they hadn't been able to understand the message.

> In genuine worship God's presence is felt, God's pardon is offered, God's purposes are revealed, and God's power is displayed.

There is an intimate connection between worship and evangelism. It is the goal of evangelism to produce worshipers of God. The Bible tells us that "the Father seeks [worshipers]" (John 4:23) so evangelism is the task of recruiting worshipers of God.

At the same time, it is worship that provides the *motivation* for evangelism. It produces a desire in us to tell others about Christ. The result of Isaiah's powerful worship experience (Isa. 6:1–8) was Isaiah saying, "Here am I. Send me!" True worship causes us to witness.

In genuine worship God's presence is felt, God's pardon is offered, God's purposes are revealed, and God's power is displayed. That sounds to me like an ideal context for evangelism! I've noticed that when unbelievers watch believers relate to God in an intelligent, sincere manner, it creates a desire in them to know God too.

6. God expects us to be sensitive to the fears, hang-ups, and needs of unbelievers when they are present in our worship services. This is the principle Paul taught in 1 Corinthians 14. In verse 23, Paul commanded that tongues be limited in public worship. His reasoning? Speaking in tongues seems like foolishness to unbelievers. Paul didn't say tongues *were* foolish, only that they *appear* foolish to unbelievers. "So if the whole church comes together and everyone speaks in tongues, and some who do not understand or some unbelievers come in, will they not say that you are out of your mind?" (1 Cor. 14:23).

I believe there is a larger principle behind this advice to the Corinthian church. The point Paul is making is that we must be willing to adjust our worship practices when unbelievers are present. God tells us to be sensitive to the hang-ups of unbelievers in our services. Being seeker sensitive in our worship is a biblical command.

Although Paul never used the term "seeker sensitive," he definitely pioneered the idea. He was very concerned about not placing any stumbling blocks in front of unbelievers. He told the Corinthian church, "Do not cause anyone to stumble, whether Jews, Greeks or the church of God" (1 Cor. 10:32). He also advised the church at Colosse, *"Be tactful with those who are not Christians* and be sure you make the best use of your time with them" (Col. 4:5 JB, italics added).

When you have guests over to your home for dinner does your family act differently than when it's just your family at the table? Of course they do! You pay attention to your guests' needs, making sure they are served first. The food may be the same, but you may use a different set of china or present the meal in a more thoughtful way. The table conversation is usually more courteous. Is this being hypocritical? No. By doing these things, you are being sensitive and showing respect to your guests. In the same way, the spiritual food is unchanged in a seeker-sensitive service, but the presentation is more thoughtful and considerate of the guests present.

7. *A worship service does not have to be shallow to be seeker sensitive. The message doesn't have to be compromised, just understandable.* Making a service "comfortable" for the unchurched doesn't mean changing your theology, it means changing the environment of the service. Changing the environment could be done through the way you greet visitors, the style of music you use, the Bible translation you preach from, and the kinds of announcements you make in the service.

> Making a service "comfortable" for
> the unchurched doesn't mean changing
> your theology. It means changing
> the environment.

The message is not always comfortable; in fact, sometimes God's truth is very uncomfortable! Still, we must teach "the whole counsel of God." Being seeker sensitive does not limit what you say, but it does affect *how you say it.*

As I mentioned in the previous chapter, the unchurched are not asking for a watered-down message—they expect to hear the Bible when they come to church. What they *do* want is to hear how the Bible relates to their lives in terms they understand and in a tone that shows you respect and care about them. They are looking for solutions, not a scolding.

Unbelievers wrestle with the same deep questions believers have: Who am I? Where did I come from? Where am I going? Does life make sense? Why is there suffering and evil in the world? What is my purpose in life? How can I learn to get along with people? These are certainly not shallow issues.

8. The needs of believers and unbelievers often overlap. They are very different in some areas but are very similar in many areas. Seeker-sensitive services focus on needs common to both believers and unbelievers. For instance, both believers and unbelievers need to know what God is really like; both need to understand the purpose of life; both need to know why and how to forgive others; both need help in strengthening their marriage and family;

> Being seeker sensitive doesn't limit what you say, but it does affect *how you say it.*

both need to know how to deal with suffering, grief, and pain; both need to know why materialism is so destructive. Christians do not stop having needs once they are saved.

9. It is best to specialize your services according to their purpose. Most churches try to evangelize the lost and edify believers in the same service. When you send mixed signals, you're going to get mixed results. Trying to aim at two targets with one gun only results in frustration.

Design one worship service to edify believers and another service to evangelize the unchurched friends brought by your members. At Saddleback, our believers' service is on Wednesday night and our seeker services are on Saturday night and Sunday morning. This way you can use different preaching styles, songs, prayers, and other elements appropriate to each target.

When I started Saddleback, I asked unchurched people *when* they would be most likely to visit a church. Every single one said, "If I ever did, it would be a Sunday morning." I also asked our members when they were most likely to bring unchurched friends. Again, they said Sunday morning. Even in today's culture, people still think of Sunday morning as "the time you go to church." So that's why we decided to use Sunday morning for evangelism and Wednesday night for edification.

Evangelistic services are nothing new; only the idea of using the Sunday morning time slot for an evangelistic service is a recent variation. Earlier in this century, Sunday *evenings* were generally recognized as the "evangelistic service" of churches. A few churches still advertise a Sunday evening evangelistic service, although it's doubtful that many unbelievers show up. Even *believers* don't like to attend Sunday evenings! They've been *voting with their feet* on that issue for decades.

10. A service geared toward seekers is meant to supplement personal evangelism, not replace it. People generally find it easier to decide for Christ when there are multiple relationships supporting that decision. Seeker services provide a group witness to enhance and confirm the personal witness of members. When an unbeliever attends a seeker service with a friend who has been witnessing to him, he sees the crowd and thinks, *Hey, there are a lot of other people who believe this. There must be something to it.*

> A service geared toward seekers is meant to supplement personal evangelism, not replace it.

There is incredible persuasive power in the witness of a crowd of believers worshiping together. For this reason, the larger your seeker service grows, the greater an evangelistic tool it will become.

11. There is no standard way to design a seeker service. This is because unbelievers are not all alike! Some want a service that makes them feel a part of it; others want to sit passively and watch. Some like quiet, meditative services; others like high-energy services. The style that works best in southern

California probably won't work in New England and vice versa. It takes all kinds of services to reach all kinds of seekers.

There are only three nonnegotiable elements of a seeker service: (1) treat unbelievers with love and respect, (2) relate the service to their needs, and (3) share the message in a practical, understandable manner. All other elements are secondary issues that churches shouldn't get hung up on.

I first began offering churches suggestions for creating seeker services nearly twenty years ago. Now that this type of service has received a lot of media attention, I sometimes find people overemphasizing minor factors. They worry about getting rid of the pulpit, not wearing a robe, or whether or not to have a drama each week, as if these things will automatically bring the unchurched flocking to their church. They are wrong. If all seekers were looking for was a quality production, they'd stay home and watch TV where millions are spent to produce half-hour programs.

> **What really attracts large numbers of unchurched to a church is changed lives!**

What *really* attracts large numbers of unchurched to a church is changed lives—a lot of changed lives. People want to go where lives are being changed, where hurts are being healed, and where hope is being restored.

At Saddleback, you see changed lives everywhere. In almost every seeker service, we include a real-life testimony from a person or couple who have been dramatically changed by the power and love of Christ. This weekly parade of "satisfied customers" is hard for skeptics to argue with.

Saddleback Church has confounded much of the conventional wisdom about seeker-sensitive churches by winning thousands of unchurched people to Christ in spite of the most unlikely and difficult circumstances. Imagine a church where the location keeps changing; where the unchurched will come and sit in a tent that is freezing in the winter, damp and leaky in the rainy spring, blisteringly hot in the summer, and has howling winds rip through it in the fall. Imagine a church where people will park three miles away when necessary and stand outside under umbrellas in the rain in order to attend. When lives are being changed, problems that otherwise might seem overwhelming to a church are treated as mere nuisances.

At every Saddleback service we invite people to fill out a registration card and sing worship songs. We take an offering, provide a message outline with Bible verses written out on it, and offer a time of commitment. Although I've heard some people claim that you can't reach the unchurched if you do these things, over 7,000 unbelievers have registered a personal commitment to Christ at Saddleback, and thousands of others are considering that decision as they return week after week. It's *how* you do these things that makes the difference.

New approaches and technologies are only tools. You don't have to use drama and multimedia or have a nice building and convenient parking to reach unbelievers. These items just make it easier. Please realize that the suggestions I give in the next two chapters are only general guidelines, suggestions from what has worked at Saddleback. Do not treat them like the Ten Commandments. Even I wouldn't do everything we do at Saddleback if I were in another part of the country. You must figure out what works best to reach seekers in your local context.

12. It takes unselfish, mature believers to offer a seeker-sensitive service. In 1 Corinthians 14:19–20, Paul says that when we think only of our own needs in worship we are being childish and immature. Members demonstrate incredible spiritual maturity when they are considerate of the needs, fears, and hang-ups of unbelievers and are willing to place those needs before their own in a service.

In every church there is constant tension between the concepts of "service" and "serve-us." Most churches end up tipping the scales toward meeting members' needs because the members pay the bills. Offering a seeker service means intentionally tipping the scales in the opposite direction, toward unbelievers. It requires members who are willing to create a safe environment for unbelievers at the expense of their own preferences, traditions, and comfort. Enormous spiritual maturity is required to voluntarily move out of a comfort zone.

Jesus said, "Your attitude must be like my own, for I, the Messiah, did not come to be served, but to serve" (Matt. 20:28 LB). Until this attitude of unselfish servanthood permeates the minds and hearts of your members, your church is not ready to begin a seeker-sensitive service.

14

Designing a Seeker-Sensitive Service

*If, therefore, the whole church comes together and
all speak in tongues, and outsiders or unbelievers enter,
will they not say that you are out of your mind?*

1 Cor. 14:23 (NRSV)

*Be wise in the way you act toward outsiders;
make the most of every opportunity.*

Col. 4:5

Growing up in a Christian home, I was often frustrated when
I brought nonbelieving friends to church. It seemed
inevitable that whenever I'd get one of my friends to attend
a service with me, that would be the Sunday my father would
preach on tithing, some guest missionary would show slides,
or we'd have a communion service — not what my unsaved
friends needed to hear or experience.

Yet it often seemed that on the weekends when I didn't
bring lost friends to church, the message would be on the plan
of salvation. I'd think, "Boy, I wish my friends were here today!"
From week to week, I didn't know if the service would be a
"safe" service to which I could bring unbelievers. The focus of
the message was always unpredictable, alternating between
evangelism and edification. I noticed this same pattern in the
churches I attended while in college. Eventually, I gave up

inviting nonbelievers to church. It wasn't a conscious decision—I just got tired of getting "burned."

Most churches rarely attract unbelievers to their services
because members are uncomfortable bringing them to church.
It doesn't matter how much the pastor encourages members to
bring friends or how many visitation programs are launched,
the results are the same: Most members never bring any lost
friends to church.

Why is this? There are three important reasons. First, as I
mentioned, the target of the messages is unpredictable. Members don't know from week to week if the pastor will be
preaching an evangelistic message or an edification message.
Second, the services are not designed for unbelievers; so much
of what goes on in them would not be understandable to an
unchurched friend. Third, members may be embarrassed by the
quality of the service.

If you were able to get the typical church member to be
completely honest about his church he'd probably say this: "I
love my church. I love my pastor. I am personally blessed by
what takes place in our ser-
vices. It meets my needs. But
... I wouldn't think of inviting
my unchurched friends from
the office because the service
wouldn't make any sense to
them. The messages are for
me, the songs are for me, the
prayers are prayed in terms I
understand, and even the announcements are for me. My
friends wouldn't understand much of our service." Ironically, at
the same time he may feel guilty for not inviting his friends.

Increasing the size of your church does not require the
intelligence of a rocket scientist: You must simply get more
people to visit! No one becomes a church member without first

> Increasing the size
> of your church is
> simple: You must get
> more people to visit!

being a visitor. If you only have a few visitors each year, you'll have even fewer new members. A crowd is not a church, but to grow a larger church you must first attract a crowd.

What is the most natural way to increase the number of visitors to your church? By making members feel guilty for not inviting friends? No. By putting up a big sign that says "Visitors Welcome"? No. By cold-calling on homes in your community? Probably not. By holding attendance contests? Unlikely. By using telemarketing or advertising? Wrong again.

The answer is quite simple: Create a service that is intentionally designed for your members to bring their friends to. And make the service so attractive, appealing, and relevant to the unchurched that your members are eager to share it with the lost people they care about.

> A crowd is not a church. But to grow a larger church you must first attract a crowd.

Saddleback has offered that kind of service from its beginning. As other churches began to develop similar approaches, the term "seeker-sensitive service" began to be used to describe this type of service. By creating a service that Christians want to bring their unsaved friends to, you don't have to use contests, campaigns, or guilt to increase attendance. Members will invite their friends week after week, and your church will experience a steady influx of unchurched visitors. In this chapter and the next one, I would like to give you a number of practical suggestions for designing a seeker-sensitive service.

Plan the Service with Your Target in Mind

Each week at Saddleback, we remind ourselves who we're trying to reach: Saddleback Sam and his wife Samantha. Once you know your target, it will determine many of the components of your seeker service: music style, message topics, testimonies, creative arts, and much more.

Most evangelical churches conclude their worship service with an altar call. This indicates that, functionally, we connect worship with evangelism. But many do not realize that it is a self-defeating strategy to focus the first fifty-eight minutes of the service on believers and suddenly switch the focus to unbelievers in the last two minutes. Unbelievers are not going to sit through fifty-eight minutes of a service that isn't in the slightest way relevant to them. The entire service, not just the invitation, must be planned with the unchurched in mind.

Make It as Easy as Possible to Attend

Americans are conditioned to expect things to be convenient. Your goal should be to remove as many barriers as possible so that the unchurched have no excuse for not attending.

Offer multiple service times. This gives people more than one opportunity to attend. Saddleback has offered four identical services each weekend for years: Saturday at 6:00 P.M., and Sunday at 8:00, 9:30, and 11:15 A.M. We've often had unbelievers visit a service, go home and call a friend, and bring them back to another service because of the sermon topic.

Offer surplus parking. In America, it takes parking to reach people. One of the first things visitors notice is parking and traffic control. I once asked several pastors of the largest churches in California what their biggest mistake was in building. Every one of them had the same answer: not enough parking. When people come to church they like to bring their cars! If you don't have a place for their car, you don't have a place for them. No matter how big your building is, you won't be able to fill it if there isn't enough parking.

Offer children's Sunday school simultaneously with the service. Unchurched people don't want to deal with squirming children, either theirs or someone else's. Saddleback offers four Sunday schools at the same time as our seeker services.

Put a map to your church on all advertising. Nothing is more frustrating than trying to find a place without a map. Saddleback has its own four-lane, half-mile entrance into our property. It's called Saddleback Parkway, and the church is the only address on it. Yet people still get lost trying to find us.

Improve the Pace and Flow of the Service

Almost all churches need to pick up the pace of their services. Television has permanently shortened the attention span of Americans. In one time-out during Monday night football you'll see a replay, three commercials, and a network news brief—they don't want you to get bored! MTV has shortened the attention span for baby busters even more. In one three-minute video alone you may be bombarded with several thousand images.

In contrast, most church services move at a snail's pace. There is a lot of "dead time" between different elements. When the minister of music finishes a song, he walks over and sits down. Fifteen seconds later, the pastor thinks about getting up. Finally, he slowly moves to the pulpit and welcomes the people. By this time, unbelievers have already fallen asleep. Work on minimizing transitional times. As soon as one element ends, another should begin.

Look for ways to save time in your service. We regularly time each element of our service: the prayers, the songs, the announcements, the message, the closing, and the transitions in between each element. Then we ask ourselves, "What took too much time and what needed more time?"

Our services usually last about seventy minutes. You can accomplish a lot in that time if you plan it wisely. For instance, your offering time can be cut in half simply by doubling the number of ushers and baskets.

Keep your pastoral prayers short in your seeker services. It is not the time to intercede for sister Bertha's ingrown toenail! The unchurched can't handle long prayers; their minds wander or they fall asleep. Pastors should be wary of using the pastoral prayer to catch up on their quiet time!

> **The difference between an average service and an outstanding service is flow.**

In addition to speeding up your service, work on improving its flow. The difference between an average service and an outstanding service is flow.

At Saddleback, we use the word IMPACT as an acronym to remind us of the flow we desire to create with our music:

Inspire Movement: This is what we want to do with the opening song. We use a bright, upbeat number that makes you want to tap your foot, clap, or at least smile. We want to loosen up the tense muscles of uptight visitors. When your body is relaxed, your attitude is less defensive.

To begin our service, we wake up the body of Christ by waking up our own bodies. When people enter a morning service they usually feel stiff, sleepy, and reserved. After our "Inspire Movement" opening song the atmosphere always changes to being more cheerful and alert. The difference this opening song makes is absolutely amazing.

Praise: We then move to joyful songs *about* God.

Adoration: We move to a more meditative, intimate song *to* God. The pace is slowed here.

Commitment: This song gives people an opportunity to affirm or reaffirm a commitment to God. It is usually a first person singular song like "I Want to Be More Like You."

Tie it all together: The very last thing we do is end the service on another short, upbeat song.

Make Visitors Feel Comfortable

Visitors have already formed an opinion about your church within the first ten minutes after they arrive. As I mentioned in chapter 12, visitors are deciding whether or not to come back long before the pastor speaks. First impressions are very difficult to change, so you need to think through what first impressions you want visitors to have. As the old saying goes, you never have a second chance to make a first impression.

In dealing with visitors, it is important to understand that their first emotional response is one of fear. If they are genuinely unchurched people they are wondering, "What is going to happen to me here?" They have the same feelings and fears you'd have if you were invited to a Moslem mosque for the first time: "Are they going to lock the doors?" "Will I have to say something?" "Will I be embarrassed by anything?"

Because visitors are filled with apprehension and anxiety, your first objective with them should be to make sure they're relaxed. Communication is blocked when a person is afraid. If you can reduce visitors' level of fear, they'll be far more receptive to the Gospel. There are many practical ways to do this.

Reserve the best parking spots for visitors. A sign as you enter Saddleback's property asks first-time visitors to turn on their headlights if they'd like the reserved parking closest to the worship center. If you have reserved parking for visitors you can station greeters there who can welcome visitors with a smile and offer them directions as soon as they get out of their cars. At Saddleback, all pastors and staff park on the dirt. Only visitors get preferred parking spots.

Station greeters outside your building. We believe that welcoming visitors is so important we have four different kinds of welcome ministers: parking attendants, greeters, hosts, and ushers. Parking attendants direct the traffic. These are the first smiles visitors will encounter. Greeters stand in our parking lots and patio areas, casually greeting people as they approach the building. Hosts are stationed at our information tables. Instead of giving directions to newcomers, they personally escort people to where they need to go. Ushers greet people inside the service, pass out programs, assist in special situations, and receive the offering.

The most important people in any organization are those who have direct contact with the customer. At Delta Airlines, the most important people to me are the ticket agent and flight attendant. Delta's president is unimportant to me. Why? I'll never have any contact with him. In your church, your welcome ministers are the most important people to visitors because they make contact in that crucial first ten minutes. Be sure to use people who project personal warmth and smile easily.

It is also important to select greeters and ushers who match your target. If you want to reach young couples, use young couples; if you want to reach teenagers, use teenagers; if you want to reach retirees, use retirees. In many churches, the greeters are the oldest members. If all the people a visitor meets in the first ten minutes are forty years older than he is, he will start wondering if he fits in your church.

One last point: Don't identify outside greeters with badges. Greeters with badges make visitors feel they're being welcomed by "officials" of the church. (One of our pastors incorrectly told a group, "We just put our greeters out there with nothing on them!") Tell the greeters to simply be themselves—friendly members.

Set up information tables outside your buildings. It's fine for the people manning these tables to wear badges because you want visitors to know where to go to ask questions.

Place directional signs everywhere. Clearly identify the main entrances to your building, the nursery, and especially the bathrooms. Visitors should not have to ask where the bathrooms are.

Have taped music playing when people enter your buildings. Most public buildings have music playing in the background. You can hear it in retail and grocery stores, doctors' offices, professional buildings, and some elevators. They even play music on many airplanes as they sit on the runway. Why? Because music relaxes people.

Silence is scary to unchurched visitors. If you were to walk into a large room filled with 200 people and no one was talking, wouldn't you wonder what was going on? You'd think, "What do they know that I don't?" But if you walked into a room where everyone was talking to each other, you would not feel self-conscious at all.

There is a place for silence in worship, but it's not at the beginning of a seeker service. Have you ever seen a sign over a church auditorium that says "Enter in Silence"? That is the last thing you want in a seeker service. You want the atmosphere before the service starts to be alive and happy and contagious with joy.

We've noticed an interesting phenomenon: The louder you play background music, the more animatedly people talk. If you play quiet music, people talk softly. When visitors walk into a building where people are talking normally to each other and upbeat music is playing, it eases their fears. They notice that people are enjoying each other and are happy to be there. They notice that there is life in the church.

Allow visitors to remain anonymous in the service. Once visitors are seated we don't bother them or single them out. We allow them to watch the service without publicly identifying themselves. We want them to feel welcomed and wanted without feeling watched.

Ironically, the way many churches welcome visitors actually makes them feel more uncomfortable than if they'd just been left alone. Visitors hate to be singled out for public recognition. (The one exception to this is visiting denominational officials!) One reason large churches attract so many visitors is because newcomers like being able to hide in a crowd. In a small church everyone knows who the visitor is—and the visitor knows they know!

In America, the most common fear people have is going to a party where they will be surrounded by strangers. The second most common fear is having to speak before a crowd, and the third most common fear is being asked a personal question in public.

The way many churches welcome visitors causes them to experience their three greatest fears all at once! The pastor, thinking he's being friendly, will say, "Please stand up; tell us your name and a little about yourself." We don't realize that when we do this, the visitor is dying a thousand deaths in his mind.

> The way many churches welcome visitors causes them to experience their three greatest fears all at once!

When I lived in Fort Worth, Kay and I belonged to a church that decided it would be better to reverse the process. So instead of having visitors stand and introduce themselves, all of the members were asked to stand each week while the visitors remained seated. Then the members were expected to turn to the seated visitors and sing a welcome song to them! Can you imagine this? The first time we visited, the members stood up all around us and all I could see was a bunch of big fat fannies. Then they began to sing to us, "We're so glad to have you here. It's so great to have you near. . . ." I wanted to die on the spot! Have you ever been sung to by a stranger? I get embarrassed if my wife sings to me! The moral to the story? Think through everything you do from a visitor's viewpoint.

Even though I refer to newcomers as "visitors" we don't call them that at Saddleback. We call them "guests." The term "visitor" implies they're not here to stay. The term "guest" implies that this is someone for whom you do everything you can to make feel comfortable.

If you use a registration card, have everyone *fill one out.* When everyone registers, visitors aren't singled out. They see that this is something that everybody does.

Saddleback's Welcome Card is a vital communication tool. We use it in at least a dozen different ways: to register attendance, record spiritual decisions, gather prayer requests, take surveys, sign up for events and programs, recruit leadership,

Welcome! Date _____

SADDLEBACK CHURCH

Mr/Mrs/Miss _____ ❏ New Address

Address _____

City _____ State _____ Zip _____

Phone (___) _____ Wk Phone (____) _____

Is this your... ❏ 1st Time? ❏ 2nd Time? ❏ 3rd Time? I am an: ❏ Attender ❏ Member

I came as a guest of _____

Current School Grade	**or**	Your Age Group

K	1	2	3	4	5	6		18-22	23-30	31-35	36-40
	7	8	9	10	11	12	College	41-45	46-50	51-60	61-70 71+

Please Indicate: ❏ Single ❏ Married

Names of children living at home & birthdates:
_____
_____

My Decision Today:
❏ I'm committing my life to Christ
❏ I want to be baptized
❏ I'm renewing my commitment to Christ
❏ Enroll me in the next...
　❏ Discovering Saddleback Membership, Class #101
　❏ Discovering Spiritual Maturity, Class #201
　❏ Discovering My Ministry, Class #301
❏ I'm willing to help where needed
❏ I'd like to talk to a staff minister

I'd Like Information On:
❏ How to Begin a Relationship with Christ
❏ How to Join this Church Family
❏ Building Program
❏ Adult Small Groups

I'd Like Information On, Con't:
❏ Business & Professional Activities
❏ Single Activities
❏ Single Parent Activities
❏ Women's Activities
❏ Men's Activities
❏ Counseling Referrals
❏ Recreation Activities
❏ Music Activities
❏ Young Adult Activities (18-30)
❏ Senior High Activities
❏ Junior High Activities
❏ Children's Activities
❏ Children's Ministry Volunteer

Comments, Requests or Prayer Needs: ❏ For Prayer Team ❏ Confidential
_____
_____
_____
_____
_____

evaluate services, update membership information, gather sermon ideas, and start new ministries, among many others. It is a vital link that allows me to keep my finger on the pulse of our growing church. These cards are worth their weight in gold.

I used to read every single card every week. They helped me memorize all the names of people until we reached 3,000 in attendance. Now I only read the cards with notes that are specifically addressed to me. But it is still a direct link to me. Everyone knows that anyone can get a message to me via the Welcome Card. I've found that people will tell you things in writing that they'd never say to you otherwise.

On the card there is also a place for visitors to indicate whether it is their first, second, or third visit to our church. In response to each of these they get a different thank-you note from me.

I urge you to not use registration books, which are passed down the rows for everyone to sign. They violate anonymity. Everyone on that row can see what a visitor has written. Also, the logistics of retrieving names from registration books are more difficult than with cards. Our cards are collected at the same time as the offering. It gives everyone something to put in the offering basket. As soon as the offering is collected, a team of data-entry people begins sorting and entering all the information from the cards into computers for use by the staff.

Offer a public welcome that relaxes people. The first words from the stage set the tone of the service. Each week one of our pastors will say something like, "Welcome to Sunday at Saddleback! We're glad you're here. If you're here for the first time, we want you to sit back, relax, and enjoy the service we've planned for you."

Let people know they can expect to enjoy the service. Tell them they won't have to say anything and nobody's going to embarrass them. Offer a disclaimer about the offering: "If you're visiting with us, please understand that you are not expected to participate in the offering. This is only for those who are a part of our church family. As our guest we want you to get something out of this service. We don't expect you to give."

Begin and end each service with people greeting each other. We are told five times in the New Testament to greet one another and show affection. So at the beginning and the end of each service we tell everyone to turn around and shake hands with three (or ten or twenty) people.

Over the years, this simple tradition has created a warm sense of camaraderie and family between people who don't even know each other. Sometimes I have people say something to each other at the end of a service like, "It was nice sitting by you today." For some people this small act of friendliness is the only affirmation they get all week.

In the early years of Saddleback, the members practiced what we called the "three-minute rule." We all agreed that for the first three minutes after the service was over, members would talk only to people they'd never met. This was based on the fact that the first people to leave after a service are the visitors. So we would wait until after all the visitors had left to fellowship with each other.

If you use name tags, make sure everybody gets one. Don't single out visitors by either making them wear one when no one else does or by not giving them one when everyone else has one.

Offer a refreshment table at each service. Visitors hang around longer after a service if you can get a cup of coffee and a donut into their hands. This also gives members a chance to meet them. Eating tends to relax people in social settings. I don't know why it works, but somehow a 300-pound guy feels more secure in an unfamiliar crowd if he has a small Styrofoam cup of coffee to hide behind.

It has always fascinated me that Jesus did so much of his teaching when people were walking or eating with him. I'm sure this was intentional. Both of those activities relax people and reduce relational barriers. When people are relaxed they listen better and they are more open to change.

Brighten Up the Environment

Facilities and physical environment have a lot to do with what happens in a service. The shape of your building will shape your service. Walk into some buildings and your mood will instantly brighten; walk into others and you'll feel depressed. Just as the shape of a room can change a mood instantly, so can its temperature and its lighting. Be aware of these factors and use them. Figure out what mood you want your service to project, and then create it.

At Saddleback we summarize the mood we want in our seeker services with the word *celebration*. Each Sunday is Easter at Saddleback, so we are fanatical about creating a light, bright, cheerful environment. Visitors can sense this the moment they enter the facility.

Look at your facilities from the eyes of a visitor and try to determine what message your building is communicating. What is it saying? Does an entrance with heavy dark wood doors give off a different message than one with glass doors? Of course it does.

> The shape of your building will shape your service.

Even before the service begins, visitors are making value judgments about your church. The moment they get out of their cars in your parking lot they begin picking up clues by looking at the grounds around your facilities. Does your landscaping appear well kept? Is the grass mowed and are the hedges trimmed? Is there trash lying around? Does the church sign need to be painted? Cleanliness is attractive. Dirty, unkempt grounds and facilities are repulsive.

Sometimes the message of the facilities contradicts the message intended by your church. You may be saying, "We're friendly!" but your buildings may be saying, "We're cold and impersonal." You may claim, "We're relevant," but your building may be screaming, "We're fifty years behind the times." It's difficult to project a "We've got it all together" image if your building is falling apart.

One of the problems faced in maintaining the church environment is that you tend to overlook defects after about four weeks. Once you become familiar with a building, you stop noticing what's wrong with it. You become oblivious to the faded paint, the frayed carpet, the chipped pulpit, the outdated rack of tracts in the vestibule, the old bulletins left inside hymnals, the stack of music on the piano, the burned-out lightbulbs overhead. Unfortunately, these things stand out immediately to visitors, who notice details.

One way to combat this tendency is to do an environmental impact report on your church. Get a photographer to walk around your facilities and take pictures from the eyes of a visitor. Then show those pictures to your leaders and determine what needs to be changed. Most pastors have never viewed their auditorium while sitting in the back row. Environmental factors that you need to pay close attention to include lighting, sound, seating, space, temperature, plants, nurseries, and restrooms.

Lighting. Lighting has a profound effect on people's moods. Inadequate lighting dampens the spirit of a service. Shadows across a speaker's face reduce the impact of any message.

Most churches are far too dark. Maybe it's conditioning from all those years Christians spent worshiping in the catacombs. Even churches with plenty of windows often cover them up. Somehow, churches have gotten the idea that dimming the lights creates a more "spiritual" mood. I completely disagree.

I believe that church buildings should be bright and full of light. God's character is expressed in light. First John 1:5 says, "God is light; in him there is no darkness at all." Light was the very first thing God created (Gen. 1:3). Today, I think God would like to say "Let there be light" to thousands of churches.

If you want to wake up your services, brighten up your environment. Take the curtains off your windows. Throw open the windows and doors. Turn on all the lights. This week, secretly replace all the lightbulbs in your worship center with twice the watts. Then study the change in mood in next Sunday's service. You may have a revival on your hands!

Sound. Invest in the best sound system you can afford. If you're trying to cut costs, do it in some other area—don't skimp here. Saddleback grew for fifteen years without our own building, but we've always had a state-of-the-art sound system.

It doesn't matter how persuasive the message is if people can't hear it in a pleasing manner. A tinny, fuzzy sound system can undermine the most gifted musician and incapacitate the most profound preacher. And nothing can destroy a holy moment faster than a loud blast of feedback. If you are a pastor, insist that your church purchase a lavaliere microphone so you are not handcuffed to the pulpit.

Seating. Both the comfort and the arrangement of your seating dramatically affect the mood of any service. The mind can only absorb what the seat can endure. Uncomfortable seating is a distraction that the devil loves to use.

If you can get away with replacing the pews, I'd advise it. In today's culture the only places people are forced to sit on benches are in church and in the cheap bleacher section at ball games. People expect to have their own individual chairs. Personal space is highly valued in our society. This is why box seats are prized at stadiums. If people are forced to sit too close to each other, they get very uncomfortable. There should be at least eighteen inches between people if you're using chairs and twenty-one inches between people if you're using pews.

If you use movable seats, set them up so that each person can see someone else's face. It will dramatically improve how people respond to the service. If you are planting a new church, always set up fewer chairs than you need. It's encouraging to your people when additional chairs must be brought in as people arrive. It's very discouraging to worship in a service when surrounded by empty chairs.

Space. The one rule about space is this: Don't have too much or too little! Either extreme will limit your growth. When your service is 80 percent filled, you need to start another service. One reason many churches plateau is that they think they don't need to add another service because there are still a few open seats available. When you run out of space, you experience what Pete Wagner calls "sociological strangulation." A small building can strangle the growth of a church.

You can also have too much space. Many churches have a building far too large for them to fill. Even if you've got 200 people attending, if your auditorium seats 750, it feels like "no one is here!" It's almost impossible to create a feeling of warmth and intimacy when there are more empty chairs than people. An important growth dynamic is lost when your building is too big for your church.

The smaller the crowd, the closer the speaker needs to be to them. As your crowd grows larger, the lectern or pulpit can be moved farther back and raised on a higher stage. If you only have fifty people in a service, put a lectern just a few feet in front of your first row. Forget the stage.

Temperature. As a pastor who has preached for years in unair-conditioned gyms and unheated tents I say this with the utmost conviction: The temperature can destroy the best-planned service in a matter of minutes! When people are too hot or too cold they stop participating. They mentally check out and start hoping for everything to end quickly.

The most common mistake churches make regarding temperature is to allow the building to become too warm. An usher sets the thermostat at a reasonable setting before the service without realizing that, when the building is actually filled with a crowd, the body heat will raise the temperature substantially. By the time the air-conditioning has cooled everything down, the service is nearly over.

Before the service begins, set the thermostat several degrees cooler than what is comfortable. Cool it down before the crowd gets there. The temperature will rise quite quickly once the service starts. Keeping the temperature on the cool side will keep everyone awake.

Plants. I encourage you to use plants, trees, and greenery as decorations in your facilities. For years we hauled plants, ferns, and small trees in and out of rented facilities each weekend. Plants say, "At least *something* is alive in this place!"

I'm sure you've heard people say, "I feel close to God when I'm out in nature." That's understandable. When God made Adam and Eve, he didn't put them in a skyscraper with concrete and asphalt all around them; he placed them in a garden. The natural beauty of God's creation inspires, relaxes, and restores people. It's no accident that Psalm 23 is the most beloved psalm. People can easily imagine the refreshing scene of still waters and green pastures.

As a side note, be careful not to overdo mystical, religious symbols in your facilities. Everyone knows what the cross is, but the unchurched are confused by chalices, crowns, and doves with fire coming out their tails.

Clean, safe nurseries. If you want to reach young families, you've got to have sanitized, safe nurseries. There should be no mop buckets in the corners, and the toys should be cleaned each week.

Clean restrooms. Visitors may forget the sermon, but the memory of a foul-smelling restroom lingers on ... and on ... and on! You can tell a lot about the morale of a church by checking out the quality of the restrooms.

The sad truth is that many churches need a completely new building. They'll never reach their community in the building they're using. One pastor told me in frustration that he was praying, "God, let the fire fall!"

When my friend Larry DeWitt was called to pastor a church in southern California, he found a small, clapboard church building in a high-tech suburban area. Larry recognized that the age and style of the building were a barrier to reaching that community. He told the church leaders he'd accept the pastorate if they'd move out of the building and start holding services in a Hungry Tiger restaurant. The members agreed.

Today, after moving to different facilities, that church has grown to several thousand in attendance. It would have never grown that large if they had stayed in their original building. As I stated in chapter 1, the shoe must never tell the foot how big it can get. Saddleback used high school campuses for our seeker services for thirteen years. In order to make the best of what we had to work with we organized two quality control crews. The first crew would come in before 6 A.M. and set up forty-two different classrooms and a gymnasium. The set-up crew would diagram each classroom's layout on the chalkboard before moving anything. That way everything could be reset in the right order by the take-down crew when they came in at 1 P.M. after all the services were over. Every classroom was vacuumed twice every Sunday—once at the beginning of the day and once after we'd finished using the rooms. It was hard work, but part of the price of growth.

The goal in all that we do to brighten up the environment is the same as what Paul said in Titus 2:10 (italics added): "...

so that in every way they will make the teaching about God our Savior *attractive*."

Create an Attractive Atmosphere

Atmosphere is that hard-to-define but unmistakable feeling you get when you enter a church service. It's often called the "spirit," the "mood," or the "tone" of the service. Regardless of what you call it, atmosphere definitely impacts what happens in your service. It can either work for your purpose or against what you're trying to accomplish.

If you don't purposely determine the type of atmosphere you want to create in a service, you are leaving it to chance. At Saddleback we use five words to describe the atmosphere we seek to create each week.

Expectation. One of the frequent comments visitors make about our services is that they feel a sense of expectancy among the people. There is a pervasive enthusiasm at the start of each service that says, "Something good is about to happen!" People feel excitement, energy, and a spirit of anticipation about being together. Members sense that God is with us and lives are going to be changed. Visitors often describe the atmosphere as "electric."

What causes this spirit of expectancy? It is produced by a number of factors: members praying for the services all week, members praying during the services, enthusiastic members who bring their unsaved friends to church, a history of life-changing services, the sheer size of the crowd, celebration-style music, and the faith of the team that leads the service.

Your opening prayer should always express the expectation that God will be in the service and that people's needs are going to be met. Expectancy is just another word for faith. Jesus said, "According to your faith will it be done to you" (Matt. 9:29).

Celebration. Psalm 100:2 says, "Worship the LORD with gladness; come before him with joyful songs." Because God wants our worship to be a celebration, we cultivate an atmosphere of gladness and joy. Too many church services resemble a funeral more than a festival. A major cause of this is often the demeanor of those leading the worship. I've visited some services where I felt like asking the worship leader, "Do you ever smile?"

Worship is a delight, not a duty. We experience joy in God's presence (Ps. 21:6). In Psalm 42:4, David remembered, "... how I used to go with the multitude ... to the house of God, with shouts of joy and thanksgiving among the festive throng." Does that describe the atmosphere of your services?

Affirmation. Hebrews 10:25 (NCV) says, "You should meet together and encourage each other. Do this even more as you see the day coming." There is so much bad news in the world, people need a place to hear good news.

We want our services to be an encouragement, not a discouragement to people. Even when the message is confrontational, we start positive and we end positive. You can change a person's behavior far more quickly through affirmation than through criticism. Study the ministry of Jesus and see how skillfully he used affirmation to bring out the best in people.

Incorporation. We work hard to create a family atmosphere in our services in spite of our size. The way we greet each other at the beginning and end of each service, the way the people on stage interact with each other, and the way the pastors speak to the crowd all say, "We are a family. We're in this together. You belong here."

I love 1 Peter 3:8 in the Living Bible: "You should be like one big happy family, full of sympathy toward each other, loving one another with tender hearts and humble minds." In a world that is becoming increasingly impersonal, people are looking for a place where they can feel they belong.

Restoration. Life is tough. Each weekend, I look into the faces of thousands of people who have been beaten up by the world all week. They arrive with their spiritual and emotional batteries depleted. My job is to reconnect them with spiritual jumper cables to the restorative power of Christ. Jesus said, "Come to me, all you who are weary and burdened, and I will give you rest. Take my yoke upon you and learn from me, for I am gentle and humble in heart, and you will find rest for your souls" (Matt. 11:28–29).

One of the purposes of weekly worship is to be spiritually restored and emotionally recharged for the new week ahead. Jesus insisted, "The Sabbath was made for man, not man for the Sabbath" (Mark 2:27). In my message preparation I always pray, "Father help me to say something on Sunday morning that will prepare people for Monday morning."

I envision the church as a spiritual oasis in the middle of a parched desert. We are called to offer the refreshing water of life to people who are dying of thirst all around us.

In southern California especially, people need relief from the rat race. For this reason we use humor in our services. "A cheerful heart is good medicine" (Prov. 17:22). It's not a sin to help people feel good. By teaching people to laugh at themselves and their problems, it not only lightens their load, it helps them to change.

I believe one of the greatest problems among evangelicals is that we've got it backward: We take ourselves too seriously and we don't take God seriously enough! He is perfect—we aren't. It is more than a coincidence that *humor* and *humility* come from the same root word. In any case, if you learn to laugh at yourself you'll always have plenty of material to enjoy.

Liberation. The Bible says, "Where the Spirit of the Lord is, there is freedom" (2 Cor. 3:17). We avoid stuffiness, formality, and any kind of pretentiousness in our services. Instead we cultivate an informal, relaxed, and friendly atmosphere. We've found that an informal, unpretentious service disarms the fears and defenses of the unchurched.

People always feel more anxious in a formal setting than they do in an informal setting. This is extremely important to remember if you are interested in changing lives. Services that are formal and ceremonial cause unchurched visitors to worry that they might do "the wrong thing." It makes them feel self-conscious. I'm sure you've had that feeling when you didn't know how to act in a strange, public setting.

When people feel self-conscious, they raise their emotional defenses. Since we want to communicate to the unchurched, our first task is to reduce their anxiety so that they *drop* their defenses. Once they relax, they stop thinking about themselves and are able to tune in to the message.

To many unchurched Americans, the word *informal* is a synonym for *authentic*, while *formality* suggests *insincere* and *phony.* Baby boomers especially are turned off by pomp and protocol. For this reason, we don't use reverential titles for our pastors at Saddleback. No one ever refers to me as "Dr. Warren" at our church; I'm just called "Rick."

We also have no dress code at Saddleback. The pastors dress casually, just like everyone else who attends. A recent survey by GQ magazine indicated that only about 25 percent of American men now own a suit. I haven't preached in a suit at Saddleback for years. (Of course, preaching in a hot tent and gym probably had something to do with that!)

What people wear to church is a cultural issue, not a theological one, so we don't make a big deal about it. One thing we know for sure: Jesus never wore a suit and tie, so it isn't required to be Christlike.

Print a Simple Order of Service

Unchurched visitors don't know what to expect when they come to your church. This makes them anxious. A printed order of service says, "There are no surprises here." Telling the unchurched what you are going to do in advance relaxes them and lowers their defenses.

Describe the service in nontechnical terms. If visitors can't understand your order of service, there is no reason to print it. In a typical bulletin you'll find terms such as *invocation*, *offertory anthem*, *invitational hymn*, *benediction*, and *postlude*. To an unbeliever, you might as well be talking pig Latin.

At Saddleback, instead of "Invocation" and "Benediction," our program simply says "Opening prayer" and "Closing prayer." Instead of "Call to worship," it says "Song"; instead of "Offering," it says "Giving back to God." You get the idea. We have the Living Bible version of the order of service. We're more interested in making it clear for the unchurched than impressing those who know what the more formal terms mean.

Include explanatory notes. When you go to an opera or play that is difficult to understand, they provide you with program notes. Tell people why you do what you're doing in the service. Our bulletin gives an explanation for our Welcome Card, the offering, the time of commitment, and other parts of our service.

Minimize Internal Church Announcements

The larger your church gets, the more announcements you'll have. If you don't establish a policy of what warrants a public announcement and what doesn't, you will end up using a significant portion of your service on internal church announcements. How do you handle this?

Train your members to read the bulletin. Say something like, "This week, there are special events for men, single adults, and junior high students. Be sure to read your bulletin to find out what's happening for you." That is all you need to say.

Announce only events that apply to everyone. Each time you announce events that only involve one segment of your church, everyone else tunes out. Pretty soon no one listens.

Don't waste everyone's time announcing events that appeal to only a small percentage of the congregation.

Avoid appeals for help from the pulpit. Pulpit appeals for volunteer help should be minimized in your seeker service. Personal recruitment works better anyway.

Do not conduct internal church business during a seeker service. Save it for your believers' service. I know of one church that asked all the visitors to leave at the end of a service so the members could conduct their business. That's being visitor-unfriendly!

Continually Evaluate and Improve

Each Monday morning after a game, NFL football players watch films from the previous Sunday to determine what they can do better next week. We should be even more concerned about what happens in our worship services each Sunday. The NFL is just playing a game; we aren't.

Growing churches should always be asking, "How can we do it better?" They are ruthless in evaluating their services and ministries. Evaluation is the key to excellence. You must continually examine each part of your service and assess its effectiveness.

At Saddleback, the three tools that aid in evaluation are the First Impression card, the Welcome card, and a Worship Evaluation sheet. All three provide us with valuable feedback, which is the secret of continuous improvement.

The First Impression card gives us feedback from first-time visitors, helping us to see the service from their perspective. The Welcome card gives us feedback from our regular attenders and members. We receive a steady flow of suggestions and tips from those in the crowd. And the Worship Evaluation sheet gives us feedback from our own staff members. It includes an evaluation for everything from parking to bulletins to refreshment tables to the music and message.

In 1 Corinthians 14:40, Paul concluded his instructions on seeker-sensitive services by saying, "Everything should be done in a fitting and orderly way." This verse implies that planning, evaluating, and improving our services is a proper thing to do. Both the worship of God and the evangelizing of people deserve our best effort.

Remember Whom You Are Serving

You may feel overwhelmed by all of the suggestions I've given you for creating a seeker-sensitive service. Remember, these are important ideas, but they aren't all essential to building a seeker-sensitive service. As I stated earlier, the only non-negotiable elements of a seeker service are to treat unbelievers with love and respect, relate the service to their needs, and share the message in a practical, understandable manner.

Seeker-sensitive services are hard work! They take enormous amounts of energy, creativity, commitment, time, money, and preparation to pull them off week after week. Why bother? Why go to all this trouble trying to bridge the cultural gap between the church and the unchurched? Because, like Paul, we do it all "for Jesus' sake" (2 Cor. 4:5).

You must know why you do what you do or else you'll be defeated by discouragement. I remember one particular Sunday morning a number of years ago. We were setting up the high school for the weekend services and about half of our setup crew had not shown up, for one reason or another. As I was carrying nursery equipment from a trailer to one of the classrooms across the campus I felt overwhelmed with a sense of discouragement.

Satan began to throw darts of self-pity at me: Why should you have to do all this setup and takedown while the only thing other pastors have to do is show up? They just walk into their own building. Most pastors don't have to mess with this at all, but you've had to do it for years!

As I was beginning to enjoy my pity party, the Holy Spirit tapped me on the shoulder and asked, "Hey, Rick, who are you doing this for anyway?" I stopped dead in my tracks in the middle of the high school parking lot, began to cry, and reminded myself that I was doing what I was doing for Jesus' sake. And what I do is nothing compared to what he's done for me.

"In all the work you are doing, work the best you can. Work as if you were doing it for the Lord, not for people. Remember that you will receive your reward from the Lord, which he promised to his people. You are serving the Lord Christ" (Col. 3:23–24 NCV).

15

Selecting Your Music

*He put a new song in my mouth. . . . Many people will see
this and worship him. Then they will trust the LORD.*

Psalm 40:3 (NCV)

I'm often asked what I would do differently if I could start Saddleback over. My answer is this: From the first day of the new
church I'd put more energy and money into a first-class music
ministry that matched our target. In the first years of Saddleback,
I made the mistake of underestimating the power of music so I
minimized the use of music in our services. I regret that now.

Music is an integral part of our lives. We eat with it, drive
with it, shop with it, relax with it, and some non-Baptists even
dance to it! The great American pastime is not baseball—it is
music and sharing our opinions about it.

A song can often touch people in a way that a sermon can't.
Music can bypass intellectual barriers and take the message
straight to the heart. It is a potent tool for evangelism. In Psalm
40:3 (NCV) David says, "He put a *new* song in my mouth. . . .
Many people will see this and worship him. Then they will trust
the LORD" (italics added). Notice the clear connection between
music and evangelism: "Then they will trust the LORD."

Aristotle said, "Music has the power to shape character."
Satan is clearly using music to do that today. The rock lyrics of
the 1960s and 1970s shaped the values of most Americans who
are now in their thirties, forties, or fifties. Today, MTV shapes

the values of most people in their teens and twenties. Music is the primary communicator of values to the younger generation. If we don't use contemporary music to spread godly values, Satan will have unchallenged access to an entire generation. Music is a force that cannot be ignored.

Not only did I underestimate the power of music when we began Saddleback, I also made the mistake of trying to appeal to everybody's taste. We covered the gamut, "from Bach to Rock," often in a single service. We'd alternate between traditional hymns, praise choruses, and contemporary Christian songs. We used classical, country, jazz, rock, reggae, easy listening, and even rap. The crowd never knew what was coming next. The result: We didn't please anybody, and we frustrated everybody! We were like the radio station I mentioned in chapter 9 that tried to appeal to everyone by playing every type of music.

Again, it's impossible to appeal to everyone's musical preference and taste. Music is a divisive issue that separates generations, regions of the country, personality types, and even family members. So we shouldn't be surprised when opinions of music differ in the church. You must decide who you're trying to reach, identify their preferred style of music, and then stick with it. You're wasting your time if you're searching for a style of music that everyone in your church will agree on.

Choosing Your Style of Music

The style of music you choose to use in your services will be one of the most critical (and controversial) decisions you make in the life of your church. It may also be *the* most influential factor in determining who your church reaches for Christ and whether or not your church grows. You must match your music to the kind of people God wants your church to reach.

The music you use "positions" your church in your community. It defines who you are. Once you have decided on the style of music you're going to use in worship, you have set the direction of your church in far more ways than you realize. It will determine the kind of people you attract, the kind of people you keep, and the kind of people you lose.

If you were to tell me the kind of music you are currently using in your services I could describe the kind of people you are reaching without even visiting your church. I could also tell you the kind of people your church will never be able to reach.

I reject the idea that music styles can be judged as either "good" or "bad" music. Who decides this? The kind of music you like is determined by your background and culture. Certain tones and scales sound pleasant to Asian ears; other tones and scales sound pleasant to Middle Eastern ears. Africans enjoy different rhythms than South Americans.

> Match your music to the kind of people God wants your church to reach.

To insist that all "good" music was written in Europe two hundred years ago is cultural elitism. There certainly isn't any biblical basis for that view. Depending on where you grew up you may love Kentucky bluegrass, Dixieland jazz, Chicago blues, Milwaukee polka, or Nashville country and western. None of these styles is any "better" music than the other.

Churches also need to admit that no particular *style* of music is "sacred." What makes a song sacred is its *message*. Music is nothing more than an arrangement of notes and rhythms; it's the words that make a song spiritual. There is no such thing as "Christian music," only Christian lyrics. If I were to play a tune for you without any words, you wouldn't know if it was a Christian song or not.

The sacred message of a song may be communicated in a wide variety of musical styles. For 2,000 years, the Holy Spirit has used all different kinds of music to bring glory to God. It takes all kinds of churches, using all kinds of music styles, to reach all kinds of people. To insist that one particular style of music is sacred is idolatry.

I'm amused whenever I hear Christians who resist contemporary Christian music say, "We need to get back to our musical roots." I wonder how far back they want to go. Back to the Gregorian chant? Back to the Jewish melodies of the Jerusalem church? They usually only want to go back about fifty to one hundred years.

> There is no such thing as "Christian music." There are only Christian lyrics.

Some people assume that the "hymns" mentioned in Colossians 3:16 refer to the same style of music we call "hymns" today. The truth is, we don't know what their hymns sounded like. But we do know that the New Testament churches used the style of music that matched the instruments and culture common to that day. Since they obviously didn't have pianos or organs back then, their music wouldn't have sounded at all like the music in our churches today.

In Psalms we read that in biblical worship they used drums, clashing cymbals, loud trumpets, tambourines, and stringed instruments. That sounds a lot like contemporary music to me!

Sing a New Song

Throughout church history, great theologians have put God's truth to the music style of their day. The tune of Martin Luther's "A Mighty Fortress Is Our God" is borrowed from a popular song of his day. (Today, Luther would probably be borrowing tunes from the local karaoke bar.) Charles Wesley used several popular tunes from the taverns and opera houses in England. John Calvin hired two secular songwriters of his day to put his theology to music. The Queen of England was so incensed by these "vulgar tunes" that she derisively referred to them as Calvin's "Geneva jigs"!

Songs that we now consider sacred classics were once as criticized as today's contemporary Christian music. When "Silent Night" was first published, George Weber, music director of the Mainz Cathedral, called it "vulgar mischief and void of all religious and Christian feelings." And Charles Spurgeon, the great English pastor, despised the contemporary worship songs of his day—the same songs we now revere.

Perhaps most impossible to believe, Handel's *Messiah* was widely condemned as "vulgar theater" by the churchmen of his day. Like the criticism of today's contemporary choruses, the *Messiah* was panned for having too much repetition and not enough message—it contains nearly one hundred repetitions of "Hallelujah!"

Even the hallowed tradition of singing hymns was once considered "worldly" in Baptist churches. Benjamin Keach, a Baptist pastor of the seventeenth century, is credited with introducing hymn singing to English Baptist churches. He began first by teaching the children to sing because they loved it. The parents, however, did not enjoy singing hymns. They were convinced that singing was "foreign to evangelical worship."

A major controversy occurred when Pastor Keach tried to introduce hymn singing to the whole congregation in his church at Horsley Down. Finally, in 1673, he got them to agree to at least sing a hymn after the Lord's Supper by using the biblical precedent of Mark 14:26. However, Keach allowed those who objected to doing this to leave before the hymn. Six years later, in 1679, the church agreed to sing a hymn on days of "public thanksgiving."

Another fourteen years passed before the church could agree that hymn singing was appropriate in worship. The controversy was costly, causing twenty-two of Benjamin Keach's members to leave and join a "non-singing church." However, the fad of hymn singing caught on with other churches, and the "non-singing church" soon called a pastor who made hymn singing a condition of his coming. How things change. You can slow progress but you can't stop it.

The amazing thing to me about this incident was Pastor Keach's incredible patience. It took him twenty years to change his congregation's worship style. In an average church it is probably easier to change the church's theology than its order of service.

One of our weaknesses as evangelicals is that we don't know church history. Because of this, we begin confusing our current traditions with orthodoxy. Many of the methods and tools we use in churches today such as hymn singing, pianos, pipe organs, altar calls, and Sunday school were once considered worldly and even heretical. Now that these tools are widely accepted as gifts from God used to enhance worship, we have a new blacklist. Today's objections are aimed against innovations such as the use of synthesizers, drums, drama, and video in worship.

The debate over what style of music should be used in worship is going to be one of the major points of conflict in local churches in the years ahead. Every church will eventually have to address this issue. Be prepared for heated disagreement. James Dobson once admitted on his "Focus on the Family" program that "Of all the subjects we've ever covered in this radio program, from abortion to pornography to whatever, the most controversial subject we've ever dealt with is music. You can make people mad about music more quickly than anything else." The debate over music styles has divided and polarized many churches. I guess that is why Spurgeon called his music ministry "the War Department"!

Why do people take disagreement over worship styles so personally? Because the way you worship is intimately connected with the way God made you. Worship is your personal expression of love for God. When someone criticizes the way you worship, you naturally take it as a personal offense.

Saddleback is unapologetically a contemporary music church. We've often been referred to in the press as "the flock that likes to rock." We use the style of music the majority of people in our church listen to on the radio. Years ago, after being frustrated with trying to please everyone, I decided to survey our church. I passed out 3 x 5 cards to everyone in the crowd service and asked them to write down the call letters of the radio station they listened to.

What we discovered is that 96 percent of our people said they listen to middle-of-the-road adult contemporary music. Most people under forty don't relate to any music before 1965. To them, a classic is an Elvis tune! They like bright, happy, cheerful music with a strong beat. Their ears are accustomed to music with a strong bass line and rhythm.

For the first time in history, there exists a universal music style that can be heard in every country of the world. It's called contemporary pop/rock. The same songs are being played on radios in Nairobi and Tokyo and Moscow. Most TV commercials use the contemporary/rock style. Even country and western has adapted it. This is the primary musical style we've chosen to use at Saddleback.

After surveying who we were reaching, we made the strategic decision to stop singing hymns in our seeker services. Within a year of deciding what would be "our sound," Saddleback *exploded* with growth. I will admit that we have lost hundreds of potential members because of the style of music Saddleback uses. On the other hand, we have attracted thousands more because of our music.

Rules for Selecting a Music Style

Realizing that I am walking into an area full of land mines, I would like to offer a few suggestions regarding music. Regardless of the style your church chooses to use, I believe there are a few rules you need to follow.

Preview all the music you use

Don't have any surprises in your service. I learned this principle the hard way. I could tell you a number of stories that would bring tears to your eyes, like the time a guest singer decided to sing a twenty-minute song on nuclear disarmament! If you don't manage your music, your music will manage your service. Set up some parameters so that music supports the purpose of the service rather than working contrary to it.

When you preview the music you intend to use, consider both the lyrics and the tune. Ask yourself whether the lyrics are doctrinally sound, whether they are understandable to the unchurched, and whether the song uses terms or metaphors that unbelievers wouldn't understand. Always identify the purpose of a song. Is it a song of edification, worship, fellowship, or evangelism?

At Saddleback we categorize songs according to target. Songs on the crowd list are appropriate when unbelievers are present (at our seeker services). Songs on the congregation list are songs that are meaningful to believers but wouldn't make sense to the unchurched (we sing them at our midweek worship service). Songs on the core list deal with service and ministry (we sing them at our SALT rallies).

Ask, "How does this tune make me feel?" Music exerts a great influence on human emotions. The wrong kind of music can kill the spirit and mood of a service. Every pastor has known the agony of trying to resurrect a service after a music number that left everyone feeling depressed and suicidal. Decide what mood you want in your service, and use the style that creates it. At Saddleback, we

> **Music sets the mood of your service.**

believe worship is to be a celebration so we use a style that is upbeat, bright, and joyful. We rarely sing a song in a minor key.

Even when we invite popular Christian artists to sing at Saddleback, we insist on previewing every song they intend to sing. The atmosphere we're trying to maintain in our seeker service is far more important than any singer's ego.

Speed up the tempo

As I pointed out in chapter 14, the Bible says, "Worship the LORD with *gladness*; come before him with *joyful songs*" (Ps. 100:2, italics added), but many worship services sound more like a funeral than a festival. John Bisagno, pastor of the 15,000-member First Baptist Church of Houston, Texas, says, "Funeral dirge anthems and stiff-collared song leaders will kill a church faster than anything else in the world!"

At Saddleback, we joke about our aerobic singing. It is lively! I recently received a First Impression card from an eighty-one-year-old visitor and his wife that said, "Thank you for stirring up our geriatric blood!" It is impossible to fall asleep when Saddleback sings. We want our music to have both a spiritual and emotional impact on people. The I, M, P, and T of the IMPACT acronym I shared in the last chapter are all songs with an upbeat tempo. A and C songs are slower and more meditative. Unbelievers usually prefer celebrative music over contemplative music because they don't yet have a relationship with Christ.

Update the lyrics

There are many good songs that can be used in a seeker service by just changing a word or two in order to make them understandable to unbelievers. References to biblical metaphors and theological terms in a song may need to be translated or reworded. If the Bible needs to be translated from seventeenth-century English for seekers, so do the obscure lyrics of older songs.

If you use hymns, this sometimes requires major editing. "Here I raise mine Ebenezer," "Beulah land," "terrestrial ball," "cherubim and seraphim," "angels prostrate fall," and "washed in the blood of the Lamb" are all confusing phrases to the unchurched. They have no idea what you're singing about. The unchurched are likely to think that "the balm in Gilead" is a song about terrorists!

> Every true revival has always been accompanied by new music.

Some members will insist that there's good theology in the old hymns. I agree. Why not edit out the archaic terms and put the lyrics to a contemporary tune? Remember, there's nothing sacred about the music. Dress up some of those old friends in new clothes. If you print congregational songs in your program, you are allowed to edit the lyrics if the song is in the public domain.

By the way, some contemporary praise choruses are just as confusing as hymns when it comes to terminology. Unbelievers have no idea what "Jehovah Jireh" means. You might as well be singing "Mumbo Magumbo!"

Encourage members to write new songs

Every congregation should be encouraged to compose worship songs. If you study church history, you'll discover that every genuine revival has always been accompanied by new music. New songs say, "God is doing something *here and now*, not just a hundred years ago." Every generation needs new songs to express its faith.

Psalm 96:1 says, "Sing to the LORD a *new* song" (italics added). Sadly, in most churches they are still singing the same *old* songs. The Columbia Record Company once did a study and discovered that after a song is sung fifty times, people no longer think about the meaning of the lyrics — they just sing it by rote.

We love old songs because of the emotional memories they stir within us. There are certain songs, like "Victory in Jesus," "I Surrender All," and "So Send I You," that automatically bring tears to my eyes because they remind me of significant spiritual turning points in my life. But these songs do not make the same impact on unbelievers, or even other believers, because they don't share my memories.

Many churches overuse certain songs due to the personal preferences of either the pastor or the music leader. The repertoire of music is held hostage by the leader. What the minister of music or pastor likes should not be the determining factor in the style of music you use. Instead, use your target to determine your style.

If you really want to know if you are using worn-out songs in your services I challenge you to try an experiment next Sunday: Videotape the faces of your congregation while they sing the songs during the service. When people sing the same old songs, apathy and boredom show up on their faces. Predictability has killed more worship services than any other factor.

A song loses its testimonial power if people aren't thinking about what they're singing. But songs can be a powerful witness to unbelievers when people sing songs they feel deeply about.

Many of the gospel songs of the first half of this century tend to glorify the Christian experience rather than Christ. In contrast, today's most effective worship songs are love songs sung directly to God. This is biblical worship. We are told at least seventeen times in Scripture to sing *to the Lord.* In contrast, most hymns are sung *about* God. The strength of many contemporary worship songs is that they are God-centered, rather than man-centered.

Replace the Organ with a MIDI Band

With today's technology any church can have the same quality and sound of music that is heard on professionally produced albums. All you need is a MIDI keyboard and some MIDI discs. The beauty of using MIDI is that you can use it to "fill in the gaps" wherever you lack instrumentalists. For instance, if you have a keyboard player, trumpet player, and a guitarist, but lack a bass player and a drummer, you can simply add the MIDI track for bass and drums to your "live" musicians. If no one in your church is familiar with using MIDI technology you can get instructions from almost any music store.

At our size, Saddleback now has a complete pop/rock orchestra, but most churches aren't large enough to assemble that. If I were beginning a new church today, I'd find a person who knew something about MIDI and give him or her a keyboard. MIDI was not around when I started Saddleback, and I sometimes wonder how many more people we might have reached in our early years if we'd had MIDI-quality music in our services.

When I took our music preference survey, I couldn't find a single person who said, "I listen to organ music on the radio." About the only place you can still hear a pipe organ is in church. What does that say to you? Think this through: We invite the unchurched to come and sit on seventeenth-century chairs (which we call pews), sing eighteenth-century songs (which we call hymns), and listen to a nineteenth-century instrument (a pipe organ), and then we wonder why they think we're out-of-date! I'm afraid that we'll be well into the twenty-first century before some churches start using the instruments of the twentieth century.

You must decide whether your church is going to be a music conservatory for the musical elite or whether your church is going to be a place where common people can bring unsaved friends and hear music they understand and enjoy. At Saddleback, we use music for the *heart*, not for the *art*.

Don't force unbelievers to sing

Use more performed music than congregational singing in your service for seekers. Visitors do not feel comfortable singing tunes they don't know and words they don't understand. It is also unrealistic to expect the unchurched to sing songs of praise and commitment to Jesus before they become believers. That's getting the cart before the horse.

Unchurched visitors often feel awkward during the congregational singing portion of your service. Since they don't know the songs, and the songs speak of praise and commitment to Jesus, they are forced to stand there while everyone else sings. This is especially embarrassing in a small church, because everyone notices if you aren't singing. On the other hand, unchurched visitors feel very comfortable *listening* to performed music, if it is in a style to which they can relate. So focus on performed music in your seeker service and save times of extended congregational praise for your believers' service. (At our believers' service we regularly spend thirty to forty minutes in uninterrupted praise and worship.)

Understand that the larger your church gets, the more congregational singing can be used in the seeker service. This is because when an unchurched visitor is surrounded by a thousand other people, no one cares if he's singing or not. He or she can hide in the crowd and listen without feeling watched, soaking up the emotion of the moment.

Although it is better not to have extended congregational praise in a seeker

> It is a mistake to remove *all* congregational singing from a seeker service.

service, I believe it is a mistake to remove it from a seeker service entirely because it is a powerful, emotional element. When believers sing in harmony together, it creates a sense of intimacy in even a large gathering. This intimacy impresses the unchurched, who can sense something good is happening even if they can't explain it.

To "harmonize" means "to bring into agreement." When believers sing in harmony together it is an audible expression of the unity and fellowship of the body. Each person is singing his part while listening to the others in order to blend. There is something profoundly attractive about believers singing together in sincere, heartfelt praise. It is a witness that these normal-looking people really do have a relationship to Christ and to each other.

Make Your Music Count

Although music is usually the most controversial element of a seeker service, it is a critical element that cannot be ignored. We need to understand the incredible power of music and harness that power by being willing to set aside our own personal preferences and use the music that will best reach the unchurched for Christ.

16

Preaching to the Unchurched

Be tactful with those who are not Christians. . . .
Talk to them agreeably and with a flavor of wit, and
try to fit your answers to the needs of each one.

Colossians 4:5–6 (JB)

[Speak] only what is helpful for building
others up according to their needs, that it may
benefit those who listen.

Ephesians 4:29

When I started Saddleback, I had about ten years of sermons stockpiled from my previous ministry as an evangelist. I could have coasted the first few years, doing little sermon preparation, by using messages I'd already written. But once I surveyed the unchurched in my community I quickly dropped that idea.

When I discovered that the greatest complaint of the unchurched in my area was "boring, irrelevant sermons," I decided I'd better seriously reexamine my preaching. I reviewed ten years' worth of sermons asking one question: Would this message make sense to a totally unchurched person?

It didn't matter if I liked the message or not. Neither was it enough for a sermon to be doctrinally correct and homiletically sound. If I was going to start a church by attracting hard-core pagans, it would have to be a message to which they could relate. I ended up throwing out every sermon I'd written in the previous ten years, except two.

Starting over from scratch, I had to develop a whole new set of preaching skills. I've already alluded to some of my convictions about preaching in chapter 12 on how Jesus attracted crowds. If you're interested in knowing the details of my style of sermon preparation and delivery, you can order the tape series "Communicating to Change Lives" from The Encouraging Word tape ministry. The fax and phone numbers are at the end of this book.

Adapt Your Style to Your Audience

The style of preaching that I use in our seeker service is very different than the style I use to teach believers. The style of communication that most church members are used to is counterproductive in reaching most of the unchurched.

When preaching to believers I like to teach through books of the Bible, verse-by-verse. In fact, at one point in Saddleback's growth, I took two and a half years teaching verse-by-verse through Romans at our believers' service. Verse-by-verse, or book, exposition builds up the body of Christ. It works great when you're speaking to believers who accept the authority of God's Word and are motivated to learn the Scriptures. But what about unbelievers who are not yet motivated to study Scripture? I do not believe verse-by-verse teaching through the books of the Bible is the most effective way to evangelize the unchurched. Instead, you must start on common ground, just as Paul did with his pagan audience at the Areopagus in Athens. Instead of beginning with an Old Testament text, he quoted one of their own poets to get their attention and establish common ground.

Our English word *communication* comes from the Latin word *communis*, which means "common." You can't communicate with people until you find something you have in common with them. With the unchurched, you will not establish common ground by saying, "Let's open our Bibles to Isaiah, chapter 14, as we continue in our study of this wonderful book."

The ground we have in common with unbelievers is not the Bible, but our common needs, hurts, and interests as human beings. You cannot start with a text, expecting the unchurched to be fascinated by it. You must first capture their attention, and then move them to the truth of God's Word. By starting with a topic that interests the unchurched and then showing what the Bible says about it, you can grab their attention, disarm prejudices, and create an interest in the Bible that wasn't there before.

Each week I begin with a need, hurt, or interest and then move to what God has to say about it in his Word. Rather than concentrating on a single passage, I will use many verses from many passages that speak to the topic. I call this type of preaching "verse-*with*-verse" exposition, or topical exposition. (In seminary, verse-*with*-verse topical exposition is called systematic theology!)

I honestly don't think God cares at all whether you teach the Bible book by book or topic by topic, as long as you teach the Bible. He doesn't care whether you start with the text and move to applying it to people's needs, or start with people's needs and move to the text.

Today, "preaching to felt needs" is scorned and criticized in some circles as a cheapening of the Gospel and a sellout to consumerism. I want to state this in the clearest way possible: Beginning a message with people's felt needs is more than a marketing tool! It is based on the theological fact that God chooses to reveal himself to man according to *our* needs! Both the Old and New Testaments are filled with examples of this.

Even the names of God are revelations of how God meets our felt needs! Throughout history when people have asked God, "What is your name?" God's response has been to reveal himself according to what they needed at that time: To those who needed a miracle, God revealed himself as Jehovah Jireh (I am your provider); to those who needed comfort, God revealed himself as Jehovah Shalom (I am your peace); to those who needed salvation, God revealed himself as Jehovah Tsidkenu (I am your righteousness). The examples go on and on. God meets us where we are, at our point of need. Preaching to felt needs is a theologically sound approach to introducing people to God.

> **Both verse-by-verse (book) exposition and verse-with-verse (topical) exposition are necessary in order to grow a healthy church.**

Preaching that changes lives brings the truth of God's Word and the real needs of people together through application. Which end of the continuum you begin with depends on your audience. But what is even more important is that you eventually bring God's truth and people's needs together through application, regardless of where the message begins.

God's Word——————>.<————People's needs
Application

Both verse-by-verse (book) exposition and verse-with-verse (topical) exposition are necessary in order to grow a healthy church. Book exposition works best for edification. Topical exposition works best for evangelism.

Make the Bible Accessible to Unbelievers

Unbelievers usually feel intimidated by the Bible. It is filled with strange names and titles, and it sounds like nothing they've read before. The King James Version is especially confusing to the unchurched. In addition, the Bible is the only book they've seen that puts numbers before each sentence and is bound in leather. This often causes many unbelievers to have a superstitious fear about reading or even holding a Bible.

Since God's Word is "the Word of life" we must do everything we can to bring the unchurched into contact with it and help them feel comfortable using it. There are several things you can do to relieve anxiety and spark interest in the Bible among the unchurched.

Read Scripture from a newer translation. With all the wonderful translations and paraphrases available today, there is no legitimate reason for complicating the Good News with four-hundred-year-old English. Using the King James Version creates an unnecessary cultural barrier. Remember, when King James authorized the new translation it was because he wanted a *contemporary* version. I once saw an advertisement that claimed if King James were alive today, he'd be reading the New International Version! That's probably true. Clarity is more important than poetry.

Use pew Bibles. In the early years of Saddleback, we purchased cheap, hardcover Bibles and placed them in every chair. Since the unchurched don't know the books of the Bible, you can simply announce the page number of your Scripture reading. This prevents visitors from being embarrassed by how long it takes them to find a text. It's intimidating to sit next to someone who turns to the text before you can even find the index!

Select your Scripture readings with the unchurched in mind. While all Scripture is equally inspired by God, it is not all equally applicable to unbelievers. Some passages are clearly more appropriate for seeker services than others. For instance, you probably won't want to read David's prayer in Psalm 58: "Break the teeth in their mouths, O God. . . . Like a slug melting away as it moves along, like a stillborn child, may they not see the sun. . . . The righteous will be glad . . . when they bathe their feet in the blood of the wicked." Save this passage for your own personal quiet time or the local pastors' breakfast!

Certain texts require more explanation than others. With this in mind, at Saddleback we like to use passages that don't require any previous understanding. We also like to use passages that show the benefits of knowing Christ.

Provide an Outline with Scriptures Written Out

I provide a printed outline of the message with all the Bible verses to be used written out on it. There are a number of reasons I do this:

- The unchurched don't own Bibles.
- It relieves embarrassment in finding texts.
- You cover more material in less time. I once counted the number of times a well-known pastor said, "Now turn to this" during his message, and I timed how long he took to find the passages. He spent seven minutes of his message just turning pages.
- Everyone can read a verse aloud together because everyone has the same translation.
- You can use and compare multiple translations.
- The audience can circle and underline words for emphasis and take notes in the margins.
- It helps people remember the message. We forget 90–95 percent of what we hear within seventy-two hours. That means by Wednesday, if they didn't take notes, your congregation has forgotten all but about 5 percent of what you said on Sunday.
- People can review the verses later by taping the notes to their refrigerators.
- It can become the basis for small-group discussion.
- Members can teach the outline to others. We have a number of businessmen at Saddleback who lead office Bible studies using the previous Sunday's outline.

The long-lasting value of a message outline that has the Scripture written out continues to amaze me. Recently a high school biology teacher told me how God used an outline in his life. He got a call from his teenage daughter, who had been in a car accident. She was fine, but the car was totaled and the accident was her fault. He went to pick up his daughter, and while they were waiting for a tow truck, he sat down on the curb and began to think how irritated he was at his daughter for being reckless.

As he was getting angrier and angrier, he noticed a piece of paper in the gutter. Recognizing it as one of my sermon outlines, he picked it up. The message and Bible verses were on the topic "Defusing Your Anger." He now keeps that outline folded in his wallet.

There are so many positive benefits to this method that I never speak without using a handout. Several thousand pastors have adopted the outline style we use at Saddleback. If you'd like a sample, just write to me.

Plan Your Titles to Appeal to the Unchurched

If you scan the church page of your Saturday newspaper, you'll see that most pastors are not attempting to attract the unchurched with their sermon titles. A sample of intriguing sermon topics from the *Los Angeles Times* includes: "The Gathering Storm," "On the Road to Jericho," "Peter Goes Fishing," "A Mighty Fortress," "Walking Instructions," "Becoming a Titus," "No Such Thing as a Rubber Clock," "River of Blood," and "The Ministry of Cracked Pots."

Do any of these titles make you want to hop out of bed and rush to church? Would any of them appeal to an unchurched person scanning the paper? What are preachers thinking? Why are they wasting money advertising titles like these?

I have been criticized for using sermon titles for our seeker services that sound like Reader's Digest articles. That is intentional. Reader's Digest is still one of the most-read magazines in America because its articles appeal to human needs, hurts, and interests.

Jesus said, "Yes, worldly people are smarter with their own kind than spiritual people are" (Luke 16:8 NCV). They understand what captures attention. Jesus expects us to be just as perceptive and strategic in our evangelism: "I am sending you out like sheep among wolves. Therefore be as shrewd as snakes and as innocent as doves" (Matt. 10:16).

My sermon titles aren't intended to impress members of other churches. In fact, if you judged Saddleback on the basis of sermon titles only, you might conclude that we're pretty shallow. But since Christians aren't our target, we're not being shallow, we're being strategic. Beneath those "felt-need" sermon titles is a hard-core biblical message. The misunderstanding of other Christians is a small price to pay for winning thousands to Christ.

Preach in Series

Few pastors understand the power of momentum. Preaching a sermon series is one example of using the power of momentum. Each message builds on the one before, creating a sense of anticipation. A series also takes advantage of word-of-mouth advertising. People know exactly where your series is going and, if you announce your sermon titles in advance, they can plan to bring friends on particular weeks that might best suit their need.

I always announce a new series on days we expect a lot of visitors, like Easter. It creates a hook that brings many first-time visitors back for the next week. The best length for a series is four to eight weeks. Anything longer than eight weeks causes your congregation to lose interest. They begin to wonder if you are knowledgeable about anything else. I once heard of a woman who complained, "My pastor has been in Daniel seventy weeks longer than Daniel was!"

Be Consistent in Your Preaching Style

You cannot switch back and forth between targeting seekers and believers in the same services. For example, don't follow up a series on "Managing Stress" with "Expository Gems from Leviticus" or follow a series on "What God Thinks About Sex" with "Unmasking the Beast in Revelation." You'll create schizophrenic members, and no one will know when it's safe to bring unchurched friends.

I'm not saying you can't preach on Christian growth themes in your seeker service. I believe you can, and I do. As I mentioned in a previous chapter, I love to teach theology and doctrine to the unchurched without telling them what it is and without using religious terminology. But when you *do* preach a series on some aspect of spiritual maturity, you must communicate it in a way that connects it somehow to the needs of unbelievers.

Choose Guest Speakers Carefully

We don't use many guest speakers anymore because I've put together a preaching team on our pastoral staff to share the load with me. The advantage of using your own staff is that they know your people, love your people, and most importantly, they will use the style of preaching that is consistent with your philosophy of ministry.

All it takes is one offbeat guest speaker to lose people you've been cultivating for months. When the unchurched have a bad experience, it's extremely difficult to get them back. If, just as they are getting comfortable and lowering their defenses, some guest speaker comes along and blows them out of the water, their worst suspicions about the church will be confirmed.

We have canceled speakers after the first service when they didn't match our beliefs or style. Once when I was away on vacation we had a well-known Christian speaker fill in for me. Unfortunately, his message was that God wanted every Christian to get rich. After the first service, my associate pastors confronted him and said, "Thank you, but we won't be using you in the next three services!" My youth pastor pulled out an old message and replaced him. Pastors must protect their flocks from heresy.

Preach for Commitment

We should always offer unbelievers an opportunity to respond to Christ in a seeker service. They may choose to not respond, and you must respect that without pressuring them, but the opportunity must always be offered. Too many pastors go fishing without ever reeling in the line or drawing up the net.

There are many different ways to draw up the net. In planning for Saddleback's first service I had intended to extend a traditional "come forward" altar call at the end of the service. As a Southern Baptist evangelist, that was the way I'd always done it.

> Too many pastors go fishing without ever reeling in the line or drawing up the net.

But as I concluded my first message in the Laguna Hills High School Theater, I suddenly realized I had two problems. First, there was no center aisle in the building. The chairs were welded together, and the building was designed to empty to side doors. Second, I realized that even if they could get to the front, all that was there was an orchestra pit that dropped off right in front of the stage. I nearly cracked up thinking about saying, "I'm going to ask you to come down and jump in the pit for Jesus!" I honestly didn't know what to do next. How could I get people to indicate their commitment to Christ if they couldn't come forward?

Over the next few weeks, we experimented with several different ways of having people indicate their commitment to

Christ. We tried setting up a counseling room where people could go after the service. But we found that once people walked out of the service they just kept walking to their car. If you decide to use a separate room, don't call it a "counseling" room. To the unchurched, it sounds like a psychiatric ward. Instead, use a nonthreatening title like "Visitor's Center" or "Reception Area."

After a number of experiments, we came up with our registration/commitment card idea. We turned the back side of our Welcome Card into a decision card. At the beginning of the service, we encourage everyone to fill out the front side. At the end of each service, I ask everyone to bow their heads and I lead in a closing prayer, during which I give an opportunity for unbelievers to make a commitment to Christ. Then, I'll pray a model prayer as an example and ask them to let me know about their decision on the commitment card. The last thing we do in our service is have a special music number and collect the cards and offering at the same time. The cards are then processed immediately for follow-up. While the next service is happening, the information on the cards collected from the previous hour's service is entered into computers.

This approach has worked so well for us that we continued to use it even after we moved to facilities that would have allowed an altar call. We have had services where 100, 200, 300, and once nearly 400, unbelievers have committed their lives to Christ and indicated it on a card.

Some might ask, "Where do people make their *public* profession of faith?" That's what baptism is—a public statement of faith in Christ. In some churches, we have overemphasized the altar call so much that baptism is almost anticlimactic.

Offering a time of commitment is an important element of a seeker service. Here are some suggestions for leading people to make that commitment.

Clearly explain exactly how to respond to Christ. Too many invitations to salvation are misunderstood. The unchurched often have no idea what's going on.

Plan out your time of commitment. Deliberately and carefully think through what you want to happen. Extending an opportunity to come to Christ is too important to just tack on to the end of a message without planning it. People's eternal destinies lie in the balance.

Be creative in inviting people to receive Christ. If you say the same thing every week the audience will disconnect out of boredom. The best way to avoid getting in a rut is to force yourself to write out your call for commitment with each message.

Lead unbelievers in a model prayer. The unchurched don't know what to say to God, so give them an example: "You might pray something like this. . . ." Ask them to repeat a simple prayer, in their hearts, after you. This helps people verbalize their faith.

Never pressure unbelievers to decide. Trust the Holy Spirit to do his work. As I said in chapter 10, if the fruit is ripe, you don't have to yank it. An overextended invitation is counterproductive. It hardens hearts rather than softening them. We tell people to take the time they need to think through their decision. I believe that if they're honest with themselves, they will make the right decision.

Keep in mind that you're asking people to make the most important decision of their lives. Evangelism is usually a process of repeated exposure to the Good News. It's pretty unrealistic to expect a forty-year-old man to completely change the direction of his life on the basis of one thirty-minute message. Would you keep going to a grocery store if every time you went there to buy milk, the clerks pressured you to buy a steak? Imagine a clerk saying, "Today is the day of steak! Now is the time for steak! You must buy steak today because you might not have steak tomorrow!" People usually aren't as closed as we think they are. They just need time to think about the decision we're asking them to make.

Offer multiple ways to indicate a commitment to Christ. If you are currently offering a traditional altar call, instead of replacing it, try adding the card approach. Put another hook in the water. The card can be an alternative for those who are shy about coming forward. Remember, Jesus never said you have to walk from Point A to Point B in a church to confess your faith.

The altar call is actually a modern invention. Asahael Nettleton began using it in 1817, and Charles Finney popularized it. They didn't have altar calls in the New Testament churches because there were no church buildings for about the first 300 years, which means there were no aisles to walk down and no altars to come to!

One of the most effective invitation approaches I've used is to take a "spiritual survey" at the end of a service. After presenting the plan of salvation and leading in a prayer of commitment, I set it up like this: "You know, there is nothing I'd rather do than to have a personal conversation with each of you about your spiritual journey. I wish I could invite each of you out for some pie and coffee and have you tell me what's going on in your life. Unfortunately, with the size of our church, that isn't possible. So I ask you to do me a favor and participate in a personal survey. I'd like you to take the welcome card you filled out earlier in the service and, on the back of it, write either the letter A, B, C, or D, based on what I'm going to explain.

"If you have already committed your life to Christ prior to this service, write down the letter 'A.' If today you are believing in Christ for the first time, write down the letter 'B.' If you say, 'Rick, I haven't made that decision yet but I'm considering it, and I want you to know that I am considering it,' write down the letter 'C.' If you feel you don't ever intend to commit your life to Christ, I'd appreciate your honesty by your writing down the letter 'D' on your card."

The results are always amazing to me. One Sunday we had nearly 400 "B"s—professions of faith in Christ. We have had as many as 800 "C"s—which gives us a great prayer list. We've never had more than seventeen "D"s.

Expect people to respond. I don't know exactly how my faith affects the spiritual battle that is waged for the souls of people, but I do know this: When I expect unbelievers to respond to Christ, more do so than when I don't expect people to be saved.

Once a young seminary student complained to Charles Spurgeon, "I don't understand it—whenever I preach, no one comes to Christ. But whenever you preach, people always come to Christ!" Spurgeon replied, "Do you expect people to come to Christ *every time* you preach?" The young man said, "Of course not." "That's your problem," said Spurgeon.

I often pray, "Father, you've said, 'According to your faith it will be done unto you.' I know it would be a waste of time to speak and not expect you to use it, so I thank you in advance that lives are going to be changed."

The Primacy of Preaching

This chapter was not intended to give a full explanation of my philosophy of preaching. That could be a book in itself. My purpose here was to just highlight some practical suggestions that can make a big difference in preaching to the unchurched, regardless of your preaching style.

Preaching seems to go in and out of fashion in many denominations. In our high-tech world, it is often criticized as being an outdated and uninteresting mode of communication. I agree that many preaching styles that once worked no longer effectively communicate to unbelievers. In terms of seeing radical life changes in individuals, however, nothing else can take the place of Spirit-anointed preaching. The message is still the most important element of a seeker service. Saddleback's fifteen years of growth in spite of hot gymnasiums, leaky tents, and crowded parking have shown that people will put up with a lot of inconveniences and limitations if the messages are genuinely meeting their needs.

Part Five
Building Up the Church

Community
Crowd
Congregation
Committed
Core
Lay Ministers
Maturing Members
Members
Regular Attenders
Unchurched

17

Turning Attenders into Members

Now you are no longer strangers to God and foreigners to heaven, but you are members of God's very own family, ... and you belong in God's household with every other Christian.

Ephesians 2:19 (LB)

In Christ we who are many form one body, and each member belongs to all the others.

Romans 12:5

Once you've gathered a crowd of attenders you must begin the important task of forming them into a congregation of members. The crowd must become a church. On our Life Development Process diagram we call this "getting people to first base," and we do it through the process of incorporation, or assimilation. Assimilation is the task of moving people from an awareness of your church to attendance at your church to active membership in your church. The community talks about "*that* church," the crowd talks about "*this* church," but the congregation talks about "*our* church." Members have a sense of ownership. They are contributors, not just consumers.

Many American Christians are what I call "floating believers." Anywhere else in the world, being a believer is synonymous with being connected to a local body of believers—you rarely find a lone-ranger Christian in other countries. Many American Christians, however, hop from one church to another without any identity, accountability, or commitment. This is a direct expression of America's rampant individualism. They have not been taught that the Christian life involves more than just *believing*—it also includes *belonging*. We grow in Christ by being in relationship to other Christians. Romans 12:10 says, "Be devoted to one another in brotherly love."

C. S. Lewis once wrote an essay on church membership, reminding us that the word *membership* is of Christian origin, but it has been taken over by the world and emptied of all its original meaning. Today, most people associate the term *membership* with paying dues, meaningless rituals, silly rules and handshakes, and having your name on some dusty roll. Paul, however, had a very different image of membership. To him, being a member of the church did not refer to some cold induction into an institution, but rather it meant becoming a vital organ of a living body (Rom. 12:4–5; 1 Cor. 6:15; 1 Cor. 12:12–27). We need to reclaim this image. *Any* organ that is detached from the body will not only miss what it was created to be, it will also shrivel and die quickly. The same is true for Christians that are uncommitted to any specific congregation.

The incorporation of new members into your church fellowship does not happen automatically. If you don't have a system and a structure to assimilate and *keep* the people you reach, they won't stay with your church. You'll have as many people going out the back door of your church as are coming in the front door.

Many churches mistakenly assume that once a person has received Christ, the sale has been consummated, and it is now up to the new believer to follow through with his commitment and join the church. This is nonsense. Baby believers don't know what they need! It is the *church's* responsibility to take the initiative in assimilating new people into the congregation.

I believe that when God wants to deliver a bunch of baby Christians, he looks around for the warmest incubator he can find. Churches that make new member assimilation a priority and have a plan for doing it are usually blessed with growth. In contrast, churches that don't care about new members, or are haphazard in assimilating them *don't grow.* In this chapter, I would like to share the strategy we use at Saddleback for incorporating and retaining the members of our congregation.

Develop a Plan to Assimilate New Members

Because your congregation has a unique history, culture, and growth rate, you need to ask some important questions. The answers will determine the assimilation plan that's best for your situation. Proverbs 20:18 says, "Make plans by seeking advice." Here are the twelve questions we ask at Saddleback:

1. What does God expect from members of his church?
2. What do we expect from our members right now?
3. What kind of people already make up our congregation?
4. How will that change in the next five to ten years?
5. What do our members value?
6. What are new members' greatest needs?
7. What are our long-term members' greatest needs?
8. How can we make membership more meaningful?
9. How can we insure that members feel loved and cared for?
10. What do we owe our members?
11. What resources or services could we offer our members?
12. How could we add value to what we already offer?

Next, you need to realize that prospective members have their own set of questions. These questions will also influence how you design your assimilation plan. Before people commit to joining your church, they want to know the answers to five unspoken questions.

Do I fit here? This is the question of *acceptance*. It is best answered by establishing affinity groups within your church so that people with similar ages, interests, problems, or backgrounds can find and relate to each other. Everyone needs a niche, and small groups play a crucial role in meeting this need. You must show people that you have a place for them.

Does anybody want to know me? This is the question of *friendship.* You can answer this question by creating opportunities for people to develop relationships within your congregation. There are unlimited ways you can do this, but it does take planning. Remember, people are not looking for a friendly *church* as much as they are looking for *friends*. People deserve individual attention.

Am I needed? This is the question of *value.* People want to make contributions with their lives. They want to feel that they matter. When you can show people they can make a difference with their gifts and talents by joining your church, they will want to be involved. Position your church as a creative place that needs the expression of all sorts of talents and abilities, not just singers, ushers, and Sunday school teachers.

What is the advantage of joining? This is the question of *benefit.* You must be able to clearly and concisely explain the reasons and benefits of membership in your church. Explain the biblical, practical, and personal reasons for membership.

What is required of members? This is the question of *expectations.* You must be able to explain the responsibilities of membership as clearly as you state the benefits of it. People have a right to know what is expected of them *before* they join.

Communicate the Value of Membership

Joining a church used to be an act of conformity in our society. You joined a church because everybody else did. Now the rules have changed and conformity is no longer a motivating factor. In fact, George Gallup has found that the vast majority of Americans believe it is possible to be a "good Christian" without joining (or even attending) a local church.

Instead, membership is now an act of commitment. The way you motivate people to join today is to show them the value-for-value benefits they will receive in return for their commitment. At Saddleback, we've found that when people understand the meaning and value of membership, they get excited about it.

There are numerous benefits to membership:

1. It identifies a person as a genuine believer (Eph. 2:19; Rom. 12:5).
2. It provides a spiritual family to support and encourage them in their walk with Christ (Gal. 6:1–2; Heb. 10:24–25).
3. It gives them a place to discover and use their gifts in ministry (1 Cor. 12:4–27).
4. It places them under the spiritual protection of godly leaders (Heb. 13:17; Acts 20:28–29).
5. It gives them the accountability they need to grow (Eph. 5:21).

In chapter 6, I suggested that you personalize the purposes of the church. This is especially important when convincing attenders in your crowd to join your congregation. You need to emphasize the fact that the church provides them with benefits they cannot find anywhere else in the world:

- Worship helps you focus on God. It prepares you spiritually and emotionally for the week ahead.
- Fellowship helps you face life's problems by providing the support and encouragement of other Christians.

- Discipleship helps you fortify your faith by learning the truth of God's Word and applying biblical principles to your lifestyle.
- Ministry helps you find and develop your talents and use them in serving others.
- Evangelism helps you fulfill your mission of reaching your friends and family for Christ.

There are many analogies for a Christian disconnected from a church: a football player without a team; a soldier without a platoon; a tuba player without an orchestra; a sheep without a flock. But the most understandable (and biblical) picture is that of a child without a family.

First Timothy 3:15 (NCV) refers to the church as "... the family of God. That family is the church of the living God, the support and foundation of the truth." God does not want his children growing up in isolation from each other, so he created a spiritual family on earth for us. Paul reminded us in Ephesians 2:19 (LB): "You are members of God's very own family, ... and you belong in God's household with every other Christian." A Christian without a church family is an orphan.

It is important to position the church as a family, rather than as an institution. Since the 1960s, Americans have become increasingly anti-institutional. The phrase "organized religion" is used contemptuously. Yet people are also longing for a sense of family and community.

A number of factors have fragmented the nuclear family in today's culture: the high divorce rate, delayed marriages, the emphasis on individuality, "alternative" lifestyles, and women working outside the home, among others. The high rate of mobility is another. In our mobile society, people have few roots. People are no longer surrounded by the extended family of aunts and uncles, grandparents, and brothers and sisters that provided a safety net for previous generations.

Today we have a record number of single adults in America. Vance Packard calls America "a nation of strangers." As a result, we're experiencing an epidemic of loneliness in society. One Gallup poll reported that four in ten Americans admit to frequent feelings of "intense loneliness." Americans are, in fact, the loneliest people in the world.

Everywhere you look there are signs that people are hungering for fellowship, community, and a sense of family. Beer commercials, for instance, don't sell beer, they sell fellowship. No one is ever portrayed drinking alone; it's always done in the context of people enjoying each other's company. Phrases accompany the commercials like: "It doesn't get any better than this!" Advertisers have discovered that independent-minded baby boomers are suddenly longing to be *connected* as they enter middle age.

This "longing for belonging" provides the church with a timely opportunity. Positioning the church as an extended family, as "a place where you are cared for," will strike a sensitive chord in many lonely hearts.

Establish a Required Membership Class

A number of studies have shown that the way people join an organization greatly influences how they function in that organization after joining. This is true of joining a church as well. The *manner* in which people join your church will determine their effectiveness as members for years to come.

I believe the most important class in a church is the membership class because it sets the tone and expectation level for everything else that follows. The very best time to elicit a strong commitment from your members is at the moment they join. If little is required to join, very little can be expected from your members later on.

Just as a weak membership class will build a weak congregation, a strong membership class will build a strong congregation. Note that a *strong* class doesn't necessarily mean a *long* class. Saddleback's membership class (Class 101) is only four hours long and is taught in one day, yet it produces a high level of commitment in our membership because those who take the class find out exactly what will be expected of them as members. The strength of a membership class is determined by its content and call for commitment, not its length.

For a number of reasons, I believe the senior pastor should teach this class, or at least a portion of it. The opportunity to see the pastor's vision for the church, feel his love for the members, and hear his personal commitment to care, feed, and lead them is very important to new members. The following note from a new member expresses what many have written about Saddleback's membership class:

> Dear Pastor Rick,
>
> Thank you for teaching the membership class (101) yourself. It was very moving to hear you express your love and commitment to your flock and your vision for our future. We wish we could have taken the class sooner. The comments and suggestions we made when we first came to Saddleback seem trivial now that we understand the philosophy, strategy, and vision of this church. It will be a privilege to follow your leadership and be under your care. We are really excited now to find our place of service at Saddleback.

Some churches' membership classes cover the wrong material. Their content is based on spiritual growth or basic doctrine. These subjects are vitally important, but they are more appropriately covered in a new believers' class or Christian doctrine class, both essential classes that should be separate from the membership class. Your membership class should answer the following questions:

- What is a church?
- What are the purposes of the church?

- What are the benefits of being a member?
- What are the requirements for membership?
- What are the responsibilities of membership?
- What is the vision and strategy of this church?
- How is the church organized?
- How can I get involved in ministry?
- What do I do now that I am a member?

If you are a church that targets the unchurched, you need to include a clear explanation of salvation in your membership class because you will have many people who want to join the church who are not believers! We always explain that trusting Christ is the first requirement for membership, and we have people who commit their lives to Christ in every membership class.

There are many elements you can use in your membership class to keep it interesting and interactive: video clips, a notebook with fill-in-the-blank curriculum, small-group interaction, and a good meal together. Be sure to include a lot of stories that personalize the history, values, and direction of your church. At Saddleback, we even include a quiz at the end of the class, testing the prospective members on how well they can state the purposes of our church and other important concepts.

Completion of a membership class should be required for membership. People who are uninterested or unwilling to learn your church's purposes, strategy, and the meaning of membership are failing to demonstrate the kind of commitment that membership implies. If they don't even care enough to understand the responsibilities of membership, they cannot be expected to fulfill those responsibilities after joining and should not be allowed to join. There are plenty of other congregations they could join that offer a meaningless membership.

It's also important to think of the different age groups when teaching a membership class. At Saddleback, we offer three ver-

Outline of Class 101:
Discovering Saddleback Membership

I.   Our Salvation

    A. Making sure you are a Christian

    B. The symbols of salvation

        1. Baptism

        2. Communion

II. Our Statements

    A. Our Purpose Statement: *Why we exist*

    B. Our Vision Statement: *What we intend to do*

    C. Our Faith Statement: *What we believe*

    D. Our Values Statement: *What we practice*

III. Our Strategy

    A. Brief history of Saddleback

    B. Who we are trying to reach (our target)

    C. Our Life Development Process to help you grow

    D. The S.A.D.D.L.E.B.A.C.K. strategy

IV. Our Structure

    A. How our church is organized for growth

    B. Our affiliation

    C. What it means to be a member

    D. What is my next step after joining?

V.   The Saddleback Quiz

sions of the membership class: a children's version for older elementary kids (taught by our children's pastor), a youth version for junior high and high school (taught by our youth pastors), and the adult membership class.

Develop a Membership Covenant

Why do churches have so many people on their membership rolls who give little or no evidence of Christian commitment or even conversion? Why do many churches find it difficult to motivate members to give, serve, pray, and share their faith? The answer is that the members were allowed to join with no expectations placed on them. You get what you ask for.

Paul mentions two different types of commitment in 2 Corinthians 8:5 (GNB): "First they gave themselves to the Lord; and then, by God's will, they gave themselves to us as well." At Saddleback, we call these the *first-base* commitments. You commit yourself to Christ for salvation and then you commit yourself to other Christians for membership in our church family. In our church we define *koinonia* (fellowship) as "being as committed to each other as we are to Jesus Christ."

Jesus said that our love for each other was to be the mark of discipleship (see John 13:34–35). I believe it's an indictment of Christianity that most believers can quote John 3:16, but they can't quote 1 John 3:16: "This is how we know what love is: Jesus Christ laid down his life for us. And we ought to lay down our lives for our brothers." When was the last time you heard a message on this verse? Most churches are silent about developing that level of commitment to each other.

The phrase "one another" or "each other" is used over fifty times in the New Testament. We are commanded to love each other, pray for each other, encourage each other, admonish each other, greet each other, serve each other, teach each other, accept each other, honor each other, bear each other's burdens, forgive each other, sing to each other, submit to each other, and be devoted to each other. All of these commands are what membership in a local body of believers is all about. They are the responsibilities of membership. At Saddleback, we expect of our members only what the Bible clearly expects of all believers. We summarize these expectations in our membership covenant.

The most important part of a marriage ceremony is when the man and woman exchange vows, making certain promises to each other before witnesses and God. This covenant between them is the essence of the marriage. In the same way, the essence of church membership is contained in the willingness to commit to a membership covenant. It is the most important element of our membership class.

Throughout biblical and church history, spiritual covenants have been made between people for mutual edification and accountability. At Saddleback we have four requirements for membership: (1) a personal profession of Christ as Lord and Savior, (2) baptism by immersion as a public symbol of one's faith, (3) completion of the membership class, and (4) a signed commitment to abide by Saddleback's membership covenant.

I urge you to prayerfully prepare and adopt a membership covenant in your congregation if you don't have one. It can revolutionize your church. You may worry, "If we adopt a membership covenant, there will be some who leave our church over it." You're right. There will be some. But people are going to leave your church *no matter what you do*. Don't be afraid of people leaving. People even walked away from Jesus. When your congregation adopts a membership covenant, at least you get to choose the kind of people that stay.

Make Your Members Feel Special

Completing a membership class does not automatically cause people to feel that they belong. They need to feel

The Saddleback Membership Covenant

Having received Christ as my Lord and Savior and been baptized, and being in agreement with Saddleback's statements, strategy, and structure, I now feel led by the Holy Spirit to unite with the Saddleback church family. In doing so, I commit myself to God and to the other members to do the following:

1. I will protect the unity of my church

    ... by acting in love toward other members

    ... by refusing to gossip

    ... by following the leaders

"So let us concentrate on the things which make for harmony, and on the growth of our fellowship together" (Rom. 14:19 PHILLIPS).

"Have a sincere love for other believers, love one another earnestly with all your heart" (1 Peter 1:22 TEV).

"Do not let any unwholesome talk come out of your mouths, but only what is helpful for building others up according to their needs" (Eph. 4:29).

"Obey your leaders and submit to their authority. They keep watch over you as men who must give an account. Obey them so that their work will be a joy, not a burden, for that would be no advantage to you" (Heb. 13:17).

2. I will share the responsibility of my church

    ... by praying for its growth

    ... by inviting the unchurched to attend

    ... by warmly welcoming those who visit

"To the church— ... We always thank God for you and pray for you constantly" (1 Thess. 1:1–2 LB).

"The Master said to the servant, 'Go out to the roads and country lanes, and urge the people there to come so my house will be full" (Luke 14:23 NCV).

"So, warmly welcome each other into the church, just as Christ has warmly welcomed you; then God will be glorified" (Rom. 15:7 LB).

3. I will serve the ministry of my church
   ... by discovering my gifts and talents
   ... by being equipped to serve by my pastors
   ... by developing a servant's heart

"Serve one another with the particular gifts God has given each of you" (1 Peter 4:10 PHILLIPS).

"[God] gave ... some to be pastors and teachers, to prepare God's people for works of service, so that the body of Christ may be built up" (Eph. 4:11–12).

"Each of you should look not only to your own interests, but also to the interests of others. Your attitude should be the same as that of Christ Jesus: Who ... [took on] the very nature of a servant" (Phil. 2:3–4, 7).

4. I will support the testimony of my church
   ... by attending faithfully
   ... by living a godly life
   ... by giving regularly

"Let us not give up meeting together ... but let us encourage one another" (Heb. 10:25).

"Whatever happens, make sure that your everyday life is worthy of the gospel of Christ" (Phil. 1:27 PHILLIPS).

"Each one of you, on the first day of each week, should set aside a specific sum of money in proportion to what you have earned and use it for the offering" (1 Cor. 16:2 LB).

"A tenth of [all your] produce ... is the Lord's, and is holy" (Lev. 27:30 NCV).

welcomed and wanted once they've joined your church. They need to be recognized and affirmed and celebrated by your congregation. They need to feel *special*. As a small church you may be able to do this informally, but as your church grows you will need to create some initiation rituals that say publicly, "You are now one of us!"

Of course, baptism for a new believer is an event that obviously fits this category. Our monthly baptisms are always big celebrations, with lots of laughter, applause, and shouts of joy. We have a professional photographer take a picture of each person just before he or she is baptized. Later we present those baptized with a photograph of their baptism and a baptism certificate together in a beautiful leatherette binding that people are proud to display.

When Saddleback was much smaller, we used to rent the Mission Viejo Country Club every three months and hold a new members' banquet. Older members would pay for the meals of the new members. Each new member would be recognized and would give a two-minute testimony in front of all those in attendance. I never made it through hearing the touching stories of changed lives without crying.

For years, Kay and I would host an informal coffee in our home on the fourth Sunday night of each month. Called the "Pastor's Chat," it was simply an opportunity for new members and visitors from the previous month to meet us face-to-face and ask any questions they had. We'd place a sign-up sheet out on the patio before Sunday services and the first thirty to sign up would get to come. The chats would last from 7 to 10 P.M. This simple act of hospitality brought in hundreds of new members and established many relationships that Kay and I cherish today. Hospitality grows a healthy church.

There are many other ways you can make members feel special, such as sending cards on their birthdays, recognizing their first anniversaries as members, recognizing other special days (births, weddings, anniversaries, graduations, achievements) in your newsletter, featuring a testimony in each service, holding staff receptions, and returning a "We prayed for you" note in response to a prayer request. The point is this: People need more than a warm handshake at the end of a service to feel like they really belong.

Create Opportunities to Build Relationships

The importance of helping members develop friendships within your church cannot be overemphasized. Relationships are the glue that holds a church together. Friendships are the key to retaining members.

A friend told me of a survey he took in a church. When he asked, "Why did you join this church?" 93 percent of the members said, "I joined because of the pastor." He then asked, "What if the pastor leaves? Will you leave?" Ninety-three percent said, "No." When he asked why they wouldn't leave, the response was, "Because I have friends here!" Notice the shift in allegiance from pastor to other members. This is normal and healthy.

Lyle Schaller has done extensive research that shows the more friendships a person has in a congregation, the less likely he or she is to become inactive or leave. In contrast, I once read about a survey where they asked 400 church dropouts why they *left* their churches. Over 75 percent of the respondents said, "I didn't feel anyone cared whether I was there or not."

It is a myth that you must know everyone in the church in order to feel like a part of a church. The average church member knows sixty-seven people in the congregation, whether the church has 200 or 2,000 attending. A member does not have to know everyone in the church in order to feel like it's their church, but he or she does have to know *some* people.

While some relationships will spontaneously develop, the friendship factor in assimilation is too crucial to leave to chance.

You can't just *hope* members will make friends in the church. You must encourage it, plan for it, structure for it, and facilitate it.

Think relationally. Create as many opportunities as you can for people to meet and get to know each other. Since so many church meetings consist solely of lectures ("Sit still while I instill"), members may very well walk in and out of church for a year without developing any friendships. Try to include some kind of relational activity in every congregation meeting. It may be as simple as saying, "Turn around and introduce yourself to one person and find out something interesting about that person."

Although we've used all kinds of events to build relationships within our church family (supper clubs, sports, game nights, picnics, and so forth), our weekend retreats have been the most effective tool for cultivating new friendships. Consider this: The amount of time a person spends with other members at a single forty-eight-hour retreat is greater than the time they will spend together on Sundays over a year. If you are a church planter and you want to develop relationships quickly in your church, take everybody on a retreat.

Since most people have a hard time remembering names, especially in a larger church, use name tags as often as you can. Nothing is more embarrassing than not knowing the name of someone you've seen at church for years.

Encourage Every Member to Join a Small Group

One of the biggest fears members have about growth is how to maintain that "small church" feeling of fellowship as their church grows. The antidote to this fear is to develop small groups within your church. Affinity groups can provide the personal care and attention every member deserves, no matter how big the church becomes.

Develop a network of small groups built around different purposes, interests, age groups, geography, or anything else. To be honest, it really doesn't matter what rationale you use to start new groups—just keep starting them. It is unlikely that very many new members will join *existing* small groups. New members assimilate best into new groups. You can even start new groups right out of your membership class. New members have their "newness" in common.

One of the sayings I quote to our staff and lay leaders repeatedly is, "Our church must always be growing larger and smaller at the same time." By that I mean there must be a balance between the large group celebrations and the small-group cells. Both are important to the health of a church.

> The church must always be growing larger and smaller at the same time.

Large group celebrations give people the feeling that they are a part of something significant. They are impressive to unbelievers and encouraging to your members. But you can't share personal prayer requests in the crowd. Small affinity groups, on the other hand, are perfect for creating a sense of intimacy and close fellowship. It's there that everybody knows your name. When you are absent, people notice.

Because Saddleback existed for so many years without owning a building, we've had to rely heavily on small groups for adult education and fellowship. Even though we now own a seventy-four-acre campus, we will continue to use homes for our small-group meetings.

There are four benefits of using homes:

- They are infinitely expandable (homes are everywhere)
- They are unlimited geographically (you can minister to a wider area)
- They are demonstrations of good stewardship (you use buildings that other people pay for, releasing more money for ministry)

• They facilitate closer relationships (people are more relaxed in a home setting)

The larger your church grows, the more important small groups become for handling the pastoral care functions. They provide the personal touch that everyone needs, especially in a crisis. At Saddleback we like to say that the whole church is like a large ship, and the small groups are the lifeboats.

I don't have the space to give a detailed explanation of our small-group strategy and structure so let me just say this: *Small groups are the most effective way of closing the back door of your church*. We never worry about losing people who are connected to a small group. We know that those people have been effectively assimilated.

Keep Communication Lines Open

It is vital that clear lines of communication are established within your church. People tend to be down on what they aren't up on. Informed members are effective members, whereas uninformed members, regardless of talent, can't do much. Build redundancy into your communication system by developing several channels for disseminating congregational information.

At Saddleback, we use anything we can to communicate important messages out to the congregation: fax machines, voice mail, video, newsletters, cassette tapes, prayer chains, CARE callers, newspaper articles, postcards—even the Internet! (For those of you on-line, you can peek in at http://www.saddleback.com for our Home Page.)

Just as important as staff-to-congregation communication is congregation-to-staff communication. It must flow both ways. Proverbs 27:23 says, "Be sure you know the condition of your flocks, give careful attention to your herds." The most important flock is God's flock, so we pay special attention to what is happening with it. We use welcome cards, CARE callers, and Lay Pastor Reports to monitor the heartbeat of our church family:

The Welcome Card. I've already discussed how we use this in our seeker service. It is an incredible communication tool, considering its simplicity. Anybody can write me a note at any time. Because our members know that we read these cards and take them seriously, we have a continuous flow of information coming in. It requires two full-time secretaries and a staff of a dozen volunteers to process all the cards we get, but it allows our pastors and staff to stay "close to the customer."

CARE Callers. CARE stands for "Contact, Assist, Relate, and Encourage." This lay ministry calls through the church directory on a systematic basis to find out what's happening in the lives of our members. They make their calls in the evenings and ask three questions: (1) How are you doing? (2) Do you have any prayer requests? (3) Is there anything you'd like for us to report to Pastor Rick or a staff member? Each CARE caller takes notes on a form to insure accurate information is recorded. Then they update the people they've called on any coming events or church news. It's just another way of keeping in touch with our members and saying "we care."

Lay Pastor Reports. These are written reports we get back from the lay pastors who lead our small groups. The reports give us feedback on the health of the group and what is happening in individual lives.

We're in This Together

In concluding this chapter on membership I want to stress the importance of *continually* emphasizing the corporate nature of the Christian life to your members. Preach it, teach it, and talk about it with individuals. We belong together. We need each other. We are connected, joined together as parts of one body. We are a family!

Almost daily, I receive letters from people who have joined our church and who have experienced the healing power of *koinonia*. I close with a recent example:

Dear Pastor Rick,

I have carried the pain of physical abuse in silence for many years. A year ago, after a devastating loss, I moved here to southern California. Disconnected from everything, I was very lonely. I cried solid for three weeks.

I finally decided that maybe I should try a church. From the moment I stepped inside my first service at Saddleback, I felt I *belonged* here.

To shorten my story, Christ became real to me, I joined our church, and am now serving in a ministry that is *very* fulfilling to me. I love being a part here!

I know everyone's pain is different, but we all need God. My pain was almost unbearable without a church family. When I took the membership class I had to hold back tears of joy when you discussed how Saddleback is a family. It really is! I am so grateful for my brothers and sisters here and for a church that I can call *home*!

18

Developing Mature Members

*...building up the church, the body of Christ,
to a position of strength and maturity.*

Ephesians 4:12 (LB)

*Our greatest wish and prayer is that you will
become mature Christians.*

2 Corinthians 13:9 (LB)

The New Testament is very clear that God's will for every believer is spiritual maturity. He wants us to grow up. Paul said in Ephesians 4:14 (PHILLIPS), "We are not meant to remain as children at the mercy of every chance wind of teaching. . . . But we are meant to speak the truth in love, and to grow up in every way into Christ, the head."

The ultimate goal of spiritual growth is to become like Jesus. God's plan for us since the beginning has been for us to be like his Son. "For those God foreknew he also predestined to be conformed to the likeness of his Son, that he might be the firstborn among many brothers" (Rom. 8:29). God wants every believer to develop the character of Christ.

The big question, then, is: How does spiritual growth happen? How do we become mature in Christ?

Myths About Spiritual Maturity

Before I share the Saddleback's strategy for developing believers to maturity, I want to dispel some popular misconceptions about spiritual growth and maturity. It is important for any strategy to be based on accurate information.

Maturity Myth #1: Spiritual growth is automatic once you are born again

Many churches have no organized plan for following up on new believers and no comprehensive strategy for developing members to maturity. They leave it all to chance, assuming that Christians will automatically grow to maturity if they attend church services. They think all they need to do is encourage people to show up at meetings and the job will get done.

Obviously, this isn't true. Spiritual growth does not just happen once you are saved, even if you attend services regularly. Churches are filled with people who have attended services for their entire lives, yet are still spiritual babies. An assimilated member is not the same as a mature member. On our Life Development Process diagram, the task of equipping people with the habits necessary for spiritual maturity is called "getting people to second base."

> We become whatever we are committed to.

Spiritual growth is not automatic with the passing of time, either. The writer of Hebrews sadly noted, "... though by this time you ought to be teachers, you need someone to teach you the elementary truths of God's word all over again" (Heb. 5:12). Millions of Christians have grown older without ever growing up.

The truth is this: Spiritual growth is intentional. It requires commitment and effort to grow. A person must want to grow, decide to grow, and make an effort to grow. Discipleship begins with a decision—it doesn't have to be a complex decision, but it does have to be sincere. The disciples certainly didn't understand all of the implications of their decision when they decided to follow Christ; they simply expressed a desire to follow him. Jesus took that simple but sincere decision and built on it.

Philippians 2:12–13 says, "Continue to work out your salvation with fear and trembling, for it is God who works in you to will and to act according to his good purpose." Notice that it says "work out," not "work on," your salvation. There is nothing you can add to what Christ did for your salvation. Paul is talking in these verses about spiritual growth to people who are already saved. The important thing is that God has a part in our growth, but so do we.

Becoming like Christ is the result of the commitments we make. We become whatever we are committed to! Just as a commitment to the Great Commandment and the Great Commission will grow a great church, it is also the way to grow a great Christian. Without a commitment to grow, any growth that occurs will be circumstantial, rather than intentional. Spiritual growth is too important to be left to circumstance.

Spiritual growth that leads to maturity begins with the kind of commitment described in Romans 6:13 (LB): "Give yourselves completely to God—every part of you—for you are back from death and you want to be tools in the hands of God, to be used for his good purposes." Later, I'll explain how to lead people to make this kind of commitment.

Maturity Myth #2: Spiritual growth is mystical, and maturity is attainable by only a select few

Mention the term "spirituality" today and many people conjure up an image of someone in a white robe, sitting in a yoga position, burning incense, and chanting *"ommmmm"* with his or her eyes closed. Others think of Christian mystics and monks who cloister themselves away from the real world, subjecting themselves to the rigors of poverty, chastity, and solitude.

Unfortunately, many Christians feel that spiritual maturity is so far out of their reach, they don't even try to attain it. They have this mystical, idealized image of what a mature Christian looks like. Maturity, they believe, is only for "super saints." Some Christian biographies have been partly responsible for this myth by glossing over the humanity of godly people and implying that if you don't pray ten hours a day, move to a jungle, and plan to die as a martyr you may as well forget aspiring to maturity. This is quite discouraging to the average believer, who feels he must be content with being a "second-class" Christian.

The truth is this: Spiritual growth is very practical. Any believer can grow to maturity if he or she will develop the habits necessary for spiritual growth. We need to take the mystery out of spiritual growth by breaking the components down into practical, everyday habits.

Paul often compared training for the Christian life to the way athletes stay in shape. I love the Phillips paraphrase of 1 Timothy 4:7: "Take time and trouble to keep yourself spiritually fit." The path to spiritual fitness is as practical as the path to physical fitness.

Anyone can become physically fit if he or she will regularly do certain exercises and practice good health habits. Likewise, spiritual fitness is simply a matter of learning certain *spiritual* exercises and being disciplined to do them until they become habits. Character is shaped by the habits we develop.

> **Character is shaped by the habits we develop.**

At Saddleback, we place a great deal of emphasis on developing spiritual habits. We have seen incredible growth occur in people when we break down the idea of spiritual growth into practical action steps and everyday habits.

Maturity Myth #3: Spiritual maturity can occur instantly if you find the right "key"

This is a popular misconception. It is obvious from the titles of some best-selling Christian books that many Christians at least *hope* this is true. Books that promise "four easy steps to maturity" or "the key to instant sainthood" reinforce the myth that Christian character can be acquired overnight.

> Believers grow faster when you provide a track to grow on.

Many sincere Christians spend their entire lives earnestly searching for an experience, a conference, a revival, a book, a tape, or a single truth that will *instantly* transform them into a mature believer. Their search is futile. Although we have instant coffee, instant potatoes, and now even instant weight-loss methods, there is no such thing as instant spiritual maturity.

The truth is this: Spiritual growth is a process that takes time. Just as God allowed Joshua and the Israelites to possess the land "little by little" (Deut. 7:22), he uses a gradual process of change to develop us into the image of Christ. There are no shortcuts to maturity. It is a slow process. Ephesians 4:13 (PHILLIPS) says, " . . . we *arrive* at real maturity—that measure of development which is meant by 'the fullness of Christ' " (italics added). Saying that maturity is a destination at which we *arrive* implies a journey. Despite our wish to speed up the process, spiritual growth is a journey that will last a lifetime.

I have spent a great deal of time trying to understand the components of this process and find a way to communicate them in a simple way that our members can grasp and remember. It is my conviction that believers grow faster when you provide a track to grow on. The result is Saddleback's philosophy of edification, which we call the Life Development Process.

The Life Development Process uses the baseball diamond as an analogy for growth because it is universally understood in America. It is easy for people to understand how we want them to mature when they see a milestone of spiritual growth assigned to each base. We explain to our members that our goal is to help them move around the bases of life. We want Saddleback Sam to *score!*

As I stated in chapter 8, you don't get credit for runners left on base at the end of the inning! For that reason, we have assigned a staff pastor to each of the bases: membership, maturity, ministry, and missions. Each pastor serves as a "base coach," — someone who helps the runners make it safely to the next base.

If you convince people of the importance of scoring and give them a coach at each base, it's much easier to get people to home plate. Likewise, if you lead people to commit to growing spiritually, teach them some basic habits, and give them guidance as they progress around the bases, you can expect to see them grow.

Maturity Myth #4: Spiritual maturity is measured by what you know

Many churches evaluate spiritual maturity solely on the basis of how well you can identify Bible characters, interpret Bible passages, quote Bible verses, and explain biblical theology. The ability to debate doctrine is considered by some as the ultimate proof of spirituality. However, while knowledge of the Bible is foundational to spiritual maturity, it isn't the total measurement of it.

The truth is this: Spiritual maturity is demonstrated more by behavior than by beliefs. The Christian life isn't just a matter of creeds and convictions; it includes conduct and character. Beliefs must be backed up with behavior. Our deeds must be consistent with our creeds.

The New Testament repeatedly teaches that our actions and attitudes reveal our maturity more than our affirmations. James 2:18 puts it bluntly: "Show me your faith without deeds, and I will show you my faith *by what I do*" (italics added). James also said, "Who among you is wise and understanding? Let him show by his good behavior" (James 3:13 NASB). If your faith hasn't changed your lifestyle, your faith isn't worth much.

> Maturity is demonstrated more by *behavior* than by beliefs.

Paul believed in connecting belief and behavior. In every one of his letters, he drives home the importance of practicing what we believe. Ephesians 5:8 (LB) says, "Though once your heart was full of darkness, now it is full of light from the Lord, and *your behavior should show it!*" (italics added).

Jesus said it most succinctly of all: "By their fruit you will recognize them" (Matt. 7:16). It is fruit, not knowledge, that demonstrates a person's maturity. If we don't put into practice what we know, we foolishly "build a house on sand" (see Matt. 7:24–27).

As I mentioned earlier, biblical knowledge is just one measurement of spiritual growth. In addition, we can measure maturity through perspective, conviction, skills, and character. These "Five Levels of Learning" are the building blocks of spiritual growth we use at Saddleback. In the next section I'll share how we seek to develop disciples that are strong in all five areas.

One real danger of having knowledge without the other four components is that it produces pride. First Corinthians 8:1 says, "Knowledge puffs up, but love builds up." Knowledge needs to be tempered by character. Some of the most carnal Christians I've known were a veritable storehouse of biblical knowledge. They could explain any passage and defend any doctrine, yet were unloving, self-righteous, and judgmental. It is impossible to have spiritual maturity and pride at the same time.

Five Levels of Learning
(Measurements of maturity)

Knowledge
Perspective
Conviction
Skills
Character

Another danger of having knowledge is that it increases responsibility. "Anyone, then, who knows the good he ought to do and doesn't do it, sins" (James 4:17). With a deeper knowledge of the Word comes a stronger judgment if we fail to apply it. That is why we must have the conviction and character to practice what we know. Any strategy your church develops to build up believers must help people not only learn the Word, but also love it and live it.

Maturity Myth #5: Spiritual growth is a personal and private matter

The idolatry of individualism in American culture has influenced even the way we think about spiritual growth. Most spiritual formation teaching tends to be self-centered and self-focused without any reference to our relationship to other Christians. This is completely unbiblical and ignores much of the New Testament.

The truth is this: Christians need relationships to grow. We don't grow in isolation from others; we develop in the context of fellowship. We find this over and over again in the New Testament. Hebrews 10:24–25 says, "Let us consider how we may spur one another on toward love and good deeds. Let us not give up meeting together, as some are in the habit of doing, but let us encourage one another." God intends for us to grow up in a family.

In the last chapter I pointed out that relationships are the "glue" that keeps people connected to your church. But relationships play an even more important role in moving people to maturity; they are absolutely essential for spiritual growth. The Bible teaches that fellowship is not optional for a Christian; it is mandatory. Christians that are not connected in loving relationships with other believers are disobeying the "one another" commands given in God's Word.

John tells us that the proof that we are walking in the light is that we have "fellowship with one another" (1 John 1:7). If you're not having regular fellowship with other believers you should seriously question whether or not you are really walking in the light.

John further suggests that we ought to question whether we really are saved if we don't love other believers. "We know that we have passed from death to life, because we love our brothers. Anyone who does not love remains in death" (1 John 3:14). If relationships with other believers are this important, why don't churches put more emphasis on them?

The quality of your relationship to Christ can be seen in the quality of your relationship to other believers. "For anyone who does not love his brother, whom he

> Christians need relationships to grow. We don't grow in isolation; we develop in the context of fellowship.

has seen, cannot love God, whom he has not seen" (1 John 4:20). Notice that John says "cannot." It is impossible to love God if you don't love his children.

Jesus also taught that if you are out of fellowship with a brother, your worship is worthless (see Matt. 5:23–24). A Christian cannot be in fellowship with God and out of fellowship with believers at the same time.

One reason many Christians never witness is because they don't know how to relate to people. Because they've never been in a small group or developed friendships, they have few relational skills. They can't relate to unbelievers because they can't even relate to *believers*. People must be taught how to develop relationships. Although this seems obvious, very few churches take time to teach their members how to relate to each other.

Maturity Myth #6: All you need is Bible study to grow

Many evangelical churches have been built on this myth. I call them "classroom churches." Classroom churches tend to be left-brain oriented and cognitive focused. They stress the teaching of Bible content and doctrine, but give little, if any, emphasis to believers' emotional, experiential, and relational development. All you need to be spiritually mature, says one well-known classroom church, is to have "doctrine in your frontal lobe."

The truth is this: It takes a variety of spiritual experiences with God to produce spiritual maturity. Genuine spiritual maturity includes having a heart that worships and praises God, building and enjoying loving relationships, using your gifts and talents in service to others, and sharing your faith with lost people. Any church strategy to bring people to maturity must include *all* of these experiences: worship, fellowship, Bible study, evangelism, and ministry. In other words, spiritual growth occurs by participating in all five purposes of the church. Mature

Christians do more than study the Christian life—they *experience* it.

Because some Christians have made the mistake of overemphasizing emotional experiences to the neglect of sound biblical doctrine, many evangelical churches have downplayed the role of experience in spiritual growth. They have overreacted to other groups' glorification of experience by removing *any* emphasis on experience and viewing every experience with suspicion, especially if it moves the emotions.

> **Spiritual growth occurs by participating in all five purposes of the church.**

Sadly, this denies the fact that God created human beings with emotions in addition to minds. God has given us feelings for a purpose. By removing all experience from the Christian-growth process, you are left with nothing but a sterile, intellectual creed that can be studied but not enjoyed or practiced.

Deuteronomy 11:2 (TEV) says, "Remember today what you have learned about the LORD *through your experiences with him*" (italics added). Experience is a great teacher. In fact, there are some lessons we can learn *only* by experience. I love the paraphrase of Proverbs 20:30 (TEV): "Sometimes it takes a painful experience to make us change our ways."

I once heard the well-known Bible teacher Gene Getz say, "Bible study *by itself* will not produce spirituality. In fact, it will produce carnality if it isn't applied and practiced." I have found this to be true. Study *without service* produces Christians with judgmental attitudes and spiritual pride.

If Christianity was a philosophy, then our primary activity might be studying. But Christianity is a relationship and a life. The words used most often to describe the Christian life are *love, give, believe,* and *serve.* Jesus did not say, "I have come that you might *study*." In fact, the word "study" appears only a couple of times in the New Testament. But if you look at the weekly schedule of many churches, you'd get the impression that attending studies is a Christian's sole duty.

The *last* thing many believers need is to go to another Bible study. They already know far more than they are putting into practice. What they need are ministry and evangelism experiences where they can *apply* what they already know, relational experiences (like a small group) where they can be *held accountable* for what they know, and meaningful worship experiences where they can *express* appreciation to God for what they know.

James had to warn the first Christians: "Do not deceive yourselves by just listening to his word; instead, put it into practice" (James 1:22 TEV). There is the old illustration of a pond that becomes stagnant because it takes in water but doesn't give any out. When any Christian's schedule consists completely of receiving biblical input with no outflow of ministry or evangelism, his or her spiritual growth will stagnate. Impression without expression leads to depression.

Churches do their members a great disservice by keeping people so busy going to the next Bible study that they don't have time to apply what they learned at the last one they attended. People file away and forget lessons before they can be internalized and put into practice, all the while thinking they are growing because their notebooks are getting fatter. This is foolishness.

Please don't think that I don't value Bible study. Actually, the opposite is true. I wrote a textbook on methods of Bible study, *Dynamic Bible Study Methods*. We must "continue in the Word" in order to be Christ's disciples. All I'm saying is that it is a mistake to assume that study *alone* will produce maturity. It is only one component of the maturity process. People need experiences in addition to study in order to grow. Churches must have a *balanced* strategy for developing disciples.

Designing Your Strategy

Saddleback's strategy for developing disciples is based on the six truths I identified in contrast to each myth. We believe that spiritual growth begins with commitment, is a gradual process, involves developing habits, is measured by five factors, is stimulated by relationships, and requires participation in all five purposes of the church.

Raise the level of commitment

I've always loved Elton Trueblood's name for the church: "The Company of the Committed." It would be wonderful if every church was known for the commitment of its members. Unfortunately, churches are often held together by *committees* rather than by commitment.

One of the ways to assess whether or not your church is maturing spiritually is if the standards for leadership keep getting tougher as time passes, requiring a deeper level of commitment to Christ and spiritual growth. For instance, when Saddleback first began, our only requirement for serving in children's Sunday school was that you had to be a warm body. Over the years, we've tightened the requirements considerably! We have done the same thing with our lay pastors, our musicians, and other ministry positions.

Each time you raise the standards for leadership, you bring everyone else in the church along a little bit. As the phrase goes, "a rising tide raises all the boats in the harbor." Focus on raising the commitment of your leadership, not those who are the least committed in your crowd, nor even the semicommitted in your congregation. You will find that whenever you raise the standard of commitment for those who are in the most visible positions of leadership, it raises the expectations for everyone else.

How do you get people to commit to a process of spiritual growth?

You must ask people for commitment. If you don't ask people for commitment, you won't get it. And, if you don't ask your members for commitment, you can be certain that other groups *will* ask for it: civic groups, service clubs, political parties, or parachurch ministries. The question isn't whether or not people are going to be committed, but rather *who* is going to get their commitment. If your church doesn't ask for and expect commitment from people, those people will conclude that what the church is doing is not as important as their other activities.

> The question isn't whether or not people are going to be committed, but rather *who* is going to get their commitment.

It's amazing to me that many community organizations require more from participants than local churches do. If you've ever been a Little League parent, you know that when your child signed up to play, *you* were required to make a major commitment in terms of providing refreshments, transportation, trophies, and victory parties in addition to your attendance. There was nothing *voluntary* about your participation!

One of the most helpful things a church can do for people is to assist them in clarifying what commitments to make and what commitments to decline. The reason we have so many weak Christians is because they are half-committed to many causes rather than being totally committed to the things that matter most. A barrier to spiritual growth for many people is not lack of commitment, but over-commitment to the wrong things. People must be taught to make wise commitments.

Ask confidently for a big commitment. Jesus always asked for commitment clearly and confidently. He was not at all reluctant to ask men and women to drop everything and follow him. It is an interesting phenomenon that, often, the greater the commitment you request, the greater response you will get.

People *want* to be committed to something that gives significance to their lives. They respond to responsibilities that give life meaning and are attracted by a challenging vision. In contrast, people are often unmoved by weak appeals and pitiful requests for help. Jesus knew this when he said in Luke 14:33, "Any of you who does not give up everything he has cannot be my disciple." He was demanding total commitment.

One Sunday, at the close of a message, I gave out a special Life Commitment card that asked people to commit their *entire* lives to Jesus Christ: their time, money, ambitions, habits, relationships, career, home, and energy. The amazing thing to me was not that we got back thousands of cards, but that 177 of those cards were signed by people who had never filled out a regular registration card although they indicated they'd been coming for years! They just had never felt it was worth their time to fill out the weekly registration card. Sometimes it's easier to elicit a big commitment than a small one.

Some pastors are afraid to ask for a big commitment, fearing that they will drive people away. But people do not resent being asked for a great commitment if there is

> People do not resent being asked for a great commitment if there is a great purpose behind it.

a great purpose behind it. An important distinction to remember is that people respond to passionate vision, not need. That's why many stewardship campaigns don't work: They focus on the needs of the church rather than the vision of the church.

Be specific in asking for commitment. Another key to developing commitment is to be specific. Tell people exactly what is expected of them. At Saddleback, instead of saying, "Be committed to Christ," we explain specifically what that involves. We ask people to commit to Christ, then to baptism, then to membership, then to the habits for maturity, then to ministry, and finally to fulfilling their life mission. As I explained earlier, we have developed four covenants that spell out exactly what each of these commitments includes.

Explain the benefits of commitment. Another key to developing commitment in people is to identify its benefits. God does this time and time again in the Bible. So many of the commands in Scripture have wonderful promises attached to them. We always end up being blessed whenever we're obedient.

Be sure to explain the personal benefits, the family benefits, the benefits to the body of Christ and society in general, and the *eternal* benefits of committing to spiritual growth. People really do have an innate desire to learn, to grow, and to improve, but sometimes you must awaken that desire by stating your learning goals and growth objectives in terms of their value and benefit.

I'm fascinated sometimes by the way advertisers make such commonplace products such as deodorant, detergent, and dishwasher soap sound as if they will give your life new meaning, energy, and joy. Advertisers are masters at packaging. How ironic that the church has the *real* secret to meaning, significance, and satisfaction in life, but we often present it in such a bland, unattractive way. Compare the quality of a church ad with an advertisement for something else and you'll see the difference right away.

At the beginning of Classes 101, 201, 301, and 401, we state the values and benefits to the participants by saying, "Here's what this class will do for you." We also clearly explain the benefits of committing to each of the four covenants.

Build on *commitment rather than* toward *commitment.* Even though you tell people where you are taking them (by challenging them with a big commitment), it is important to start with whatever commitment they are able to give, regardless of how weak it may seem.

We challenge people to make a commitment and then grow into it. It's like choosing to become a parent. Very few couples feel competent to parent before they have their first child. But somehow, after the decision is made and a baby is born, the couple grows into their parenting role.

It is also okay to break big commitments into smaller steps and lead people gradually along. As you've already seen, that's the idea behind our Life Development Process (the baseball diamond). We don't expect people to grow from being new believers to the commitment level of Billy Graham or Mother Teresa overnight—we let them take baby steps. By using the baseball diamond as a visual illustration of spiritual progress, people can see how far they've come and how far they have to go.

It's important to celebrate each time someone commits to moving forward to the next base. The ability to make and keep commitments is a sign of maturity that people deserve to be recognized and rewarded for. Create celebration events, like rites of passage, where you can publicly acknowledge that growth. We hold a party at the end of each year where we congratulate all who have signed the maturity covenant and have renewed their commitments for another year.

Celebration events give people a sense of accomplishment and motivate them to keep making progress. A man once commented to me, "I've attended a Sunday school class for over thirty years. Do I ever get to graduate?" At celebration events, allow people to share testimonies of how their increased commitment has blessed their lives.

I've read a number of articles and books that state that the baby boomer and baby buster generations will not commit to anything. This simply isn't true! What they *do* expect is to receive value equal to their commitment. They are more particular in their commitments because there are so many more options available now. Baby boomers and baby busters are desperately seeking something worth committing their lives to.

Help people develop spiritual growth habits

The most practical and powerful way to get believers headed in the direction of spiritual maturity is to help them establish habits that promote spiritual growth. Often called *spiritual disciplines*, we use the term *habits* because it is less threatening to new believers. While we teach that being a disciple certainly requires discipline, we believe these habits are to be *enjoyed* rather than endured. We don't want people to be afraid of spiritual exercises that will strengthen and develop them.

Dostoyevski once said, "The second half of a man's life is made up of the habits he acquired during the first half." And Pascal said, "The strength of a man's virtue . . . is measured by his habitual acts." Human beings are creatures of habit. If we don't develop good habits, we will develop bad ones.

> You cannot talk about character without talking about habits.

There are dozens of good habits we need to develop as we grow to spiritual maturity. In designing Class 201, I spent a lot of time thinking about the foundational habits that must be learned first in order to grow. What are the minimum requirements? What are the core habits that give birth to all the others? As I studied, I kept coming back to habits that influence our time, our money, and our relationships. If Christ's lordship is recognized over these three areas of life, then he will truly be in control.

Class 201, "Discovering Spiritual Maturity," focuses on how to establish four basic habits of a disciple: the habit of time with God's Word, the habit of prayer, the habit of tithing, and the habit of fellowship. These are based on statements made by Jesus that define discipleship: a disciple follows God's Word (see John 8:31–32); a disciple prays and bears fruit (see John 15:7–8); a disciple is not possessed by his possessions (see Luke 14:33); and a disciple expresses love for other believers (see John 13:34–35).

After teaching the what, why, when, and how of these four habits, the class covers the practical steps to starting and maintaining other habits. In Nehemiah 9:38, the entire nation made a spiritual covenant together, put it in writing, and then asked their leaders to sign it as witnesses. At the end of Class 201, we close with everyone signing a maturity covenant. The signed covenant cards are collected, I sign them as a witness, we laminate them, and then they are returned so people can carry them in their wallets. Every year we renew our commitments and issue new cards. We've found that an annual recommitment emphasis helps people who got discouraged or quit the habits to make a fresh start.

Do people come out of Class 201 as mature Christians? Of course not. That's why it's called *Discovering* Spiritual Maturity." The purpose is to get people started on the journey. They leave committed to the process and to the basic habits that are necessary for growth. Although they will struggle along the way, people leave the class permanently changed. It is always a very moving moment when the people in each class commit their time, money, and relationships to Christ. Their faces are full of hope and expectation that they will grow—and they do!

My 1992 Growth Covenant

☐ A Daily Time With God
Mark 1:35

☐ A Weekly Tithe To God
1 Corinthians 16:2

☐ A Committed Team For God
Hebrews 10:25

Personal Bible
reading
and prayer

Giving the
first 10%
of my income

Fellowship with
Believers in a
small group

Signature ·   Pastor

Take the time and trouble to keep yourself spiritually fit. Bodily fitness has a limited value, but spiritual fitness is of unlimited value, for it holds promise both for this present life and for the life to come.

1 Tim. 4:7 (ph)

Name: (print)_____

Address:_____

_____

Build a Balanced Christian Education Program

I mentioned earlier that I believe there are five measurements of spiritual growth: knowledge, perspective, conviction, skills, and character. These five levels of learning are the building blocks of spiritual maturity.

At Saddleback, our Christian education program is built around these levels of learning. There is not space to tell about all of the different training courses offered through our Life Development Institute, but I do want to explain how we've developed a key program to facilitate each level of learning.

Knowledge of the Word. To begin building a spiritual growth curriculum you need to ask two questions: "What do people already know?" and "What do they need to know?" A church that has grown primarily by biological growth (conversion of members' children) or transfer growth may have many members who already have a working knowledge of the Bible. But that is not the case in a church designed to reach the unchurched. You cannot assume your new members know *anything* about the Bible. You must start from ground zero.

At a recent monthly baptism, we baptized sixty-three new believers including a former Buddhist, a former Mormon, a man with a Jewish background, and a former Catholic nun. When you add in ex-New Agers and plain old pagans, you have quite a mixture to deal with. Biblical illiteracy is almost universal among unbelievers. They do not even recognize the most well-known stories or personalities of the Bible.

Tom Holladay, our pastor who leads the Maturity team, told me of a recent conversation he had with a brand-new believer who was struggling with trials in his life. Tom opened his Bible to James 1 and explained the purpose of trials. The man seemed satisfied. As he started to leave Tom's office he said, "I thought maybe my trials were a result of some sins from a previous life." Tom realized the man needed more than an explanation of trials; he needed to understand the biblical view of life.

At the knowledge level, your church needs to regularly offer "new believer" Bible studies and surveys of the Old Testament and New Testament. We once took twenty-seven Wednesday nights to cover each of the twenty-seven New Testament books. There are a number of excellent Bible survey curricula available, including the well-known Walk Thru the Bible seminars.

Saddleback's largest program to develop knowledge of the Word is a nine-month inductive Bible study course, written and taught by our lay teachers. It is called the WORD study.

WORD is an acronym for the four activities of this Bible study: *Wonder* about it (ask questions about the text), *Observe* it, *Reflect* on it, and *Do* it! It is based on the methods described in my book *Dynamic Bible Study Methods*. Each session includes homework assignments for self-discovery, lectures, and break-out small groups for discussion of the homework. The course begins in September each year and ends the following June. WORD for Women is offered twice a week, and WORD for Men is offered once a week.

While every book of the Bible is important, at Saddleback we want our members to study five "core" books before they branch out into other studies. These books are Genesis, John, Romans, Ephesians, and James.

Perspective. Perspective is understanding something because you are seeing it from a larger frame of reference. It is the ability to perceive how things are interrelated and then judge their comparative importance. In a spiritual sense, it means seeing life from God's point of view. In the Bible, the words *understanding, wisdom,* and *discernment* all have to do with perspective. The opposite of perspective is *hardness of heart, blindness,* and *dullness.*

> ## Perspective answers the "why" questions of life.

Psalm 103:7 says, "[God] made known his *ways* to Moses, his *deeds* to the people of Israel" (italics added). The people of Israel got to see *what* God did, but Moses got to understand *why* God did it. This is the difference between knowledge and perspective. Knowledge is learning what God has said and done. Perspective is understanding why God said it or did it. It answers the "why" questions of life.

The Bible teaches that unbelievers have no spiritual perspective, and that a lack of perspective is evidence of spiritual immaturity. God's recurring complaint about the nation of Israel was that they lacked perspective, and many of the prophets rebuked the people for this weakness. In contrast, having perspective is a characteristic of spiritual maturity. Hebrews 5:14 (NASB) says, "Solid food is for the mature, who because of practice have their *senses trained to discern good and evil*" (italics added). There are many benefits of learning to see everything from God's perspective, but I'll only mention four of them.

First, *perspective causes us to love God more.* The better we understand the nature and ways of God, the more we love him. Paul prayed, "May you be able to feel and understand, as all God's children should, how long, how wide, how deep, and how high his love really is" (Eph. 3:18 LB).

Second, *perspective helps us resist temptation.* When we look at a situation from God's viewpoint, we realize that the long-term consequences of sin are greater than any short-term pleasure sin might provide. Without perspective we follow our own natural inclinations. "There is a way that *seems* right to a man, but in the end it leads to death" (Prov. 14:12, italics added).

Third, *perspective helps us handle trials.* When we have God's perspective on life we realize that ". . . in all things God works for the good of those who love him" (Rom. 8:28) and that "the testing of your faith develops perseverance" (James 1:3). Perspective was one of the reasons Jesus was able to endure the cross (see Heb. 12:2). He looked past the pain to the joy that was set before him.

Fourth, *perspective protects us from error.* If there was ever a time Christians needed to be grounded in the truth, it is today. We live in a society that rejects absolute truth and accepts each opinion as equally valid. Pluralism has created a very confused culture. The problem is not that our culture believes nothing, but that it believes *everything.* Syncretism, not skepticism, is our greatest enemy.

Life Perspectives I

Doctrine	Primary Perspective
God	God is bigger and better than I can imagine.
Jesus	Jesus is God showing himself to us.
Holy Spirit	God lives in and through me now.
Revelation	The Bible is God's inerrant guidebook for life.
Creation	Nothing "just happened." God created it all.
Salvation	Grace is the only way to have a relationship with God.
Sanctification	God's will is for us to grow in Christlikeness.
Good and Evil	God has allowed evil to provide a choice. God can bring good even out of evil events.
The Afterlife	Death is not the end but the beginning. Heaven and hell are real places.
The Church	The only true world "superpower" is the church. It will last forever.
Prayer	Prayer can do anything God can do.
Second Coming	Jesus is coming again to judge the world and gather his children.

What is desperately needed today are pastors and teachers who will clearly teach God's perspective—about work, money, pleasure, suffering, good, evil, relationships, and all the other key issues of life. When we have perspective, "we will no longer be like children, forever changing our minds about what we believe because someone has told us something different, or has cleverly lied to us and made the lie sound like the truth" (Eph. 4:14 LB). Perspective is what produces stability in people's lives.

Saddleback's program to teach perspective is called "Life Perspectives." It is essentially a systematic theology course that was written by my wife, Kay, and our Pastor of Spiritual Maturity, Tom Holladay. "Life Perspectives" covers twelve essential Christian doctrines and is taught twice a week for twenty-seven weeks by Kay and lay teachers in our church. The format is a combination of lectures and discussion groups.

> Knowing what to do (knowledge), why to do it (perspective), and how to do it (skill) is all worthless if you don't have the conviction to motivate you to do it!

Conviction. Dictionaries usually define conviction as "a fixed or strong belief," but it is really much more than that. Your convictions include your values, commitments, and motivations. I like the definition I once heard Howard Hendricks give: "A belief is something you will argue about. A *conviction* is something you will die for." Knowing *what* to do (knowledge), *why* to do it (perspective), and *how* to do it (skill) is all worthless if you don't have the conviction to motivate you to actually do it.

When you first become a Christian, you often do things simply because other Christians around you suggest them or model them. You may pray, read the Bible, and attend services because you are following the examples of others. This is fine for a new Christian—little children learn the same way. However, as you grow, you must eventually develop your own reasons for doing what you do. These reasons are *convictions.* Biblical convictions are essential for spiritual growth and maturity.

> Without convictions about growth, people become discouraged and give up.

One of the biggest hit songs of the 1980s was "Karma Chameleon" by Boy George. One key line said it all: "I'm a man without conviction." Sadly, there are many people whose values are blurred, whose priorities are jumbled, and whose commitments are diffused. James Gordon once said, "A man without conviction is as weak as a door hanging on one hinge."

A person without conviction is at the mercy of circumstances. If you don't determine what is important and how you'll live, other people will determine it for you. People without conviction often mindlessly follow the crowd. I believe Paul was talking about conviction when he said in Romans 12:2 (PHILLIPS), "Don't let the world squeeze you into its own mold, but let God remake you so that your whole attitude of mind is changed."

The church *must* teach biblical convictions in order to counter the secular values to which believers are constantly exposed. As the old cliché goes, "If you don't stand for something, you'll fall for anything." What is ironic is that people often have strong convictions about weak issues (football, fashions, etc.) while having weak convictions about major issues (what is right and what is wrong).

Conviction helps us be diligent in continuing to grow spiritually. Growth requires time and effort. Without conviction about growth, people become discouraged and give up. No one stays with a difficult task unless they are convinced there is a good reason for doing so. A church can teach people how to pray, how to study the Bible, and how to witness, but unless they impart the corresponding convictions, people will not stick with it.

The people who have made the greatest impact on this world, for good or evil, have not been necessarily the smartest, wealthiest, or best-educated people; they have been the people with the strongest, deepest convictions. Marx, Ghandi, Buddha, Columbus, and Luther are just a few of the people who changed the face of the world because of their convictions.

In 1943, 100,000 young people in brown shirts filled the Olympic stadium in Munich, Germany, the largest stadium in the world at that time. They formed with their bodies a sign for a fanatical man standing behind the podium. The message read, "Hitler, we are yours." Their commitment allowed them to conquer Europe. Years later, a group of young Chinese students committed to memorizing and living the philosophy of a little red book, *The Sayings of Chairman Mao.* The result was the Cultural Revolution that to this day keeps one billion people in the world's largest country under the slavery of communism. That is the power of conviction!

Jesus' life was dominated by his conviction that he was sent to do the Father's will. This conviction produced a deep awareness of his life's purpose that kept him from being distracted by the agenda of others. To gain insight into the convictions that he held, study all the times Jesus used the phrase "I must . . ." When people develop Christlike convictions, they too will develop a sense of purpose in life.

Conviction has an attractive quality to it, which explains the popularity of many cults. A cult's beliefs may be erroneous and often illogical, but they are believed with intense conviction. Churches without clear, strong convictions will never attract the level of commitment that Christ deserves. We must burn with the conviction that the kingdom of God is the greatest cause in the world. Vance Havner used to say, "Jesus demands greater allegiance than any dictator that ever lived. The difference is that Jesus has a *right* to it!"

At Saddleback, we teach biblical convictions in every program, class, seminar, and message but conviction is *caught* as much as it is taught. It spreads best through relationships. Conviction is contagious: People acquire it by being around other people who have it. This is a major reason we emphasize small groups as a part of our Life Development Process. Close association with people of conviction will often have a greater influence than merely listening to a message delivered with conviction.

Skills. Skill is the ability to do something with ease and accuracy. You develop a skill, not by listening to a lecture, but by practice and experience. In the Christian life there are certain skills you must develop in order to mature: Bible study skills, ministry skills, witnessing skills, relational skills, time management skills, and many others.

> Skills are the "how-to steps" of spiritual growth.

Skills are the "how-to steps" of spiritual growth. Knowledge and perspective are concerned with *knowing*. Conviction and character are concerned with *being*. Skills are related to *doing*. We are to be "doers of the word, not hearers only" (James 1:22 KJV). Our actions prove we belong to God's family. Jesus said, "My mother and brothers are those who hear God's word and *put it into practice*" (Luke 8:21, italics added).

Many believers are frustrated today because they know *what* to do but they've never been taught *how* to do it. They have heard numerous messages on the importance of studying their Bibles, but no one shows them how to do it. They are made to feel guilty for a weak prayer life, but no one takes the time to explain how to make a prayer list, how to praise God's character by using his names, or how to intercede for others. Exhortation without explanation leads to frustration. Whenever we exhort people to do something, we are responsible to explain exactly how to do it.

If you want your church to produce effective Christians, you *must* teach the necessary skills for Christian living and ministry. Skill is the secret of effectiveness. Remember the verse I shared in chapter 2: "If the ax is dull and its edge unsharpened, more strength is needed but *skill will bring success*" (Eccl. 10:10, italics added).

Saddleback's program for developing skills is called Life Skills Seminars. These seminars are usually four to eight hours in length and are normally taught in a single day. We've discovered that people usually find it easier to block out an extended period on time of one day instead of attending an hour a week over six weeks. Sometimes, however, we do stretch out a Life Skills Seminar over a period of weeks because there is too much content to cover in a single day.

Each Life Skills Seminar focuses on a single, specific skill, such as how to study the Bible, how to pray more effectively, how to handle temptation, how to make time for ministry, and how to get along with other people. We have identified nine basic skills that we believe every Christian needs, but we also offer seminars on other skills whenever we perceive a particular need in our church.

Character. Christlike character is the ultimate goal of all Christian education. To settle for anything less is to miss the point of spiritual growth. We are to ". . . become mature, attaining to the whole measure of the fullness of Christ" (Eph. 4:13).

Developing the character of Christ is life's most important task because it is the only thing we'll take with us into eternity. Jesus made it quite clear in his Sermon on the Mount that eternal rewards in heaven will be based on the character we develop and demonstrate here on earth.

> Character is *never* built in a classroom; it is built in the circumstances of life.

This means the objective of all our teaching must be to change lives, not to merely provide information. Paul told Timothy that the purpose of his teaching was to develop character in those he taught: "The goal of our instruction is love from a pure heart and a good conscience and a sincere faith" (1 Tim. 1:5 NASB). Paul told Titus to do the same thing: "Now you must tell them the sort of character which should spring from sound teaching" (Titus 2:1 PHILLIPS).

Character is never built in a classroom; it is built in the circumstances of life. The classroom Bible study is simply the place to *identify* character qualities and learn how character is developed. When we understand how God uses circumstances to develop character, we can respond correctly when God places us in character-building situations. Character development always involves a choice. When we make the right choice, our character grows more like Christ.

Whenever we choose to respond to a situation in God's way instead of following our natural inclination we develop character. I once wrote a book on the fruit of the Spirit called *The Power to Change Your Life* that explains this concept more fully.

If you want to know what *Christlike* character looks like, a good place to start is the list of nine character qualities Paul enumerates in Galatians 5:22–23: "The fruit of the Spirit is love, joy, peace, patience, kindness, goodness, faithfulness, gentleness and self-control." The fruit of the Spirit is a perfect picture of Christ; he embodied all nine qualities. If you are going to develop Christlike character, you must have these qualities in your life as well.

How does God produce the fruit of the Spirit in our lives? By putting us in the exact opposite circumstances so we have a choice to make! God teaches us how to really love by putting us around unlovable people. (It doesn't require any character to love people who have it all together.) He teaches us joy in times of sorrow. (Joy is internal. Happiness depends on what's happening, but joy is independent of circumstances.) He develops peace within us by placing us in the midst of chaos so we can learn to trust him. (It doesn't require character to be at peace when everything is going your way.)

God is far more concerned with our character than he is with our comfort. His plan is to perfect us, not to pamper us. For this reason he allows all kinds of character-building circumstances: conflict, disappointment, difficulty, temptation, times of dryness, and delays. A major responsibility of your church's Christian education program is to prepare your people with the knowledge, perspective, convictions, and skills needed to handle these situations. If you do, people will develop character.

A century ago, Samuel Smiles made this observation:

Sow a thought and you reap an act;
Sow an act and you reap a habit;
Sow a habit and you reap a character;
Sow a character and you reap a destiny.

There is a logical order to building knowledge, perspective, conviction, skills, and character. You must start with a foundation of knowledge. Since spiritual growth is based on God's Word, the first level of learning is to gain a working knowledge of the Bible. Perspective and convictions must be Bible based.

On top of knowledge of the Word, you add perspective. The better you know God's Word, the more you'll begin to see life from God's viewpoint. Conviction naturally grows out of perspective. Once you begin to see things from God's perspective, you begin developing biblical convictions. An understanding of God's purpose and plan changes your motivations.

Conviction then gives you the motivation to maintain spiritual habits. Eventually, through repetition, these habits become skills. You no longer have to consciously focus when you do them.

When you put knowledge of the Word, perspective, conviction, and the corresponding skills together, the resulting product is character! First you *know* it; then you *understand* it; then you *believe* it with your whole heart; then you *do* it. The result of these four is character.

Here are five questions you need to ask about your Christian education program:

- Are people learning the content and meaning of the Bible?
- Are people seeing themselves, life, and other people more clearly from God's perspective?
- Are people's values becoming more aligned with God's values?
- Are people becoming more skilled in serving God?
- Are people becoming more like Christ?

At Saddleback, these are the objectives we continually work toward. As Paul said in Colossians 1:28 (NCV): "So we continue to preach Christ to each person, using all wisdom to warn and to teach everyone, in order to bring each one into God's presence as a mature person in Christ."

Our vision for spiritual maturity is to bring glory to God by presenting Jesus Christ with as many Christlike disciples as we possibly can before he returns.

Saddleback's 2020 Vision for a Mature Church

We dream of 15,000 members who have committed themselves to the Maturity Covenant: Having a daily time with God, giving a weekly tithe to God, and participating in a weekly team (small group) for God.

We dream of a network of 1,000 small groups within our church providing support, encouragement, and accountability to our members as they seek to grow in Christlikeness. These groups will continue to be led by trained lay pastors and leaders who lovingly lead, feed, and care for those in their group.

We dream of our Life Development Institute for our members, offering a balanced program of Bible studies, classes, topical seminars, and annual conferences for building knowledge, perspective, conviction, skills, and character. We expect 7,500 members to receive the LDI basic diploma by 2020.

We dream of our midweek believers' service involving 5,000 adults, children, and youth who are not involved in a small-group fellowship.

We dream of a faculty of 250 gifted lay teachers, equipped with the vision, character, knowledge, and expertise to feed our flock. We dream of a teacher-training program that produces experts in individual Bible books, doctrine, apologetics, and Christian growth. We dream of the day that it can be said, "The best Bible teachers in the country are the lay teachers at Saddleback."

We dream of an age-appropriate Life Development Process that leads our children and youth to love Jesus and his church, grow spiritually, discover their shape for ministry, and understand their life mission in the world.

We dream of Saddleback as a model of Christian education that focuses on life change, not just comprehension. We intend to make available resources, tools, and training to thousands of other purpose-driven churches.

We dream of working with seminaries to establish a church-based training program for pastors. We intend to train leaders for the twenty-first century church in how to start, develop, and lead purpose-driven churches.

The goal of this vision is to bring glory to God by presenting Jesus Christ with as many Christlike disciples as we possibly can before he returns (see Col. 1:28)!

19

Turning Members into Ministers

We are God's workmanship, created in Christ Jesus to do good works, which God prepared in advance for us to do.

Ephesians 2:10

... to prepare God's people for works of service, so that the body of Christ may be built up.

Ephesians 4:12

Napoleon once pointed to a map of China and said, "There lies a sleeping giant. If it ever wakes up, it will be unstoppable." I believe the church is a sleeping giant. Each Sunday, church pews are filled with members who are doing nothing with their faith except "keeping" it.

The designation "active" member in most churches means those who attend regularly and financially support the church. Not much more is expected. But God has far greater expectations for every Christian. He expects every Christian to use his or her gifts and talents in ministry. If we can ever awaken and unleash the massive talent, resources, creativity, and energy lying dormant in the typical local church, Christianity will explode with growth at an unprecedented rate.

The greatest need in evangelical churches is the release of members for ministry. A Gallup survey discovered that only 10 percent of American church members are active in any kind of personal ministry and that 50 percent of all church members have no interest in serving in any ministry. Think about that! No matter how much a church promotes involvement in lay ministry, half of its members will remain spectators. These are the people who say, "I just don't feel *led* to get involved." (Actually, it's another kind of "lead"—in the seat of their pants!)

The encouraging news that Gallup uncovered is this: 40 percent of all members *have* expressed an interest in having a ministry, but they have never been asked or they don't know how. This group is an untapped gold mine! If we can mobilize this 40 percent and add them to the current 10 percent already serving, your church could have 50 percent of its members active in a ministry. Wouldn't you be happy if half of your church were fully functioning lay ministers? Most pastors would think they had died and gone to heaven if that occurred.

While large churches have many advantages over smaller churches, one thing I greatly dislike about them is that it is easy for talent to hide in the crowd. Unless they take the initiative to reveal their giftedness or expertise, talented members could be sitting in the crowd every week and you will have no idea what they are capable of doing. This worries and deeply disturbs me, because talent that sits on the shelf will rot from disuse. Like a muscle, if you don't use it, you'll lose it.

I was talking to some people on the patio after a service once and I mentioned that we really needed someone to create a multimedia videotape for an event. The person I was talking to said, "Why don't you get her?" and pointed to a woman standing a few feet away. I walked over to the woman, found out her name, and asked what she did. She replied, "I'm the chief video production director for Walt Disney." She had been attending for about a year.

Another time, I mentioned that we needed a flower designer to decorate our tent for Mother's Day. Someone pointed out a person in the crowd to me and said, "He designs many of the prize-winning floats for the Rose Parade." It scares me to realize that talent like that could go unused due to my ignorance.

Your church will never be any stronger than its core of lay ministers who carry out the various ministries of the church. Every church needs an intentional, well-planned system for uncovering, mobilizing, and supporting the giftedness of its members. You must set up a process to lead people to deeper commitment and greater service for Christ—one that will move your members from the committed circle into your core of lay ministers. On our Life Development Process diagram we call this "getting people to third base."

Most evangelical churches believe in the concept that every member is a minister. Many even give it a major emphasis in their preaching and teaching. Still, most members do nothing but attend and give. What does it take to turn an audience into an army? How do you transform spectators into participators? In this chapter I want to explain the system we've set up to equip, empower, and release our members for ministry.

Teach the Biblical Basis for Every-Member Ministry

I've tried to emphasize in this book the importance of laying a biblical foundation for everything you do. People always need to know "why" before you teach them "how." Invest time in teaching your members the biblical basis for lay ministry. Then teach it in classes, sermons, seminars, home Bible studies, and any other way you can emphasize it. In fact, you should *never* stop teaching on the importance of every Christian having a ministry.

We have summarized what we believe about ministry in a Ministry Mission Statement. Based on Romans 12:1–8, we believe the church is built on four pillars of lay ministry. We teach these four pillar truths over and over again so that they will be deeply ingrained in the hearts of our members.

Pillar #1: Every believer is a minister

Every believer isn't a pastor, but every believer *is* called into ministry. God calls *all* believers to minister to the world and the church. Service in the body isn't optional for Christians. In God's army, there are no volunteers — he's drafted all of us into service.

To be a Christian is to be like Jesus. Jesus said, "For even the Son of Man did not come to be served, but *to serve*, and *to give* his life as a ransom for many" (Mark 10:45, italics added). Service and giving are the defining characteristics of the Christlike lifestyle expected of every believer.

At Saddleback, we teach that every Christian is *created* for ministry (see Eph. 2:10), *saved* for ministry (see 2 Tim. 1:9), *called* into ministry (see 1 Peter 2:9-10), *gifted* for ministry (see 1 Peter 4:10), *authorized* for ministry (see Matt. 28:18-20), *commanded* to minister (see Matt. 20:26-28), to be *prepared* for ministry (see Eph. 4:11-12), *needed* for ministry (see 1 Cor. 12:27), *accountable* for ministry, and will be *rewarded* according to his or her ministry (see Col. 3:23-24).

Pillar #2: Every ministry is important

There are no "little people" in the body of Christ, and there are no "insignificant" ministries. *Every* ministry is important.

> God has arranged the parts in the body, every one of them, just as he wanted them to be. . . . The eye cannot say to the hand, "I don't need you!" And the head cannot say to the feet, "I don't need you!" On the contrary, those parts of the body that seem to be weaker are indispensable.
>
> (1 Cor. 12:18-22)

Some ministries are visible and some are behind the scenes, but all are equally valuable. At SALT, our monthly ministry training rally, we emphasize and recognize all of our ministries equally.

Small ministries often make the greatest difference. The most important light in my home is not the large chandelier in our dining room but the little nightlight that keeps me from stubbing my toe when I get up to use the bathroom at night. It's small, but it's more useful to me than the show-off light. (My wife says that my *favorite* light is the one that comes on when I open the refrigerator!)

Pillar #3: We are dependent on each other

Not only is every ministry important, every ministry is also intertwined with all the others. No ministry is independent of the others. Since no single ministry can accomplish all the church is called to do, we must depend on and cooperate with each other. Like a jigsaw puzzle, each piece is required to complete the picture. You always notice the missing piece first.

When one part of your body malfunctions, the other parts don't work as well. One of the missing components in the contemporary church is this understanding of interdependence. We *must* work together. Our culture's preoccupation with individualism and independence must be replaced with the biblical concepts of interdependence and mutuality.

Pillar #4: Ministry is the expression of my SHAPE

This is a distinctive of Saddleback's teaching on ministry. SHAPE is an acronym I developed years ago to explain the five elements (spiritual gifts, heart, abilities, personality, and experiences) that determine what a person's ministry should be.

When God created animals, he gave each of them a specific area of expertise. Some animals run, some hop, some swim, some burrow, and some fly. Each animal has a particular role to play based on the way they were shaped by God. The same is true with humans. Each of us was uniquely designed, or shaped, by God to do certain things.

Wise stewardship of your life begins by understanding your shape. You are unique, wonderfully complex, a composite of many different factors. What God made you to *be* determines what he intends for you to *do*. Your ministry is determined by your makeup.

How God Shapes You for Ministry

S piritual gifts

H eart

A bilities

P ersonality

E xperiences

If you don't understand your shape, you end up doing things that God never intended or designed you to do. When your gifts don't match the role you play in life, you feel like a square peg in a round hole. This is frustrating, both to you and to others. Not only does it produce limited results, it is also an enormous waste of your talents, time, and energy.

God is consistent in his plan for our lives. He would not give each of us inborn abilities, temperaments, talents, spiritual gifts, and life experiences and then not use them! By identifying and understanding the five SHAPE factors, we can discover God's will for our lives—the unique way he intends for each of us to serve him. When it comes to ministry, your function flows out of the way God formed you.

God has been molding and shaping you for ministry since you were born. In fact, God began shaping you *before* you were born:

> You made all the delicate, inner parts of my body and knit them together in my mother's womb. Thank you for making me so wonderfully complex! It is amazing to think about. Your workmanship is marvelous—and how well I know it. You were there while I was being formed in utter seclusion! You saw me before I was born and scheduled each day of my life before I began to breathe.
>
> (Psalm 139:13–16 LB)

Spiritual gifts. The Bible clearly teaches that God gives each believer certain spiritual gifts to be used in ministry (see 1 Cor. 12; Rom. 8; Eph. 4). However, spiritual gifts are only one part of the picture. Spiritual gifts are often overemphasized to the neglect of other equally important factors. Natural abilities that you were born with also came from God. So did your experiences and inborn personality traits. Spiritual gifts reveal a *part* of God's will for your ministry, but not all of it.

Most churches say, "Discover your spiritual gift and then you'll know what ministry you're supposed to have." This is backwards. I believe the exact opposite: Start experimenting with different ministries and *then* you'll discover your gifts! Until you actually get involved in serving, you're not going to know what you're good at. You can read all the books in print and still be confused about what you are gifted to do.

I do not place much stock in the many "spiritual gift inventories" or tests that are available today. In the first place, inventories and tests require standardization, which denies the unique way God works in every life. Those who have the gift of evangelism in our church may express it much differently than Billy Graham expresses his gift of evangelism. Second, there are no definitions of most of the spiritual gifts listed in the New Testament, so today's definitions are arbitrary, highly speculative, and usually represent a denominational bias.

A third problem is that the more mature a believer becomes, the more he or she is likely to manifest the characteristics of a number of gifts. He may demonstrate a servant's heart, or she may demonstrate liberal giving, out of maturity rather than giftedness.

When I was a teenager, I took a spiritual gift inventory and discovered the only gift I had was martyrdom! I thought, "Oh, great. That's the gift you get to use only one time." I could have taken a hundred gift tests and never discovered I was gifted at preaching and teaching. It would have never occurred to me because I had never done it. It was only *after* I began accepting opportunities to speak that I saw the results, received confirmation from others, and realized, "God has gifted me to do this!"

Heart. The Bible uses the term *heart* to represent the center of your motivation, desires, interests, and inclinations. Your heart determines why you say the things you do (see Matt. 12:34), why you feel the way you do (see Ps. 37:4), and why you act the way you do (see Prov. 4:23).

Physiologically, each of us has a unique heartbeat. Each person's heart beats in a slightly different pattern. Likewise, God has given each of us a unique emotional "heartbeat" that races when we encounter activities, subjects, or circumstances that interest us. We instinctively feel deeply about some things and not about others. Another word for heart is *passion*. There are certain subjects that you feel passionate about and others you couldn't care less about. That is an expression of your heart.

Your God-given motivational bent serves as an internal guidance system for your life. It determines what interests you and what will bring you the most satisfaction and fulfillment. It also motivates you to pursue certain activities, subjects, and environments. Don't ignore your natural interests. People rarely excel at tasks they don't enjoy doing. High achievers are most often those who enjoy what they do.

God had a purpose in giving you your inborn interests. Your emotional heartbeat reveals a very important key to understanding his intentions for your life. God gave you your heart, but it is your choice to use it for good or evil, for selfish reasons or to serve God and others. First Samuel 12:20 says, ". . . serve the LORD with all your heart."

Abilities. Abilities are the natural talents that you were born with. Some people have a natural ability with words: They come out of the womb talking! Other people have natural athletic abilities: They excel in physical coordination. (All the basketball coaching in the world will never allow you to match the talent of Michael Jordan on the court.) Some people are naturally good with numbers: They think mathematically and can't understand why you don't understand calculus!

Exodus 31:3 gives an example of how God gives people "skill, ability and knowledge in all kinds of crafts" in order to accomplish his purposes. In this case, it was artistic ability to be used in building the tabernacle. It's interesting to me that musical talent is not listed as a "spiritual gift," but it certainly is a natural ability God uses in worship. It is also interesting that God gives people the ability to make money: "But remember the LORD your God, for it is he who gives you the ability to produce wealth" (Deut. 8:18).

One of the most common excuses people give for not getting involved in ministry is that they just don't have any abilities to offer. Nothing could be farther from the truth: Many national studies have proven that the average person possesses from five hundred to seven hundred skills! The real problem is twofold. First, people need some process of skill identification. Most people are using abilities that they are unaware that they have. Second, they need a process to help them match their abilities with the right ministry.

There are people in your church who have all kinds of abilities that are not being put to use: recruiting, researching, writing, landscaping, interviewing, promoting, decorating, planning, entertaining, repairing, drawing, even cooking. These abilities should not be wasted. "There are different kinds of service, but the same Lord" (1 Cor. 12:5).

Personality. It's obvious that God does not use a cookie cutter to create people. He loves variety. He made introverts and extroverts. He made people who love routine and those who love variety. He made some people "thinkers" and others "feelers." He made people who work best when given an individual assignment, and some who work better with a team.

The Bible gives us plenty of proof that God uses all types of personalities. Peter had a sanguine personality. Paul had a choleric personality. And Jeremiah's personality was definitely melancholy. When you look at the personality differences in the twelve disciples Jesus selected, it's easy to understand why they sometimes had interpersonal conflict!

There is no "right" or "wrong" temperament for ministry. We need all kinds of personalities to balance the church and give it flavor. The world would be a very boring place if we were all plain vanilla. Fortunately, people come in more than thirty-one flavors.

Your personality will affect how and where you use your spiritual gifts and abilities. For instance, two people may have the same gift of evangelism, but if one is introverted and the other is extroverted, that gift will be expressed in different ways.

Woodworkers know that it's easier to work *with* the grain than against it. In the same way, when you are forced to minister in a manner that is out of character for your temperament, it creates tension and discomfort, requires extra effort and energy, and produces less than the best results. This is why mimicking someone else's ministry never works—you don't have their personality. God made you to be you! You can learn from the examples of others, but you must filter the lessons you learn through your own shape.

When you minister in a manner that is consistent with the personality God gave you, you will experience fulfillment, satisfaction, and fruitfulness. It feels good when you do exactly what God made you to do.

Experiences. God never wastes an experience. Romans 8:28 reminds us, "We know that in all things God works for the good of those who love him, who have been called according to his purpose."

At Saddleback, we help people consider five areas of experience that will influence the kind of ministry they are best shaped for: (1) Educational experiences: What were your favorite subjects in school? (2) Vocational experiences: What jobs have you enjoyed and achieved results while doing? (3) Spiritual experiences: What have been the meaningful or decisive times with God in your life? (4) Ministry experiences: How have you served God in the past? and (5) Painful experiences: What are the problems, hurts, and trials that you've learned from?

Because your shape was sovereignly determined by God for his purpose, you shouldn't resent it or reject it. "What right have you, a human being, to cross-examine God? The pot has no right to say to the potter: Why did you make me this shape? Surely a potter can do what he likes with the clay?" (Rom. 9:20–21 JB). Instead of trying to reshape yourself to be like someone else, you should celebrate the shape God has given you.

You will be most effective and fulfilled in ministry when you use your spiritual gifts and abilities in the area of your heart's desire in a way that best expresses your personality and experiences. Fruitfulness is the result of a good ministry fit. (If you are interested in a more detailed explanation of SHAPE, you may want to hear my tape series "You Are Shaped for Significance.")

Streamline Your Organizational Structure

The next step in building your lay ministry, after teaching the biblical basis for it, is to streamline your organizational structure. One major reason many church members aren't active in ministry is because they are so busy attending meetings that they have no time left for real ministry. I've often wondered what we'd have left in Christianity if we cut out all the meetings. After all, Jesus did not say, "I have come that you might have meetings." But if you ask typical unchurched people what they notice most about their Christian neighbors' lifestyles, they are likely to say, "They go to a lot of meetings." Is this what we want to be known for?

My guess is that the average church would be healthier if it eliminated half of its meetings to allow more time for ministry and relational evangelism. One of the reasons church members don't witness to their neighbors is because they don't know them! They are always at church, attending meetings.

A few years ago, the Roper Organization did a survey of leisure time in America. They discovered that Americans have less discretionary time in the 1990s than they had in the 1970s. The average American had 26.2 hours a week in leisure time in 1973. By 1987, it had dropped to 16.6 hours per week, a loss of 10 hours a week in leisure time. Today it is even lower.

The most valuable asset people can give to your church is their time. Since people have less discretionary time, we'd better make sure we use their time in the best way when they offer it. If a layperson comes to me and says, "Pastor, I have four hours a week to give to my church in ministry," the *last* thing I would do would be to put him on some committee. I want to get him involved in ministry, not maintenance.

Teach your people the difference between maintenance and ministry. Maintenance is "church work": budgets, buildings, organizational matters, and so forth. Ministry is "the work of the church." The more people you involve in maintenance decisions, the more you waste their time, keep them from ministry, and create opportunities for conflict. Maintenance work also conditions people to think that their responsibility is fulfilled by simply voting on church business.

A common mistake made by many churches is to take their brightest and best people and turn them into bureaucrats by giving them more meetings to attend. You can drain the life out of people by scheduling a constant string of committee meetings. We have no committees at Saddleback. We do, however, have seventy-nine different lay ministries.

What is the difference between a committee and a lay ministry? Committees discuss it, but ministries do it. Committees argue, ministries act. Committees maintain, ministries minister. Committees talk and consider, ministries serve and care. Committees discuss needs, ministries meet needs.

Committees also make decisions that they expect other people to implement. At Saddleback, the implementers are the decision makers. The people who do the ministry get to make their own decisions about that ministry. We do not separate authority from responsibility, but trust people with both. This makes committees irrelevant. We don't give decision-making authority to those who don't minister.

Who, then, does the maintenance at Saddleback? The paid staff does it. This way we don't waste any of our members' valuable time. People really appreciate the fact that the time they volunteer is given to actual ministry.

I'm sure you realize how radical this approach is. Saddleback is structured in the *exact opposite way* of most churches. In the typical church, the members handle the maintenance (administration) of the church and the pastor is supposed to do all the ministry. No wonder the church can't grow! The pastor becomes a bottleneck. There is no way one man can minister to all the needs in a church. He will eventually burn out or have to move to another church for relief.

It is not within the scope of this book for me to share *all* my convictions about biblical church structure. (The details are included in a tape called "Simple Structure.") But let me just ask you to consider this question: What do the words *committees, elections, majority rule, boards, board members, parliamentary procedures, voting, and vote* have in common? None of these words are found in the New Testament! We have imposed an American form of government on the church and, as a result, most churches are as bogged down in bureaucracy as our government is. It takes forever to get anything done. Man-made organizational structures have prevented more churches from healthy growth than any of us could imagine.

While the kind of structure a church has does not *cause* growth, it does control the *rate* and the *size* of the growth. And every church must eventually decide whether it is going to be structured for *control* or structured for *growth*. This is one of the most crucial decisions your church will ever face. For your church to grow, both the pastor and the people must give up control: The people must give up control of the *leadership*, and the pastor must give up control of the *ministry*. Otherwise either party can become a bottleneck for growth.

Once a church grows beyond about 500 people, no single person or board can know everything that's going on in the church. I haven't known about everything that happens at Saddleback for years. I don't need to know about it all! You might ask, "Then how do you control it?" My answer is: "I don't. It's not my job to control the church. It's my job to *lead* it." There is a very big difference between leading and controlling. Our pastors and staff are responsible to keep the church doctrinally sound and headed in the right direction, but the day-to-day decisions are made by the people actually doing the ministries of the church.

> Every church must eventually decide whether it will be structured for *control* or structured for *growth*.

If you are serious about mobilizing your members for ministry, you must streamline your structure to maximize ministry and minimize maintenance. The more organizational machinery your church sets up, the more time, energy, and money it takes to maintain it—precious time, energy, and money that could be invested in ministry to people instead.

If you release people for ministry and relieve them of the maintenance, you'll create a far happier, more harmonious church with a much higher morale. Fulfillment comes from ministry, not maintenance. Having God use you to change lives will change your whole attitude.

In a war, you always find the highest morale and sense of camaraderie among those serving on the front line. You don't have time to argue and complain when you're dodging bullets. Ten miles back, however, soldiers in the rear echelon grumble about the food, the showers, and the lack of entertainment. The conditions aren't nearly as bad as those on the front line, but people are critical because

> **Streamline your structure to maximize ministry and minimize maintenance.**

they're not occupied with the battle. When I meet cantankerous and critical Christians, I usually discover that they're not involved in a ministry. The biggest complainers in any church are usually committee members with nothing else to do.

In those few times when you really do need a committee of people to study something, create an ad hoc study committee that has a specific assignment with a beginning and ending to it. Set a time limit after which the committee disbands. Most standing committees waste an enormous amount of brain power in scheduled, but unnecessary, meetings.

Don't vote on ministry positions

There are a number of reasons that Saddleback never votes to approve people for lay ministry positions.

You avoid a personality contest. If you vote to approve anyone who serves in a ministry, you will exclude all of the people who fear rejection. Those who are shy and lack confidence will never volunteer to serve, out of fear that they might be turned down by the congregation or board.

New ministries often need to develop slowly. If you put a public spotlight on a new ministry in the early days, it may die. All it takes is one influential negative voice to uproot a ministry idea before it has a chance to sprout.

New members can get involved more quickly. Voting puts new members at a disadvantage. A new member may be the best qualified to serve, but he or she may be unknown to the committee that controls the appointment process. I've seen gifted people shut out of ministry for years because they were not part of the church's inner circle of old-timers.

You avoid attracting people who are only interested in a position for its power or prestige. By eliminating voting, you attract the people who are genuinely interested in serving instead of those who just want a title. A man once complained to me, "I'm leaving the church because I want to be the chairman of the board, and Saddleback doesn't have a board!" At least he was honest. He found a small church where he could have an impressive title and be a big fish in a little pond. He wasn't at all interested in ministry; he was interested in power.

If people fail, it makes removal easier. If you publicly elect people, then you have to publicly remove them if they become incompetent or have failed morally. In today's world that kind of public removal can be a political, relational, and legal hot potato. Some carnal people would rather split a church than give up a position. They may line up support for a showdown. If you don't vote on ministry positions, failure can be dealt with privately.

You can respond more quickly to the Holy Spirit's leading. When any member comes up with a great ministry idea, the church shouldn't have to wait until the next business meeting to begin it. At our church, a ministry has sometimes been formed immediately after a service due to something I said in a message. Interested people gather on the patio and the work begins right away.

One time a woman came to me and said, "We need a prayer ministry." I said, "I agree! You're it!" She said, "Don't I have to be elected or go through some approval process?" She had imagined she would have to jump through all kinds of political hoops first. I said, "Of course not! Just announce a formation meeting in the bulletin and start it." She did.

Another time a person came to me and said, "We need a support group for terminally ill cancer patients." I said, "Great idea! Just start it yourself." He did. Still another man once said to me, "I can't teach and I can't sing, but I'm good at home repairs and small carpentry jobs. I'd like to start a ministry called Home Helps and do free home maintenance for widows in our church." The point is, you shouldn't have to vote on whether or not a person can use the gifts God has given him or her in the body of Christ. Whenever anyone expresses a desire to minister we immediately start them through our placement process.

Establish a Ministry Placement Process

Moving members into ministry should be an ongoing process, not a special emphasis. There are three essential parts to Saddleback's Ministry Development Center.

A monthly class. Each month, we offer Class 301: "Discovering My Ministry," a four-hour class that exposes people to the biblical basis for ministry, the SHAPE concept, and the various ministry opportunities at Saddleback. It is taught on the second Sunday afternoon of each month, from 4 to 8:30 P.M., and includes a thirty-minute meal provided free to those who take the class. It is taught simultaneously with Classes 101 (membership) and 201 (maturity). We give these classes a lot of visibility and promotion.

A placement process. Our placement process involves six steps: (1) attend Class 301, (2) commit to serving in ministry and sign Saddleback's Ministry Covenant, (3) complete a personal SHAPE profile, (4) have a personal interview with a ministry consultant to identify three or four possible areas of ministry, (5) meet with the staff person or lay leader who oversees the ministry you are interested in, and (6) be publicly commissioned at a SALT meeting.

Your placement process should focus on empowering people, not on filling positions. You'll have a much higher success rate with those you place in ministry if you focus on the shape of the individual, not the needs of the institution. Remember, ministry is about people, not programs.

Staff to administer the process. People need individual attention and guidance as they attempt to discover the ministry they are shaped for. Simply taking them through a class won't accomplish this. Each member deserves personal consultation.

Having committed myself to membership and the habits essential for spiritual maturity and agreeing with Saddleback's Ministry Statement, I commit to...

Discover my unique *Shape* for ministry and serve in the area that best expresses what God made me to be.

Prepare for ministry by participating in S.A.L.T. and C.L.A.S.S.

Demonstrate a servant's heart by serving in secondary ministries as the Body needs me.

Cooperate with other ministries and place the greater good of the whole Body over the needs of my ministry.

Signed _____   Date _____

This certifies that

_____

is a commissioned minister of Jesus Christ through

Saddleback Valley Community Church

and is entrusted with the related responsibilities and privileges.

_____

Rick Warren, Pastor

Saddleback's Ministry Development Center is led by our Pastor of Ministries and by volunteers who serve on his team. They interview members who've completed a SHAPE profile, helping them find the best place to serve. They also assist members who want to begin new ministries. If I was starting a new church today, one of the first things I'd do would be to find a volunteer shaped for interviewing people and train him or her to help with this vital task. It doesn't have to be a paid position, but you do need to find someone with the right personality and skills for the task.

Provide On-the-Job Training

Once people begin serving in a ministry, they need on-the-job training. On-the-job training is far more important and effective than preservice training. At Saddleback we require only minimal preservice training because we feel that people don't even know the right questions to ask until they are actually involved in ministry.

Another reason we don't use preservice training is that we want to involve people as quickly as possible in actual ministry. A long, drawn-out preservice training course causes most people to lose their initial enthusiasm: It wears them out before they get started! I've found that the kind of people who are willing to train for fifty-two weeks *before* beginning to serve are usually not very effective when they finally start serving. They tend to be professional students who enjoy learning about ministry more than doing it. We want people to dive right in and get wet, because only then will they be highly motivated to learn how to swim. The best way to begin is to begin.

The centerpiece of our lay ministry training program is SALT. This is a two-hour training rally held on the first Sunday evening of each month for the core of our church. The agenda for SALT includes an extended time of focused worship, recognition of all ministries, testimonies from the field, commissioning of new lay ministers, prayer in groups, "insider" church news, ministry training, and a "vision" message by me on our values, our vision, and the character qualities and skills needed for ministry. These monthly messages to our lay leaders are called "Leadership Lifters" and are taped so anyone who misses SALT can hear them later. We also make these messages available to other churches through The Encouraging Word tape ministry. At SALT, we also present a monthly "Giant-Killer" award to the lay ministry that has tackled the biggest problem in the previous month.

In addition to SALT, we also offer a variety of training classes for specific ministries through our Life Development Institute. The 300-level classes teach different ministry skills and equip people to serve in the various ministries of our church. For instance, Class 302 is called "So You Want to Be a Small-Group Leader." There are other training courses for youth ministry, children's ministry, music ministry, counseling ministry, and lay pastoring, to name just a few.

Never Start a Ministry Without a Minister

We never create a ministry position and then try to fill it. It doesn't work. The most critical factor in a new ministry isn't the *idea,* but the *leadership.* Each ministry rises or falls on the leadership. Without the right leader, a ministry will just stumble along, possibly doing more harm than good.

Trust God's timing. The staff at Saddleback never starts new ministries. We may suggest an idea, but we let the idea percolate until God provides the right person to lead it. I shared earlier that we didn't have an organized youth ministry until the church was running nearly 500 in attendance, and we didn't have an organized singles ministry until we had nearly 1,000 in attendance. Why? God had not provided the leadership until then.

It is important never to push people into a ministry. If you do, you'll be stuck with a motivation problem for the life of the ministry. Most small churches get in a hurry and try to do too much. Instead, pray and wait for God to bring you the person best shaped to lead a particular ministry. Then, let them start it. Don't worry if there's no interest in a particular ministry. It's important for church leaders to have a long-term perspective concerning their church's development. Solid growth takes time.

Study the book of Acts and you'll discover that any organizing always followed what the Holy Spirit was doing. Not once in Acts do you find people organizing a ministry and then praying, "Now, God, please bless our idea." Instead, God would begin moving in people's hearts, a ministry would spontaneously spring up in a small way, and, as it grew larger, they would add some structure to it.

This is how every one of our ministries at Saddleback has developed. Our women's ministry, for example, started as a Bible study that Kay taught in our home. It just kept growing and expanding until some structure, and eventually staff, was added. This pattern has been repeated over and over.

Establish Minimum Standards and Guidelines

It's important to decide on certain minimum standards for ministry because best intentions are not enough when working with human beings. At Saddleback, we have a job description for every position in each ministry that clarifies issues like time commitment required, what resources are provided, any restrictions, lines of authority and communication, and what kinds of results are expected.

Keep the standards clear and brief; don't bury people with procedures and committees. Allow as much freedom as possible. In our church, any member that has completed Class 301 and a SHAPE interview can begin a new ministry as long as they agree to follow three basic guidelines.

Guideline #1: Don't expect the staff to run your ministry. People often say things like, "I've got a great idea for our church" or "*We* should do something about . . ." I always ask them to clarify what they mean by "we." When people say, "The church should . . ." they usually mean "The pastor or staff should . . ."

Someone once told me, "I've been feeling so burdened for the people in prison that I've been going out there to lead a Bible study. I think *the church* should do something for those people!" I said to him, "It sounds to me like the church *did* do something. You are the church!" The next week I told the whole congregation, "I release all of you to visit those in prison, feed the hungry, clothe the poor, and shelter the homeless—and you don't even have to tell me. Just do it! Represent the church in Jesus' name." This ministry didn't require any staff supervision. Help people realize that they are the church.

Guideline #2: The ministry must be compatible with our church's beliefs, values, and philosophy of ministry. If you allow ministries to start that are not headed in the same direction your church is headed, you're asking for conflict. Rather than helping the church, such ministries will actually hinder what you are trying to do and may even harm your church's testimony.

At Saddleback, we are especially cautious with ministries that are cosponsored by organizations outside our local church. These organizations often have agendas very different than our church's agenda, which tends to produce divided loyalties.

Guideline #3: No fund-raising is allowed. If you allow every ministry to do their own fundraising, your church patio will turn into a bazaar. There will be car washes and cookie sales all over the place. Competition for dollars will become intense, and your members will resent all of the appeal letters and sales gimmicks. A unified budget is essential to having a unified church. Leaders of each ministry should submit their financial needs for consideration in the total church budget.

Allow People to Quit or Change Ministries Gracefully

To resign from a ministry in some churches, you've either got to die, leave the church, or be willing to live with intense guilt. We need to allow people to take sabbaticals or change ministries without feeling guilty. Sometimes people become stale in a ministry. Or they may need a change of pace. Or maybe they just need time off. Whatever the reason, you need to have replacements ready to fill in.

We never handcuff people to a ministry. A decision to serve in a particular ministry is not written in stone. If someone doesn't enjoy or fit a particular ministry, they're encouraged to change to another one without any shame or embarrassment.

Give people the freedom to experiment. Let them try several alternative places of service. As I said earlier, we believe that experimenting with different ministries is the best way to discover your gifts. Although we usually ask for a one-year commitment to a ministry, we never enforce it. If people realize they are mismatched, we don't make them feel guilty for resigning. By calling it an "experiment," we can encourage them to try something else. Every year, during our Lay Ministry Month, everyone is encouraged to try a new ministry if they are unsatisfied where they are currently serving.

Trust People: Delegate Authority with Responsibility

The secret of motivating people into serving over an extended period of time is to give them a sense of ownership. I want to repeat that as much as possible, you need to allow the people leading each ministry to make their own decisions without interference from some governing board or committee. For instance, allow those in the nursery ministry to decide what the rooms look like, the type of cribs to be used, how many are purchased, and the system used to check children in or out. The people actually involved in the ministry will make more informed decisions than some general board that is trying to control everything from a distance.

People respond to responsibility. They thrive and grow when you trust them. But if you treat people like incompetent babies, you'll have to diaper and feed them the rest of your life. When you give authority with responsibility, you'll be amazed at the creativity of your people. People are always as creative as the structure allows them to be. At Saddleback, each lay ministry is assigned a staff liaison, but, as much as possible, we stay out of their way.

> **People will be as creative as the structure allows them to be.**

Expect the best of your people and trust them with ministry. Many churches are so afraid of *wildfire,* that they spend all their time putting out every little campfire that'll warm up the church! If you're a pastor, let others make some of the mistakes! Don't insist on making them all yourself. You bring out the best in people by giving them a *challenge*, giving them *control,* and giving them the *credit*.

At the beginning of Saddleback, Kay and I literally helped with every job in the church: Setting up the facilities, taking them down, printing bulletins, cleaning bathrooms, making coffee, making name tags, and on and on. I stored all our equipment—cribs, sound system, and so forth—in my garage. Every Sunday morning I borrowed a truck to haul that equipment to the school we were renting. In the first year I often worked fifteen hours a day—and I loved every minute of it.

But by the time Saddleback was just a few years old I found myself running out of energy. The church had grown to several hundred people and I was still trying to be involved in every aspect and detail of the ministry. I was burning out, physically and emotionally.

At a midweek service, I confessed to our congregation that I was exhausted and that I couldn't continue to lead the church and be involved in all the ministry at the same time..I went on to say that God didn't expect me to do all the ministry. The Bible was very clear that the pastor's job is to equip members for *their* ministry. I said, "I'll make you a deal. If you agree to do the ministry of this church, I'll make sure you're well fed!" The people liked the deal, and that night we signed a covenant that, from that day forward, they would do the ministry and I would feed and lead them. After making this decision, Saddleback exploded with growth.

From the first day of Saddleback, my plan had always been to give the ministry away. Whenever a new church is started, the pastor usually holds it together in the early days. But the goal must be to wean the church from dependence on the pastor for ministry as quickly as possible. As our church grew, I released one responsibility after another to lay ministers and to staff members. Today, I only have two primary responsibilities: To *lead* and to *feed*—and even these responsibilities are now shared with six other pastors. Our pastors' management team helps me lead the church and our preaching team shares in the speaking responsibilities. Why? Because I deeply believe the church was never meant to be a one-man superstar show!

We have all seen what happens when a prominent ministry is built around a single individual. If that person dies, moves, or has a moral failure, the ministry collapses. If I were to die today, Saddleback would continue growing because it is *purpose driven*, not personality driven. We'd probably lose a thousand of what I call "gospel groupies"—fringe attenders in the crowd who like to hear me speak. But that would still leave thousands of dedicated members of the congregation, committed, and core.

Provide the Necessary Support

Don't expect people to succeed without support. Every lay ministry requires an investment of some kind.

Provide material support. Lay ministries need access to copy machines, paper, various materials and resources, a telephone, and, most likely, space to meet. In one of our future buildings, we're planning on having a large room to hold our "ministry incubators"—small, private areas for lay ministry coordinators that are equipped with a table, phone, computer, and fax for their ministries. Archimedes said, "Give me a place to stand and I will move the world." We consider lay ministers as important as paid staff. Providing space tells people, "What you are doing is important."

Provide communication support. Develop ways to stay in touch with your lay ministers. The same tools that are used to keep in touch with our members (Welcome Cards, CARE Callers, Lay Pastor Reports) are useful here too.

Provide promotional support. It is important to keep your ministries visible to the congregation. There are countless ways you can promote the ministries of your church. Here are a few suggestions:

- Have each ministry set up a table outside your auditorium or in the foyer every Sunday so people have an opportunity to see what's available. If space is a problem, rotate the ministries that are highlighted.
- Give each lay minister a name tag so members can see who's involved in what ministries.
- Hold a ministry fair. At least twice a year, we have a ministry fair where every ministry advertises its focus, programs, and events.

- Print a brochure for every ministry and publish articles on different ministries if you have a newsletter.
- Refer to the various ministries in your messages. Use testimonies that tell how a particular ministry has made a difference.

Provide moral support. Continually express appreciation, in both public and personal ways, to those who serve in your church. Plan special events such as appreciation banquets or leadership retreats to reward your core group of ministers. Present a monthly "Giant-Killer" award for outstanding service.

Throughout this chapter I have repeatedly used the term "lay ministry" so that readers would not think I am talking about paid staff. I actually don't like the term "lay minister" because it can connote a second-class form of citizenship and competence. Do you want a "lay doctor" operating on you or a "lay lawyer" defending you?

There are no laypeople in a biblical church; there are only ministers. The idea of two classes of Christians, clergy and laity, is the creation of Roman Catholic tradition. In God's eyes, there is no difference between volunteer ministers and paid ministers. We should treat those who serve without pay with the same respect we treat those who are paid for their service.

Renew the Vision Regularly

Always keep the vision of ministry before your people. Communicate the importance of their ministries. When you recruit to ministry, always emphasize the eternal significance of ministering in Jesus' name. Never use guilt or pressure to motivate people for ministry. It's *vision* that motivates; guilt and pressure only discourage people. Help people see that there's no greater cause than the kingdom of God.

Do you remember the Nehemiah Principle I talked about in chapter 6? It states that vision must be renewed every twenty-six days, which is about once a month. This is why our monthly SALT meeting for our core is so important. It is where the lay ministers need to hear the vision and values continually restated. If I'm feeling ill, I do not hesitate giving up speaking to the 10,000 in the crowd, but I have to be dying to miss being with the core at SALT. It is my opportunity to reemphasize the privilege of serving Christ.

> **The Nehemiah Principle: Vision must be renewed every twenty-six days.**

I've often said to the members of our congregation, "Imagine dying, and fifty years from now somebody in heaven comes up to you and says, 'I want to thank you.' You reply, 'I'm sorry, I don't think I know you.' Then they explain: 'You were a lay minister at Saddleback. You served and sacrificed and built the church that reached me for Christ after you died. I'm in heaven because of you.' Do you think your effort is worth that?"

If I knew a more significant way to invest my life than in service for Jesus Christ, I'd be doing it. There is nothing more important. So I make no apology for telling people that the most important thing they may do with their lives is to join Saddleback Church, get involved in a ministry, and serve Christ by serving others. The effect of their ministry for Christ will outlast by far their career, hobby, or anything else they do.

The church's best-kept secret is that people are dying to make a contribution with their lives. We are made for ministry! The church that understands this and makes it possible for every member to express his or her shape in ministry will experience amazing vitality, health, and growth. The sleeping giant will be awakened, and it will be unstoppable.

20

God's Purpose
for Your Church

*To him be glory in the church and in Christ Jesus
throughout all generations, for ever and ever! Amen.*

Ephesians 3:21

*When David had served God's purpose in his own
generation, he [died].*

Acts 13:36

One of my hobbies is gardening. I think one reason I enjoy it
so much is because it fits the way God wired up my personality: I love to watch things grow. I have always been fascinated by the different ways plants develop. No two plants
grow in the same way, at the same rate, or to the same size. Each
plant's growth pattern is unique. The same is true of churches.
No two churches will ever grow in identical ways. God intends
for your church to be unique.

Of all the growth patterns I've observed as a gardener, the
growth of the Chinese bamboo tree is the most amazing to me.
Plant a bamboo sprout in the ground, and for four or five years
(sometimes much longer) nothing happens! You water and fertilize, water and fertilize, water and fertilize—but you see no
visible evidence that anything is happening. Nothing! But about

the fifth year things change rather dramatically. In a six-week period the Chinese bamboo tree grows to be a staggering ninety feet tall! World Book Encyclopedia records that one bamboo plant can grow three feet in a single twenty-four-hour period. It seems incredible that a plant that lies dormant for years can suddenly explode with growth, but it happens without fail with bamboo trees.

As I conclude this book I want to offer you this final advice: Don't worry about the growth of your church. Focus on fulfilling the purposes of your church. Keep watering and fertilizing and cultivating and weeding and pruning. God will grow his church to the size he wants it, at the rate that's best for your situation.

God may allow you to labor for years with little visible results. Don't be discouraged! Underneath the surface things are happening that you can't see. Roots are growing down and out, preparing for what is ahead. Even when you may not see the wisdom of what God is doing, you must trust God. Learn to live with the assurance that he knows what he's doing.

> **Don't worry about the growth of your church. Focus on the purposes of your church.**

Remember Proverbs 19:21: "Many are the plans in a man's heart, but it is the Lord's purpose that prevails." If you are building a ministry on God's eternal purpose, you cannot fail. It will prevail. Keep on doing what you know is right, even when you feel discouraged. "Let us not become weary in doing good, for at the proper time we will reap a harvest if we do not give up" (Gal. 6:9). Just as with a bamboo tree, when the time is right God can change things overnight. What is most important is that you remain faithful to his purposes.

Be a Purpose-Driven Person

Purpose-driven churches are led by purpose-driven leaders. Acts 13:36, one of my life verses, tells us that David was purpose driven: "When David had served God's purpose in his own generation, he [died]." I cannot think of a greater epitaph. Imagine having that statement inscribed on *your* tombstone: "He served God's purpose in his own generation." My prayer is that God will be able to say that about me when I die. And my motivation for writing this book is that God will be able to say that about *you* when you die. The secret of effective ministry is to fulfill both parts of this statement.

He served God's purpose

The main thrust of this book has been to define God's purposes for the church and identify the practical implications of those purposes. God's purposes for the church are also his purposes for every Christian. As individual followers of Christ we are to use our lives in worship, ministry, evangelism, discipleship, and fellowship. Having the church allows us to do this together; we are not alone.

I hope you have felt my passion for the church as you have read these pages. I love the church with all of my heart. It is the most brilliant concept ever created. If we intend to be like Jesus, we must love the church as he does, and we must teach others to love the church as well. "Christ loved the church and gave himself up for her. . . . After all, no one ever hated his own body, but he feeds and cares for it, just as Christ does the church—for we are members of his body" (Eph. 5:25, 29–30). Too many Christians use the church, but don't love it.

> Too many Christians use the church, but don't love it.

As best as I can discern God's will, I have only two aspirations for my ministry: to be the pastor of one local church for my entire life, and to encourage other pastors. Pastoring a congregation of Christ's followers is the greatest responsibility, the grandest privilege, and the highest honor I can imagine. I've already stated that if I knew a more strategic way to invest my life I would do it, because I do not intend to waste my life. The task of bringing people to Christ and into membership in his family, developing them into mature disciples, empowering and equipping them for personal ministry, and sending them out to fulfill their life mission is the greatest purpose on earth. I have no doubt that it is worth living for and dying for.

In his own generation

The second half of David's epitaph is just as crucial as the first half. He served God's purpose "in his own generation." The fact is, we *can't* serve God in any other generation except our own. Ministry must always be done in the context of the current generation and culture. We must minister to people in the culture as it really is — not in some past form that we may have idealized in our minds. We can benefit from the wisdom and experiences of great Christian leaders who lived before us but we cannot preach and minister the way they did because we don't have the same culture.

David's ministry was both relevant and timely. He served God's purpose (which is eternal and unchanging) in his generation (which was current and changing). He served the timeless in a timely way. He was both orthodox and contemporary, biblical and relevant.

Being contemporary without compromising the truth has been our objective at Saddleback since we began. With every new generation, the rules change a little. If we always do what we've always done, we'll always be where we've always been. The past is behind us. We can only live in today and prepare for tomorrow. We must live the words of Charles Wesley's poem that Lowell Mason put to music over one hundred years ago:

A charge to keep I have, a God to glorify
A never dying soul to save, and fit it for the sky
To serve the present age, my calling to fulfill
O may it all my powers engage, to do my Master's will!

Measuring Success

How do you measure success in ministry? One well-known definition of successful evangelism reads like this: "Sharing the gospel in the power of the Holy Spirit and leaving the results to God." I'd like to adapt that statement and offer a definition of successful ministry: Successful ministry is "building the church on the purposes of God in the power of the Holy Spirit and *expecting* the results from God."

I don't know how the final chapters of Saddleback's story will be written, but I am confident of this: "that he who began a good work in [us] will carry it on to completion until the day of Christ Jesus" (Phil. 1:6). God finishes whatever he starts. He is Alpha and Omega, the beginning and the end. He will continue to fulfill his purposes at Saddleback and in every other church that is purpose driven.

Jesus said, "According to your faith will it be done to you" (Matt. 9:29). I call this the "faith factor." There are many factors that influence your ministry which you have no control over: your background, nationality, age,

> Successful ministry is building the church on the purposes of God in the power of the Holy Spirit and *expecting* the results from God.

giftedness. These were determined by the sovereignty of God. But there is one important factor that you do have control over: how much you choose to believe God!

As I have studied growing churches over the years, I have discovered one great common denominator in every growing church, regardless of denomination or location: *leadership that is not afraid to believe God.* Growing churches are led by leaders who expect their congregation to grow. They are people of faith who believe the promises of God, even in discouraging times. This is the secret behind everything that has happened at Saddleback Church. We have believed God for big miracles, and we've expected him to use us—by grace through faith. That is our choice. It's your choice too.

Sometimes a church's situation may look hopeless from a human standpoint. But I am firmly convinced, as Ezekiel's experience (Ezekiel 37) proved, that no matter how dry the bones may be, God can breathe new life into them. Any church can come alive if we allow the Spirit to infuse us with a new sense of his purpose. That is what the purpose-driven church is all about.

My hope is that this book has strengthened your faith, stretched your vision, and deepened your love for Christ and his church. I hope you will share it with those who care about your congregation. Accept the challenge of becoming a purpose-driven church! The greatest churches in history are yet to be built. Are you available for that task? I pray that God will use you to fulfill his purposes in your generation. There is no greater use of your life.

Resources

For information on
Tapes of the complete *Purpose-Driven Church Seminar*
Class 101, 201, 301, & 401 tapes and curriculum
Leadership Lifter training tapes
Other books by Rick Warren
A catalogue of Saddleback sermons & outlines
contact
THE ENCOURAGING WORD
20131 Ellipse
Foothill Ranch, CA 92610
Phone: 949–829–0300
Fax: 949–829–0400
Web Site: www.pastors.com
e-mail: info@pastors.com

For information on
The Purpose-Driven Church Seminar
contact
SADDLEBACK SEMINARS
#1 Saddleback Parkway
Lake Forest, CA 92630
Phone: 949-586-2000
Fax: 949-581-7614
http://www.saddleback.com